VOICES
FROM THE
ASYLUM

Edited by
MICHAEL GLENN

HARPER COLOPHON BOOKS
Harper & Row, Publishers
New York, Evanston, San Francisco, London

A hardcover edition of this book is available from Harper & Row, Publishers, Inc.

VOICES FROM THE ASYLUM.
Copyright © 1974 by Michael Glenn.
For information address Harper & Row, Publishers, Inc., 10 East 53d Street, New York, N.Y. 10022. Published simultaneously in Canada by Fitzhenry & Whiteside Limited, Toronto.

First HARPER COLOPHON edition published 1974.

LIBRARY OF CONGRESS CATALOG CARD NUMBER: 73–17606

STANDARD BOOK NUMBER: 06–090340–6 (PAPERBACK)

STANDARD BOOK NUMBER: 06–136137–2 (HARDCOVER)

CONTENTS

Introduction

I can hear readers complaining already: "What? *Another* book on mental illness? *Another* book on being crazy? What do we need *that* for?"

They're right. We don't need any more books on the myth of mental illness; or on how groovy it is to "get into" your own psychosis; or on a bag of "new," "radical" techniques for psychotherapy; or on a variety of other intellectual, abstract concerns. That's not what this book is.

This book is about what goes on in mental hospitals, day after day. It is about oppression. It's written by people who have firsthand knowledge of hospitals—patients primarily, but also attendants, doctors, and others. Its purpose is to help the public understand the relation of oppression to our capitalist system. The oppression of mental patients will go on as long as mental hospitals are capitalist institutions. Capitalism is, in part, the oppression of the masses of working and poor people in this country, carried out in the interests of the few rich people who run the show.

Most of what is called "mental illness" comes from daily life in a brutalizing society. It's not some "disease" detached from people's struggles to survive—not something to be summed up by "ego defenses" or "family dynamics."

Over a million people are now living in mental institutions—mostly working people, poor people, third-world people, women. The people running this country first create conditions which drive people frantic and make it impossible for them to live decent lives; then they create institutions in which to lock these people up, "treat" them, and process them. This is the hypocrisy of the ruling class. The "treatment," worse than the original problem, includes restraints and forced commitment, tranquilizers, electroshock, lobotomy. The mental institutions contain the victims of capitalist society, but under the medical model, the victims are blamed for their own suffering. They are labeled mentally ill, people with character disorders. Their misery is covered up by a society that refuses to admit that it itself is the major cause of emotional distress, not the "ego deficits" of the people who suffer.

Hospital conditions are degrading and cruel. They follow a bureaucratic pattern, in which M.D. administrators make decisions without ever seeing the patients affected. At the lower staff levels, working people carry out the detention and "treatment" of the patients. The hierarchy lives off its patients: mental illness is its business.

There's been a lot of talk recently about patients' legal rights, about putting an end to involuntary commitment or drugging patients without their consent. Yet, with all the protests, there's little sign that the situation is changing. In fact, with recent federal cuts in social services, including mental health, it's likely the trend will be in the opposite direction: less personal treatment, fewer rights, less consideration, and greater reliance on drugs, electroshock, and the like. In addition, the increasingly fascist trend in this country suggests that even those people pushing for reforms will find it tougher going.

The contradiction between therapy as a *service* to people and therapy as the *control and oppression* of people is sharpening. The rhetoric will make it seem that the former is being sought; in reality, the latter is being strengthened.

This book will inject some raw experience into the struggle for change. It would be illusory, of course, to pretend that real change will occur as long as the country remains a capitalist/imperialist power. Yet it is important to advance the struggle on many levels, and the struggle for the democratic (civil) rights of mental patients is an important part of maintaining some democratic rights in this society. We should be clear, though, that people's political oppression goes beyond the denial of their civil rights; it involves the struggle between classes in a society controlled from top to bottom by the ruling class. Liberation is achieved by remolding society, by a socialist revolution, not by putting a few more permissive or protective laws on the books.

The politics of mental institutions is the same as the politics of medical hospitals and clinics, schools, jails, universities, factories. It should not be seen as isolated from what's happening elsewhere. Hopefully people who read this book will move past commiseration to a commitment to change.

A lot of theories have come up to explain why people flip out and become "psychotic." Virtually every theory proposed in the past several centuries has been *one-sided*. Presented as "objective" or "scientific," they have been in fact rigid, dogmatic, and marked with the stamp of the bourgeoisie.[1]

The early advocates of the organic origin of "insanity" felt that an abnormality in the brain was responsible for erratic mental behavior. They focused on an intrinsic physical factor and excluded everything else. Freud and the psychoanalytic school which followed him elaborated the notion that neurosis and other mental problems resulted from internal conflicts. Thus, the psychoanalysts also concentrated exclusively on intrinsic factors, though these were abstract mental constructs instead of the concrete physical structures of the organicists. Later, "psychodynamic" formulations of emotional difficulties began opening the door to extrinsic factors—the family, the social group, the society. This was an advance, but these formulations remained professional and abstract.

As therapy became a pragmatic activity, therapists began developing a body of experience. They came to understand that both intrinsic and extrinsic factors were at work in emotional disorders. They could not, however, explore the extent to which extrinsic (social/political) factors influence people's behavior. Their own vested

1. Every kind of thinking reflects a class stand. Bourgeois psychology is no exception. For a good discussion of the two ways of looking at the world —idealist versus materialist—see Friedrich Engels, *Ludwig Feuerbach and the Outcome of Classical German Philosophy* (New York: International Publishers, 1941) and Mao Tse-tung, *On Contradiction* in *Selected Works*, 4 vols. (New York: China Books, 1961, 1965).

interest in the society kept them from doing this. After all, they derived great prestige from being at the top of an authoritarian, capitalist society. Their "business" was like other entrepreneurs' work. They had monopolized, professionalized, and mystified their work. Mental health was an industry, and they had no material base for expanding a critique of capitalist society. So they kept their mouths shut and focused instead on more manageable internal and individualist sources of emotional pain. They developed psychotherapy and psychology as bourgeois fields of work, serving the interests of the ruling class.

The recent "radical therapy" movement has a progressive side. It attacks professionalism and the monopoly of the therapy elite, and points to the political nature of therapy in a capitalist society. Where radical therapy attacks sex-role stereotypes, exposes mental patients' oppression, and urges people with skills to share them, it is progressive. But there has been a negative aspect to radical therapists, located in their persistent professionalism, even as they attack the therapy establishment for its elitism. They still put themselves forth as "therapists," and basically they work for reforms in therapy institutions.[2] They even use their professional credentials to bolster their own personal credibility.

Ideologically, they have often replaced the psychoanalysts' one-sided reliance on intrinsic factors with a reliance on extrinsic ones. Thus, they claim that we are all blameless, that it is only the society which has created our suffering. This view, while correctly pointing to the main factors in emotional distress—United States capitalism and its institutions—manages to liquidate the important intrinsic factors which often play a decisive role in emotional problems, often shaping the specific, particular pattern someone follows. It is not enough to attack the extrinsic factors if one does not appreciate the intrinsic factors, or worse, scorns them.

A more correct, dialectical understanding of emotional problems takes both intrinsic and extrinsic factors into account. Mao has pointed out that

2. For a fuller discussion of this see Michael Glenn and Richard Kunnes, *Repression or Revolution? Therapy in the United States Today* (New York: Harper & Row, 1973).

external causes are the condition of change and internal causes are the basis of change, and . . . external causes become operative through internal causes.[3]

Avoiding one-sidedness, we need to understand the interplay of both intrinsic and extrinsic factors. The fundamental conflict in a person's life is internal. In American society, that conflict will reflect the fundamental contradiction in the whole society—between the private ownership of the means of production and the social nature of production, between bosses and workers. But it will also reflect other contradictions, such as between the national minorities and the ruling class, between men and women, between petty bourgeois interests and the ruling class. The inner conflicts a person faces are related to society, but not wholly explained by that relationship; factors such as one's parents, family situation, genetic predisposition, and so on, can affect one's mental outlook.

External factors—a person's employment, family financial situation, myths and stereotypes of male and female behavior—shape and influence the internal conflicts. Living in an imperialist rather than in a socialist country, for example, makes a lot of difference in the people's mental health. In a socialist country like the People's Republic of China there are far fewer contradictions between the masses of people and the way the country is run, and thus the factors leading to emotional distress are reduced.

Emotional problems are to be understood as the result of this dialectical interplay of internal and external forces. Each specific situation should be analyzed in those terms. That is what "therapy" should consist of: clarifying both the internal and external factors at work.

What happens instead is that therapists usually focus on internal factors, which become the basis for a "diagnosis." Patients are labeled according to their type of "upsetness," and then treated. The radical therapists often err in the other direction, assuming that people's problems are always a result of an oppressive society, and have nothing to do with the individuals themselves.

People become upset in different ways and most don't need

3. Mao Tse-tung, *On Contradiction*, 1:314.

to be hospitalized. Usually, people who become upset get some kind of "therapy" on an out-patient basis (if they get any therapy at all). This is usually counseling, drugs, and so forth. Hospitalization in this country is reserved for people who can't cope for themselves, or who are felt to jeopardize the system by remaining outside mental institutions.

Mental hospitals are thus used as prisons. And mental hospitals for prisoners function to detain and control these people even more completely. Mental institutions are great bins, storing people who are relegated to "medical" control while they are inside. Every so often, people are discharged; every so often, people are admitted. The doctors carry on their duties of processing and treating, in a situation of nearly total control.

Traditionally it was "psychotics" who were institutionalized. They were people who had "degenerated" in their mental functioning or who were uncontrollable in their behavior. They were the stereotypes of asylum cases—"crazy people," ranting and raving, beating at themselves, running around naked, imagining themselves to be other people, possessed by strange sensations and thoughts.

Gradually, though, asylums became more than treatment bins for aberrant members of the middle class. They became public houses of detention for people who acted oddly, especially poor people who had no place to go.[4] They became filled with alcoholics, depressives, old people, manics, paranoids, people who were flipped out.

At first, in the nineteenth century, these institutions were dedicated to "moral" (physical, persuasive) treatment. Gradually, as they became more and more overburdened, less and less staffed and funded, they were used simply to house great numbers of misfits. Although there are stories of kindness and cure, there are also stories of cruelty and violence, and of the growth of a class system within these asylums—authoritarian, sadistic, supported by humanitarian bureaucrats at the highest levels.

It's true that there has been some hospital reform recently. But

4. Much of this is documented in Michel Foucault, *Madness and Civilization,* trans. Richard Howard (New York: Pantheon, 1965).

it has been thin; the abuses still exist. Mental patients still have no assurance of their rights. Standards of cleanliness and appropriate treatment, of consent to procedures, of only voluntary commitment are still lacking. More upsetting, new incursions on people's minds and bodies are on the rise—with psychosurgery and lobotomy being developed in chronic facilities and, more ominously, in the prisons. The mental health professionals, backing the established order, have unquestioned authority and unchallenged sway over patients' lives.

It's interesting that at the same time there is a more or less romantic interest in "madness," which seems totally cut off from the realities of institutional life and experience. The students, the young, and the intelligentsia are fascinated with going crazy. The experience of going psychotic is ballyhooed by some as a healthy, regenerative experience, even to be sought by those tired and frustrated chronic sufferers usually found in the middle and upper classes.

Unfortunately, such popular interest has little to do with changing the mental health institutions, or with understanding the role of labeling people as psychotic, or even with setting up new, more humane institutions which could heal distress and educate politically. The followers of R. D. Laing have talked about setting up many new Kingsley Halls, but they have not done so. The most "audacious" plans seem to be setting up halfway homes— modeled on asylums from the 1850s. These alternatives have scarcely made a dent in the overall system, and they have been a haven, if for anyone, for the well-to-do and hip, alienated young. The bulk of the private and state mental institutions have only gotten more oppressive. Actual hospital reform is lagging far behind the rhetoric.

And that is only natural, considering who these institutions serve and whose interests they reflect. The weakness of "an alternative approach," the hippy-dippy, let-it-all-hang-out philosophy, is that it ignores the basic fact: that every institution in a class society is stamped with the mark of one class or another. This reality makes the institutions weapons in the class struggle. No alternative exists: a place is either part of the problem or part of the solution.

In the hospitals, abuses are commonplace. Shock treatment is given for punishment, or for "incorrect" behavior. Lobotomies are used to calm troublesome, chronic, or violent patients. Billions of dollars worth of tranquilizers and antidepressants are poured down people's throats or into their buttocks; these drugs were not known two decades ago, but are now a thriving industry. And the usual modes of "treatment" are still used—beatings, cold packs, detention, strait jackets, quiet rooms, strippings. The patients are in a Catch-22 situation: if they cooperate, they are medicated and brutalized; if they don't cooperate, they are seen as in need of even more medication and/or electroshock. In most mental institutions there is no court of appeals. The doctor's (or attendant's) word is law.

Criticism of the United States therapy establishment has come from many directions. *The Radical Therapist* (now *Rough Times*) began its course with a hard-hitting critique of the therapy business, which it has continued to the present day. Books by people within the establishment itself—Thomas Szasz, Seymour Halleck, Ronald Leifer, and others—have pointed out the need for change and have abolished the myth that therapy is value-free, objective, and clinical. They have shown how the notion of mental illness is used politically to deal with people whose difference threatens the system. The critique can be summed up as follows: therapy is a bourgeois institution in a society controlled by the bourgeoisie.[5] While pretending to advance personal liberation by solving emotional problems, it in fact supports the values of the ruling class, and sells them to the public. Therapy does indeed work on people's problems; but often it sees as "problems" what upsets the established order. It fosters individualism, competitiveness, and the sense that "my problems are in me." It has supported women's subjugation, and has gone along with the hypocrisy of the ruling class in creating conditions for homosexuality, and then declaring it an individual "illness" that it must treat. Private therapy provides its more affluent clients with "treatment" so they

5. I'm using "bourgeoisie" here not to refer to the middle class, but in the Marxist sense of those who own the means of production, and their closest lackeys.

can maintain their position in society and keep their values intact. It also acts as consultant to a whole variety of governmental and industrial groups, to contain the "psychopathology" of workers and poor people, and to increase their productive worth to the capitalist system. The public sector of mental health is concerned with treating (oppressing) the masses of working and poor people. It does this through total control of psychiatric labeling; through out-patient clinics which offer middle-class advice ("treatment") and medication; through the state mental hospitals which tranquilize and otherwise contain people who cannot function on the outside; and through the use of therapists as consultants to the layman via the media. Therapy has, of course, a human side: many of its practitioners genuinely want to help people, and genuinely think they are doing so. Objectively, though, one has to consider whose interests are really served by therapy, and who is really helped. The overwhelming amount of help ultimately supports the system.

First, the capitalists/imperialists create conditions which drive people batty; then, they provide "therapy" to deal with the "problems." The way to health, in in-patient or out-patient treatment, is to accept the ruling-class ideology: blame yourself, take your medicine, readjust your goals to conform to the way-things-are. All that is very clear to the people who get treated in state mental institutions, prisons, clinics, and so forth. The only place it's not so clear is in the private offices of posh shrinks, whose clients share their values.

It's true that many people in mental institutions are casualties. Their lives have been shattered by their experiences. Many have been broken by repeated psychiatric treatment in addition to life under capitalism: rapes, beatings, trauma, lack of jobs, poverty, constant oppression. Certainly "emotional distress" exists. It cripples many people in this country, just as capitalism does.

No one questions that the United States system of capitalism/ imperialism/racism/sexism maims people. It has wrecked the land of Indochina, committed genocide against Asian and native American peoples, and it brutalizes and destroys its own people day after day in cities and towns.

Each of us has been affected by this, some more than others. Conditions have been created for the development of criminals, addicts, sex perverts, sadists, and so on. The people who have been beaten into madness need help from somewhere, but they don't get it from the therapists.

The solution to this is twofold: (1) therapy for the people who need it, in a political context, controlled by the people themselves; and (2) a socialist revolution in this country to change control from the bourgeoisie to the working masses.

The mental patients' liberation movement today has arisen from the need of oppressed mental patients to defend themselves against their oppressors. Most mental patients come from the ranks of poor and working people. Mental patients' liberation is thus an aspect of the class struggle, and deserves to be carried out with that in mind. At times, however, this movement has been aware only of its own cause; it has sought reformist solutions (changing a law or two), or has mistaken the hospital attendant or nurse for the real enemy—the ruling class. When its appeal is still to bourgeois laws and bourgeois morality, mental patients' liberation makes demands which can be satisfied and co-opted. While we should all support the growing mental patients' liberation groups in their efforts to fight the oppression of mental patients, we should also maintain a critical stance toward their ideology; we should struggle with these groups so they will develop deeper roots in revolutionary theory and understand how their own oppression is related to the class struggle in this country, just as the struggle of women and of black people is both distinct from and part of the class struggle today.

The system has responded to the new outcry about mental institution abuses predictably: a few reforms, a few resignations, the promise to do better. It's the same nonsense. Community mental health centers continue to be colonial outposts and mental hospitals continue to be collecting bins. At the same time, the legitimate problems of the people—alcoholism, drug abuse, despair and depression—are being neglected principally because to deal with them means dealing with the real social/political forces which create them, not with each isolated, "messed up" person.

The mental health establishment exists because of mental illness. It is an industry designed to create the myth of mental illness in the society at large (rather than deal with the by-products of oppression) and then to live by treating it. The group of professionals makes its living from mental illness. When you get down to it, it has no stake in "curing" anybody; its main concern is perpetuating itself.

This anthology won't romanticize the experience of going crazy. It won't declare that psychosis is the cure for all our alienation. Rather, it seeks only to present the day-to-day oppression and suffering which goes on in mental institutions today, the constant degradation, the total control. Hopefully, it will help people, through understanding what's going on, to become more resolute in the struggle against such abuses and the people who create and support them.

I. THE PAST

Introduction

Oppression of mental patients is, of course, nothing new. The selections in this section provide some historical perspective on what's happening today.

Edgar Allan Poe's short story reflects many people's view of "lunatics." It also presents the revolutionary potential of inmates, which is being realized today in mental patients' liberation movements.

Clifford Beers is famous as the man who created the "mental hygiene movement" in the United States in the early part of this century. His book, *A Mind That Found Itself*, was a startling, candid, and dramatic description of his own psychosis and treatment. His description of what went on in mental hospitals is still true today, as later accounts in this book will show. Although some institutions have been changed over the years, the authoritarian/sadistic mentality Beers describes is still found on many hospital wards—and will continue to be found so long as mental institutions give their staff complete control over the inmates' lives and bodies.

Antonin Artaud was a French poet, actor, and dramatist who was institutionalized for the latter part of his life. His description of electroshock is evocative and chilling; the practice is on the rise in institutions in the United States.

Attitudes toward mental patients have historically revolved

1

around how unusual and dangerous they are—how their behavior threatens the rest of us and "civilized society" in general. The selections here show that these attitudes are not wholly accurate, that mental patients are oppressed, that "treatment" is a way of talking about containing and defusing people who threaten a cruel and barbaric "civilized" society. The "fantasies" of some patients may be closer to the truth than the doctors-wardens wish to acknowledge.

In an age when paranoia is justified, what do we say about those who are "healthy"?

1. EDGAR ALLAN POE:

The System of Dr. Tarr and Prof. Fether

During the autumn of 18—, while on a tour through the extreme southern provinces of France, my route led me within a few miles of a certain *Maison de Santé* or private mad-house, about which I had heard much, in Paris, from my medical friends. As I had never visited a place of the kind, I thought the opportunity too good to be lost; and so proposed to my travelling companion (a gentleman with whom I had made casual acquaintance a few days before), that we should turn aside, for an hour or so, and look through the establishment. To this he objected— pleading haste, in the first place, and, in the second, a very usual horror at the sight of a lunatic. He begged of me, however, not to let any mere courtesy toward himself interfere with the gratification of my curiosity, and said that he would ride on leisurely, so that I might overtake him during the day, or, at all events, during the next. As he bade me good-by, I bethought me that there might be some difficulty in obtaining access to the premises, and mentioned my fears on this point. He replied that, in fact, unless I had personal knowledge of the superintendent, Monsieur Maillard, or some credential in the way of a letter, a difficulty might be found to exist, as the regulations of these private mad-houses were more rigid than the public hospital laws. For himself, he added, he had, some years since, made the acquaintance of Maillard, and would so far assist me as to ride up to the door and introduce me; although his feeings on the subject of lunacy would not permit of his entering the house.

I thanked him, and, turning from the main road, we entered a grass-grown by-path, which, in half an hour, nearly lost itself in a dense forest, clothing the base of a mountain. Through this dank and gloomy wood we rode some two miles, when the *Maison de Santé* came in view. It was a fantastic *château,* much dilapidated, and indeed scarcely tenantable through age and neglect. Its aspect inspired me with absolute dread, and checking my horse, I half resolved to turn back. I soon, however, grew ashamed of my weakness, and proceeded.

As we rode up to the gate-way, I perceived it slightly open and the visage of a man peering through. In an instant afterward, this man came forth, accosted my companion by name, shook him cordially by the hand, and begged him to alight. It was Monsieur Maillard himself. He was a portly, fine-looking gentleman of the old school, with a polished manner, and a certain air of gravity, dignity, and authority which was very impressive.

My friend, having presented me, mentioned my desire to inspect the establishment, and received Monsieur Maillard's assurance that he would show me all attention, now took leave, and I saw him no more.

When he had gone, the superintendent ushered me into a small and exceedingly neat parlor, containing, among other indications of refined taste, many books, drawings, pots of flowers, and musical instruments. A cheerful fire blazed upon the hearth. At a piano, singing an aria from Bellini, sat a young and very beautiful woman, who, at my entrance, paused in her song, and received me with graceful courtesy. Her voice was low, and her whole manner subdued. I thought, too, that I perceived the traces of sorrow in her countenance, which was excessively, although to my taste, not unpleasingly, pale. She was attired in deep mourning, and excited in my bosom a feeling of mingled respect, interest, and admiration.

I had heard, at Paris, that the institution of Monsieur Maillard was managed upon what is vulgarly termed the "system of soothing"—that all punishments were avoided—that even confinement was seldom resorted to—that the patients, while secretly watched, were left much apparent liberty, and that most of them were permitted to roam about the house and grounds in the ordinary apparel of persons in right mind.

Keeping these impressions in view, I was cautious in what I said before the young lady; for I could not be sure that she was sane; and, in fact, there was a certain restless brilliancy about her eyes which half led me to imagine she was not. I confined my remarks, therefore, to general topics, and to such as I thought would not be displeasing or exciting even to a lunatic. She replied in a perfectly rational manner to all that I said; and even her original observations were marked with the soundest good sense; but a long acquaintance with the metaphysics of *mania,* had taught me to put no faith in such evidence of sanity, and I continued to practise, throughout the interview, the caution with which I commenced it.

Presently a smart footman in livery brought in a tray with fruit, wine, and other refreshments, of which I partook, the lady soon afterward leaving the room. As she departed I turned my eyes in an inquiring manner toward my host.

"No," he said, "oh, no—a member of my family—my niece, and a most accomplished woman."

"I beg a thousand pardons for the suspicion," I replied, "but of course you will know how to excuse me. The excellent administration of your affairs here is well understood in Paris, and I thought it just possible, you know—"

"Yes, yes—say no more—or rather it is myself who should thank you for the commendable prudence you have displayed. We seldom find so much of forethought in young men; and, more than once, some unhappy *contre-temps* has occurred in consequence of thoughtlessness on the part of our visitors. While my former system was in operation, and my patients were permitted the privilege of roaming to and fro at will, they were often aroused to a dangerous frenzy by injudicious persons who called to inspect the house. Hence I was obliged to enforce a rigid system of exclusion; and none obtained access to the premises upon whose discretion I could not rely."

"While your *former* system was in operation!" I said, repeating his words—"do I understand you, then, to say that the 'soothing system' of which I have heard so much is no longer in force?"

"It is now," he replied, "several weeks since we have concluded to renounce it forever."

"Indeed! you astonish me!"

"We found it, sir," he said, with a sigh, "absolutely necessary to return to the old usages. The *danger* of the soothing system was, at all times, appalling; and its advantages have been much overrated. I believe, sir, that in this house it has been given a fair trial, if ever in any. We did every thing that rational humanity could suggest. I am sorry that you could not have paid us a visit at an earlier period, that you might have judged for yourself. But I presume you are conversant with the soothing practice—with its details."

"Not altogether. What I have heard has been at third and fourth hand."

"I may state the system, then, in general terms, as one in which the patients were *ménagés*—humored. We contradicted *no* fancies which entered the brains of the mad. On the contrary, we not only indulged but encouraged them; and many of our most permanent cures have been thus effected. There is no argument which so touches the feeble reason of the madman as the *reductio ad absurdum*. We have had men, for example, who fancied themselves chickens. The cure was, to insist upon the thing as a fact—to accuse the patient of stupidity in not sufficiently perceiving it to be a fact—and thus to refuse him any other diet for a week than that which properly appertains to a chicken. In this manner a little corn and gravel were made to perform wonders."

"But was this species of acquiescence all?"

"By no means. We put much faith in amusements of a simple kind, such as music, dancing, gymnastic exercises generally, cards, certain classes of books, and so forth. We affected to treat each individual as if for some ordinary physical disorder; and the word 'lunacy' was never employed. A great point was to set each lunatic to guard the actions of all the others. To repose confidence in the understanding or discretion of a madman, is to gain him body and soul. In this way we were enabled to dispense with an expensive body of keepers."

"And you had no punishments of any kind?"

"None."

"And you never confined your patients?"

"Very rarely. Now and then, the malady of some individual growing to a crisis, or taking a sudden turn of fury, we conveyed him to a secret cell, lest his disorder should infect the rest, and there kept him until we could dismiss him to his friends—for with the raging maniac we have nothing to do. He is usually removed to the public hospitals."

"And you have now changed all this—and you think for the better?"

"Decidedly. The system had its disadvantages, and even its dangers. It is now, happily, exploded throughout all the *Maisons de Santé* of France."

"I am very much surprised," I said, "at what you tell me; for I made sure that, at this moment, no other method of treatment for mania existed in any portion of the country."

"You are young yet, my friend," replied my host, "but the time will arrive when you will learn to judge for yourself of what is going on in the world, without trusting to the gossip of others. Believe nothing you hear, and only one half that you see. Now about our *Maisons de Santé,* it is clear that some ignoramus has misled you. After dinner, however, when you have sufficiently recovered from the fatigue of your ride, I will be happy to take you over the house, and introduce to you a system which, in my opinion, and in that of everyone who has witnessed its operation, is incomparably the most effectual as yet devised."

"Your own?" I inquired—"one of your own invention?"

"I am proud," he replied, "to acknowledge that it is—at least in some measure."

In this manner I conversed with Monsieur Maillard for an hour or two, during which he showed me the gardens and conservatories of the place.

"I cannot let you see my patients," he said, "just at present. To a sensitive mind there is always more or less of the shocking in such exhibitions; and I do not wish to spoil your appetite for dinner. We will dine. I can give you some veal *à la St. Menehoult,* with cauliflowers in *velouté* sauce—after that a glass of *Clos de Vougeôt*—then your nerves will be sufficiently steadied."

At six, dinner was announced; and my host conducted me into a large *salle à manger,* where a very numerous company were assembled—twenty-five or thirty in all. They were, apparently, people of rank—certainly of high breeding—although their habiliments, I thought, were extravagantly rich, partaking somewhat too much of the ostentatious finery of the *ville cour.* I noticed that at least two-thirds of these guests were ladies; and some of the latter were by no means accoutred in what a Parisian would consider good taste at the present day. Many females, for example, whose age could not have been less than seventy, were bedecked with a profusion of jewelry, such as rings, bracelets, and ear-rings, and wore their bosoms and arms shamefully bare. I observed, too, that very few of the dresses were well made—or, at least, that very few of them fitted the wearers. In looking about, I discovered the interesting girl to whom Monsieur Maillard had presented me in the little parlor; but my surprise was great to see her wearing a hoop and farthingale, with high-heeled shoes, and a dirty cap of Brussels lace, so much too large for her that it gave her face a ridiculously diminutive expression. When I had first seen her, she was attired most becomingly, in deep mourning. There was an air of oddity, in short, about the dress of the whole party, which, at first, caused me to recur to my original idea of the "soothing system," and to fancy that Monsieur Maillard had been willing to deceive me until after dinner, that I might experience no uncomfortable feelings during the repast, at finding myself dining with lunatics; but I remembered having been informed, in Paris, that the southern provincialists were a peculiarly eccentric people, with a vast number of antiquated notions; and then, too, upon conversing with several members of the company, my apprehensions were immediately and fully dispelled.

The dining-room itself, although perhaps sufficiently comfortable and of good dimensions, had nothing too much of elegance about it. For example, the floor was uncarpeted; in France, however, a carpet is frequently dispensed with. The windows, too, were without curtains; the shutters, being shut, were securely fastened with iron bars, applied diagonally, after the fashion of our shop-shutters. The apartment, I observed, formed, in itself, a wing of the *château,* and thus the windows were on three sides of the parallelogram, the door being at the other. There were no less than ten windows in all.

The table was superbly set out. It was loaded with plate, and more than loaded with delicacies. The profusion was absolutely barbaric. There were meats enough to have feasted the Anakim. Never, in all my life, had I witnessed so lavish, so wasteful an expenditure of the good things of life. There seemed very little taste, however, in the arrangements; and my eyes, accustomed to quiet lights, were sadly offended by the prodigious glare of a multitude of wax candles, which, in silver *candelabra,* were deposited upon the table, and all about the room, wherever it was possible to find a place. There were several active servants in attendance; and, upon a large table, at the farther end of the apartment, were seated seven or eight people with fiddles, fifes, trombones, and a drum. These fellows annoyed me very much, at intervals, during the repast, by an infinite variety of noises, which were intended for music, and which appeared to afford much entertainment to all present, with the exception of myself.

Upon the whole, I could not help thinking that there was much of the *bizarre* about every thing I saw—but then the world is made up of all kinds of persons, with all modes of thought, and all sorts of conventional customs. I had travelled, too, so much, as to be quite an adept at the *nil admirari;* so I took my seat very coolly at the right hand of my host, and, having an excellent appetite, did justice to the good cheer set before me.

The conversation, in the meantime, was spirited and general. The ladies, as usual, talked a great deal. I soon found that nearly all the company were well educated; and my host was a world of good-humored anecdote in himself. He seemed quite willing to speak of his position as superintendent of a *Maison de Santé;* and, indeed, the topic of lunacy was, much to my surprise, a favorite one with all present. A great many amusing stories were told, having reference to the *whims* of the patients.

"We had a fellow here once," said a fat little gentleman, who sat at my right—"a fellow that fancied himself a tea-pot; and by the way, is it not especially singular how often this particular crotchet has entered the brain of the lunatic? There is scarcely an insane asylum in France which cannot supply a human tea-pot. *Our* gentleman was a Britannia-ware tea-pot, and was careful to polish himself every morning with buckskin and whiting."

"And then," said a tall man just opposite, "we had here, not long ago, a person who had taken it into his head that he was a donkey—which, allegorically speaking, you will say, was quite true. He was a troublesome patient; and we had much ado to keep him within bounds. For a long time he would eat nothing but thistles; but of this idea we soon cured him by insisting upon his eating nothing else. Then he was perpetually kicking out his heels—so—so—" .

"Mr. De Kock! I will thank you to behave yourself!" here interrupted an old lady, who sat next to the speaker. "Please keep your feet to yourself! You have spoiled by brocade! Is it necessary, pray, to illustrate a remark in so practical a style? Our friend here can surely comprehend you without all this. Upon my word, you are nearly as great a donkey as the poor unfortunate imagined himself. Your acting is very natural, as I live."

"Mille pardons! Ma'm'selle!" replied Monsieur De Kock, thus addressed—"a thousand pardons! I had no intention of offending. Ma'm'selle Laplace—Monsieur De Kock will do himself the honor of taking wine with you."

Here Monsieur De Kock bowed low, kissed her hand with much ceremony, and took wine with Ma'm'selle Laplace.

"Allow me, *mon ami,*" now said Monsieur Maillard, addressing myself, "allow me to send you a morsel of this veal *à la St. Menehoult*—you will find it particularly fine."

At this instant three sturdy waiters had just succeeded in depositing safely upon the table an enormous dish, or trencher, containing what I supposed to be the *"monstrum, horrendum, informe, ingens, cui lumen ademptum."* A closer scrutiny assured me, however, that it was only a small calf roasted whole, and set upon its knees, with an apple in its mouth, as is the English fashion of dressing a hare.

"Thank you, no," I replied; "to say the truth, I am not particularly partial to veal *à la St.*——what is it?—for I do not find that it altogether agrees with me. I will change my plate, however, and try some of the rabbit."

There were several side-dishes on the table, containing what appeared to be the ordinary French rabbit—a very delicious *morceau,* which I can recommend.

"Pierre," cried the host, "change this gentleman's plate, and give him a side-piece of this rabbit *au-chat.*"

"This what?" said I.

"This rabbit *au-chat.*"

"Why, thank you—upon second thoughts, no. I will just help myself to some of the ham."

There is no knowing what one eats, thought I to myself, at the tables of these people of the province. I will have none of their rabbit *au-chat*—and, for the matter of that, none of their *cat-au-rabbit* either.

"And then," said a cadaverous-looking personage, near the foot of the table, taking up the thread of the conversation where it had been broken off—"and then, among other oddities, we had a patient, once upon a time, who very pertinaciously maintained himself to be a Cordova cheese, and went about, with a knife in his hand, soliciting his friends to try a small slice from the middle of his leg."

"He was a great fool, beyond doubt," interposed some one, "but not to be compared with a certain individual whom we all know, with the exception of this strange gentleman. I mean the man who took himself for a bottle of champagne, and always went off with a pop and a fizz, in this fashion."

Here the speaker, very rudely, as I thought, put his right thumb in his left cheek, withdrew it with a sound resembling the popping of a cork, and then, by a dexterous movement of the tongue upon the teeth, created a sharp hissing and fizzing, which lasted for several minutes, in imitation of the frothing of champagne. This behavior, I saw plainly, was not very pleasing to Monsieur Maillard; but that gentleman said nothing, and the conversation was resumed by a very lean little man in a big wig.

"And then there was an ignoramus," said he, "who mistook himself for a frog; which, by the way, he resembled in no little degree. I wish you could have seen him, sir"—here the speaker addressed myself—"it would have done your heart good to see the natural airs that he put on. Sir, if that man was *not* a frog, I can only observe that it is a pity he was not. His croak thus—o-o-o-o-gh—o-o-o-o-gh! was the finest note in the world—B flat; and when he put his elbows upon the table thus—after taking a glass or two of wine—and distended his mouth, thus, and rolled up his eyes, thus, and winked them with excessive rapidity, thus, why then, sir, I take it upon myself to say, positively, that you would have been lost in admiration of the genius of the man."

"I have no doubt of it," I said.

"And then," said somebody else, "then there was Petit Gaillard, who thought himself a pinch of snuff, and was truly distressed because he could not take himself between his own finger and thumb."

"And then there was Jules Desoulières, who was a very singular genius, indeed, and went mad with the idea that he was a pumpkin. He persecuted the cook to make him up into pies—a thing which the cook indignantly refused to do. For my part, I am by no means sure that a pumpkin pie *à la Desoulières* would not have been very capital eating indeed!"

"You astonish me!" said I; and I looked inquisitively at Monsieur Maillard.

"Ha! ha! ha!" said that gentleman—"he! he! he!—hi! hi! hi!—ho! ho! ho!—hu! hu! hu!—very good indeed! You must not be astonished, *mon ami;* our friend here is a wit—a *drôle*—you must not understand him to the letter."

"And then," said some other one of the party—"then there was

Bouffon Le Grand—another extraordinary personage in his way. He grew deranged through love, and fancied himself possessed of two heads. One of these he maintained to be the head of Cicero; the other he imagined a composite one, being Demosthenes' from the top of the forehead to the mouth, and Lord Brougham's from the mouth to the chin. It is not impossible that he was wrong; but he would have convinced you of his being in the right; for he was a man of great eloquence. He had an absolute passion for oratory, and could not refrain from display. For example, he used to leap upon the dinner-table thus, and—and—"

Here a friend, at the side of the speaker, put a hand upon his shoulder and whispered a few words in his ear; upon which he ceased talking with great suddenness, and sank back within his chair.

"And then," said the friend who had whispered, "there was Boullard, the tee-totum. I call him the tee-totum because, in fact, he was seized with the droll, but not altogether irrational, crotchet, that he had been converted into a tee-totum. You would have roared with laughter to see him spin. He would turn round upon one heel by the hour, in this manner—so—"

Here the friend whom he had just interrupted by a whisper, performed an exactly similar office for himself.

"But then," cried an old lady, at the top of her voice, "your Monsieur Boullard was a madman, and a very silly madman at best; for who, allow me to ask you, ever heard of a human tee-totum? The thing is absurd. Madame Joyeuse was a more sensible person, as you know. She had a crotchet, but it was instinct with common sense, and gave pleasure to all who had the honor of her acquaintance. She found, upon mature deliberation, that, by some accident, she had been turned into a chicken-cock; but, as such, she behaved with propriety. She flapped her wings with prodigious effect—so—so—so—and, as for her crow, it was delicious! Cock-a-doodle-doo!—cock-a-doodle-doo!—cock-a-doodle-de-doo-doo-dooo-do-o-o-o-o-o-o!"

"Madame Joyeuse, I will thank you to behave yourself!" here interrupted our host, very angrily. "You can either conduct yourself as a lady should do, or you can quit the table forthwith—take your choice."

The lady (whom I was much astonished to hear addressed as Madame Joyeuse, after the description of Madame Joyeuse she had just given) blushed up to the eyebrows, and seemed exceedingly abashed at the reproof. She hung down her head, and said not a syllable in reply. But another and younger lady resumed the theme. It was my beautiful girl of the little parlor.

"Oh, Madame Joyeuse *was* a fool!" she exclaimed, "but there was really much sound sense, after all, in the opinion of Eugénie Salsafette. She was a very beautiful and painfully modest young lady, who thought the ordinary mode of habiliment indecent, and wished to dress herself, always, by getting outside instead of inside of her clothes. It is a thing very easily done, after all. You have only to do so—and then so—so—so—and then so—so—so—and then—"

"Mon dieu! Ma'm'selle Salsafette!" here cried a dozen voices at once. "What *are* you about?—forbear!—that is sufficient!—we see, very plainly, how it is done!—hold! hold!" and several persons were already leaping from their seats to withhold Ma'm'selle Salsafette from putting herself upon a par with the Medicean Venus, when the point was very effectually and suddenly accomplished by a series of loud screams, or yells, from some portion of the main body of the *château*.

My nerves were very much affected, indeed, by these yells; but the rest of the company I really pitied. I never saw any set of reasonable people so thoroughly frightened in my life. They all grew as pale as so many corpses, and, shrinking within their seats, sat quivering and gibbering with terror, and listening for a repetition of the sound. It came again—louder and seemingly nearer—and then a third time *very* loud, and then a fourth time with a vigor evidently diminished. At this apparent dying away of the noise, the spirits of the company were immediately regained, and all was life and ancedote as before. I now ventured to inquire the cause of the disturbance.

"A mere *bagatelle,*" said Monsieur Maillard. "We are used to these things, and care really very little about them. The lunatics, every now and then, get up a howl in concert; one starting another, as is sometimes the case with a bevy of dogs at night. It occasionally happens, however, that the *concerto* yells are succeeded by a simultaneous effort at breaking loose; when, of course, some little danger is to be apprehended."

"And how many have you in charge?"

"At present we have not more than ten, all together."

"Principally females, I presume?"

"Oh, no—every one of them men, and stout fellows, too, I can tell you."

"Indeed! I have always understood that the majority of lunatics were of the gentler sex."

"It is generally so, but not always. Some time ago, there were about twenty-seven patients here; and, of that number, no less than eighteen were women; but, lately, matters have changed very much, as you see."

"Yes—have changed very much, as you see," here interrupted the gentleman who had broken the shins of Ma'm'selle Laplace.

"Yes—have changed very much, as you see!" chimed in the whole company at once.

"Hold your tongues, every one of you!" said my host, in a great rage. Whereupon the whole company maintained a dead silence for nearly a minute. As for one lady, she obeyed Monsieur Maillard to the letter, and thrusting out her tongue, which was an excessively long one, held it very resignedly, with both hands, until the end of the entertainment.

"And this gentlewoman," said I, to Monsieur Maillard, bending over and addressing him in a whisper—"this good lady who has just spoken, and who gives us the cock-a-doodle-de-doo—she, I presume, is harmless—quite harmless, eh?"

"Harmless!" ejaculated he, in unfeigned surprise, "why—why, what *can* you mean?"

"Only slightly touched?" said I, touching my head. "I take it for granted that she is not particularly—not dangerously affected, eh?"

"*Mon dieu!* what *is* it you imagine? This lady, my particular old friend, Madame Joyeuse, is as absolutely sane as myself. She has her little eccentricities, to be sure—but then, you know, all old women—all *very* old women—are more or less eccentric!"

"To be sure," said I—"to be sure—and then the rest of these ladies and gentlemen—"

"Are my friends and keepers," interrupted Monsieur Maillard, drawing himself up with *hauteur*—"my very good friends and assistants."

"What! all of them?" I asked—"the women and all?"

"Assuredly," he said—"we could not do at all without the women; they are the best lunatic nurses in the world; they have a way of their own, you know; their bright eyes have a marvellous effect—something like the fascination of the snake, you know."

"To be sure," said I—"to be sure! They behave a little odd, eh? —they are a little *queer*, eh?—don't you think so?"

"Odd!—queer!—why, do you *really* think so? We are not very prudish, to be sure, here in the South—do pretty much as we please —enjoy life, and all that sort of thing, you know—"

"To be sure," said I—"to be sure."

"And then, perhaps, this *Clos de Vougeôt* is a little heady, you know—a little *strong*—you understand, eh?"

"To be sure," said I—"to be sure. By the by, Monsieur, did I understand you to say that the system you have adopted in place of the celebrated soothing system, was one of very rigorous severity?"

"By no means. Our confinement is necessarily close; but the treatment—the medical treatment, I mean—is rather agreeable to the patients than otherwise."

"And the new system is one of your own invention?"

"Not altogether. Some portions of it are referable to Doctor Tarr, of whom you have, necessarily, heard; and, again, there are modifications in my plan which I am happy to acknowledge as belonging of right to the celebrated Fether, with whom, if I mistake not, you have the honor of an intimate acquaintance."

"I am quite ashamed to confess," I replied, "that I have never even heard the names of either gentleman before."

"Good heavens!" ejaculated my host, drawing back his chair abruptly, and uplifting his hands. "I surely do not hear you aright!

You did not intend to say, eh? that you had never *heard* either of the learned Doctor Tarr, or of the celebrated Professor Fether?"

"I am forced to acknowledge my ignorance," I replied; "but the truth should be held inviolate above all things. Nevertheless, I feel humbled to the dust, not to be acquainted with the works of these, no doubt, extraordinary men. I will seek out their writings forthwith, and peruse them with deliberate care. Monsieur Maillard, you have really—I must confess it—you have *really*—made me ashamed of myself!"

And this was the fact.

"Say no more, my good young friend," he said kindly, pressing my hand—"join me now in a glass of Sauterne."

We drank. The company followed our example without stint. They chatted—they jested—they laughed—they perpetrated a thousand absurdities—the fiddles shrieked—the drum row-de-dowed—the trombones bellowed like so many brazen bulls of Phalaris—and the whole scene, growing gradually worse and worse, as the wines gained the ascendancy, became at length a sort of pandemonium *in petto*. In the meantime, Monsieur Maillard and myself, with some bottles of Sauterne and Vougeôt between us, continued our conversation at the top of the voice. A word spoken in an ordinary key stood no more chance of being heard than the voice of a fish from the bottom of Niagara Falls.

"And, sir," said I, screaming in his ear, "you mentioned something before dinner about the danger incurred in the old system of soothing. How is that?"

"Yes," he replied, "there was, occasionally, very great danger indeed. There is no accounting for the caprices of madmen; and, in my opinion, as well as in that of Dr. Tarr and Professor Fether, it is *never* safe to permit them to run at large unattended. A lunatic may be 'soothed,' as it is called, for a time, but, in the end, he is very apt to become obstreperous. His cunning, too, is proverbial and great. If he has a project in view, he conceals his design with a marvellous wisdom; and the dexterity with which he counterfeits sanity, presents, to the metaphysician, one of the most singular problems in the study of mind. When a madman appears *thoroughly* sane, indeed, it is high time to put him in a strait-jacket."

"But the *danger,* my dear sir, of which you were speaking—in your own experience—during your control of this house—have you had practical reason to think liberty hazardous in the case of a lunatic?"

"Here?—in my own experience?—why, I may say, yes. For example:—no *very* long while ago, a singular circumstance occurred in this very house. The 'soothing system,' you know, was then in operation, and the patients were at large. They behaved remarkably well—especially so—any one of sense might have known that some devilish scheme was brewing from that particular fact, that the fellows behaved so *remarkably* well. And, sure enough, one fine morning the keepers found themselves pinioned hand and foot, and thrown into the cells, where they were attended, as if *they* were the lunatics, by the lunatics themselves, who had usurped the offices of the keepers."

"You don't tell me so! I never heard of anything so absurd in my life!"

"Fact—it all came to pass by means of a stupid fellow—a lunatic—who, by some means, had taken it into his head that he had invented a better system of government than any ever heard of before—of lunatic government, I mean. He wished to give his invention a trial, I suppose, and so he persuaded the rest of the patients to join him in a conspiracy for the overthrow of the reigning powers."

"And he really succeeded?"

"No doubt of it. The keepers and kept were soon made to exchange places. Not that exactly either, for the madmen had been free, but the keepers were shut up in cells forthwith, and treated, I am sorry to say, in a very cavalier manner."

"But I presume a counter-revolution was soon effected. This condition of things could not have long existed. The country people in the neighborhood—visitors coming to see the establishment—would have given the alarm."

"There you are out. The head rebel was too cunning for that. He admitted no visitors at all—with the exception, one day, of a very stupid-looking young gentleman of whom he had no reason to be afraid. He let him in to see the place—just by way of variety—

to have a little fun with him. As soon as he had gammoned him sufficiently, he let him out, and sent him about his business."

"And *how* long, then, did the madmen reign?"

"Oh, a very long time, indeed—a month certainly—how much longer I can't precisely say. In the meantime, the lunatics had a jolly season of it—that you may swear. They doffed their own shabby clothes, and made free with the family wardrobe and jewels. The cellars of the *château* were well stocked with wine; and these madmen are just the devils that know how to drink it. They lived well, I can tell you."

"And the treatment—what was the particular species of treatment which the leader of the rebels put into operation?"

"Why, as for that, a madman is not necessarily a fool, as I have already observed; and it is my honest opinion that his treatment was a much better treatment than that which it superseded. It was a very capital system indeed—simple—neat—no trouble at all—in fact it was delicious—it was—"

Here my host's observations were cut short by another series of yells, of the same character as those which had previously disconcerted us. This time, however, they seemed to proceed from persons rapidly approaching.

"Gracious heavens!" I ejaculated—"the lunatics have most undoubtedly broken loose."

"I very much fear it is so," replied Monsieur Maillard, now becoming excessively pale. He had scarcely finished the sentence, before loud shouts and imprecations were heard beneath the windows; and, immediately afterward, it became evident that some persons outside were endeavoring to gain entrance into the room. The door was beaten with what appeared to be a sledge-hammer, and the shutters were wrenched and shaken with prodigious violence.

A scene of the most terrible confusion ensued. Monsieur Maillard, to my excessive astonishment, threw himself under the sideboard. I had expected more resolution at his hands. The members of the orchestra, who, for the last fifteen minutes, had been seemingly too much intoxicated to do duty, now sprang all at once to their feet and to their instruments, and, scrambling upon their table, broke out, with one accord, into, "Yankee Doodle," which they performed, if not exactly in tune, at least with an energy superhuman, during the whole of the uproar.

Meantime, upon the main dining-table, among the bottles and glasses, leaped the gentleman who, with such difficulty, had been restrained from leaping there before. As soon as he fairly settled himself, he commenced an oration, which, no doubt, was a very capital one, if it could only have been heard. At the same moment, the man with the tee-totum predilection, set himself to spinning around the apartment, with immense energy, and with arms outstretched at right angles with his body, so that he had all the air of a tee-totum in fact, and knocked everybody down that happened to get in his way. And now, too, hearing an incredible popping and fizzing of champagne, I discovered at length that it proceeded from the person who performed the bottle of that delicate drink during dinner. And then, again, the frog-man croaked away as if the salvation of his soul depended upon every note that he uttered. And, in the midst of all this, the continuous braying of a donkey arose over all. As for my old friend, Madame Joyeuse, I really could have wept for the poor lady, she appeared so terribly perplexed. All she did, however, was to stand up in a corner, by the fireplace, and sing out incessantly at the top of her voice, "Cock-a-doodle-de-dooooooh!"

And now came the climax—the catastrophe of the drama. As no resistance, beyond whooping and yelling and cock-a-doodling, was offered to the encroachments of the party without, the ten windows were very speedily, and almost simultaneously, broken in. But I shall never forget the emotions of wonder and horror with which I gazed, when, leaping through these windows, and down among us *pêle-mêle,* fighting, stamping, scratching, and howling, there rushed a perfect army of what I took to be chimpanzees, ourang-outangs, or big black baboons of the Cape of Good Hope.

I received a terrible beating—after which I rolled under a sofa and lay still. After lying there some fifteen minutes, however, during which time I listened with all my ears to what was going on in the room, I came to some satisfactory *dénouement* of this tragedy. Monsieur Maillard, it appeared, in giving me the account of the lunatic who had excited his fellows to rebellion, had been merely relating his own exploits. This gentleman had, indeed, some two or three years before, been the superintendent of the establishment; but grew crazy himself, and so became a patient. This fact was unknown to the travelling companion who introduced me. The keepers, ten in number, having been suddenly overpowered, were first well tarred, then carefully feathered, and then shut up in underground cells. They had been so imprisoned for more than a month, during which period Monsieur Maillard had generously allowed them not only the tar and feathers (which constituted his "system"), but some bread and abundance of water. The latter was pumped on them daily. At length, one escaping through a sewer, gave freedom to all the rest.

The "soothing system," with important modifications, has been resumed at the *château;* yet I cannot help agreeing with Monsieur Maillard, that his own "treatment" was a very capital one of its kind. As he justly observed, it was "simple—neat—and gave no trouble at all—not the least."

I have only to add that, although I have searched every library in Europe for the works of Doctor *Tarr* and Professor *Fether,* I have, up to the present day, utterly failed in my endeavors to procure a copy.

2. CLIFFORD BEERS:
A Mind That Found Itself*

I

Choice of a sanatorium by people of limited means is, unfortunately, very restricted. Though my relatives believed the one in which I was placed was at least fairly well conducted, events proved otherwise. From a modest beginning made not many years previously, it had enjoyed a mushroom growth. About two hundred and fifty patients were harbored in a dozen or more small frame buildings, suggestive of a mill settlement. Outside the limits of a city and in a state where there was lax official supervision, owing in part to faulty laws, the owner of this little settlement of woe had erected a nest of veritable fire-traps in which helpless sick people were forced to risk their lives. This was a necessary procedure if the owner was to grind out an exorbitant income on his investment.

The same spirit of economy and commercialism pervaded the entire institution. Its worst manifestation was in the employment of the meanest type of attendant—men willing to work for the paltry wage of eighteen dollars a month. Very seldom did competent attendants consent to work there, and then usually because of a scarcity of profitable employment elsewhere. Providentially for me, such an attendant came upon the scene. This young man, so long as he remained in the good graces of the owner-superin-

* SOURCE: Clifford Beers, from *A Mind That Found Itself*. Pp. 41–50, 98–101, 128–140, 160–163, 168–171. Copyright 1907, 1917, 1921, 1923, 1931, 1932, 1934, 1935, 1937, 1939, 1940, 1942, 1944, 1948, 1953 by the American Foundation for Mental Hygiene, Inc. Reprinted by permission of Doubleday & Company, Inc.

tendent, was admittedly one of the best attendants he had ever had. Yet aside from a five-dollar bill which a relative had sent me at Christmas and which I had refused to accept because of my belief that it, like my relatives, was counterfeit—aside from that bill, which was turned over to the attendant by my brother, he received no additional pecuniary rewards. His chief reward lay in his consciousness of the fact that he was protecting me against injustices which surely would have been visited upon me had he quitted his position and left me to the mercies of the owner and his ignorant assistants. To-day, with deep appreciation, I contrast the treatment I received at his hands with that which I suffered during the three weeks preceding his appearance on the scene. During that period, no fewer than seven attendants contributed to my misery. Though some of them were perhaps decent enough fellows outside a sickroom, not one had the right to minister to a patient in my condition.

The two who were first put in charge of me did not strike me with their fists or even threaten to do so; but their unconscious lack of consideration for my comfort and peace of mind was torture. They were typical eighteen-dollar-a-month attendants. Another of the same sort, on one occasion, cursed me with a degree of brutality which I prefer not to recall, much less record. And a few days later the climax was appropriately capped when still another attendant perpetrated an outrage which a sane man would have resented to the point of homicide. He was a man of the coarsest type. His hands would have done credit to a longshoreman—fingers knotted and nearly twice the normal size. Because I refused to obey a peremptory command, and this at a time when I habitually refused even on pain of imagined torture to obey or to speak, this brute not only cursed me with abandon, he deliberately spat upon me. I was a mental incompetent, but like many others in a similar position I was both by antecedents and by training a gentleman. Vitriol could not have seared my flesh more deeply than the venom of this human viper stung my soul! Yet, as I was rendered speechless by delusions, I could offer not so much as a word of protest. I trust that it is not now too late, however, to protest in behalf of the thousands of outraged patients in private and state hospitals whose mute submission to such indignities has never been recorded.

Of the readiness of an unscrupulous owner to employ inferior attendants, I shall offer a striking illustration. The capable attendant who acted as my protector at this sanatorium has given me an affidavit embodying certain facts which, of course, I could not have known at the time of their occurrence. The gist of this sworn statement is as follows: One day a man—seemingly a tramp—approached the main building of the sanatorium and inquired for the owner. He soon found him, talked with him a few minutes, and an hour or so later he was sitting at the bedside of an old and infirm man. This aged patient had recently been committed to the institution by relatives who had labored under the common delusion that the payment of a considerable sum of money each week would insure kindly treatment. When this tramp-attendant first appeared, all his visible worldly possessions were contained in a small bundle which he carried under his arm. So filthy were his person and his clothes that he received a compulsory bath and another suit before being assigned to duty. He then began to earn his four dollars and fifty cents a week by sitting several hours a day in the room with the aged man, sick unto death. My informant soon engaged him in conversation. What did he learn? First, that the uncouth stranger had never before so much as crossed the threshold of a hospital. His last job had been as a member of a section-gang on a railroad. From the roadbed of a railway to the bedside of a man about to die was indeed a change which might have taxed the adaptability of a more versatile being. But coarse as he was, this unkempt novice did not abuse his charge—except in so far as his inability to interpret or anticipate wants contributed to the sick man's distress. My own attendant, realizing that the patient was suffering for the want of skilled attention, spent a part of his time in this unhappy room, which was but across the hall from my own. The end soon came.

My attendant, who had had training as a nurse, detected the unmistakable signs of impending death. He forthwith informed the owner of the sanatorium that the patient was in a dying condition, and urged him (a doctor) to go at once to the bedside. The doctor refused to comply with the request on the plea that he was at the time "too busy." When at last he did visit the room, the patient was dead. Then came the supervisor, who took charge of the body. As it was being carried from the room the supervisor, the "handy man" of the owner, said: "There goes the best paying patient the institution had; the doctor" (meaning the owner) "was getting eighty-five dollars a week out of him." Of this sum not more than twenty dollars at most, at the time this happened, could be considered as "cost of maintenance." The remaining sixty-five dollars went into the pocket of the owner. Had the man lived for one year, the owner might have pocketed (so far as this one case was concerned) the neat but wicked profit of thirty-three hundred and eighty dollars. And what would the patient have received? The same privilege of living in neglect and dying neglected.

II

For the first few weeks after my arrival at the sanatorium, I was cared for by two attendants, one by day and one by night. I was still helpless, being unable to put my feet out of bed, much less upon the floor, and it was necessary that I be continually watched lest an impulse to walk should seize me. After a month or six weeks, however, I grew stronger, and from that time only one person was assigned to care for me. He was with me all day, and slept at night in the same room.

The earliest possible dismissal of one of my two attendants was expedient for the family purse; but such are the deficiencies in the prevailing treatment of the insane that relief in one direction often occasions evil in another. No sooner was the expense thus reduced than I was subjected to a detestable form of restraint which amounted to torture. To guard me at night while the remaining attendant slept, my hands were imprisoned in what is known as a "muff." A muff, innocent enough to the eyes of those who have never worn one, is in reality a relic of the Inquisition. It is an instrument of restraint which has been in use for centuries and even in many of our public and private institutions is still in use. The muff I wore was made of canvas, and differed in construction from a muff designed for the hands of fashion only in the inner partition, also of canvas, which separated my hands, but allowed them to overlap. At either end was a strap which buckled tightly around the wrist and was locked.

The assistant physician, when he announced to me that I was to be subjected at night to this restraint, broke the news gently—so gently that I did not then know, nor did I guess for several months, why this thing was done to me. And thus it was that I drew deductions of my own which added not a little to my torture.

The gas jet in my room was situated at a distance, and stronger light was needed to find the keyholes and lock the muff when adjusted. Hence, an attendant was standing by with a lighted candle. Seating himself on the side of the bed, the physician said: "You won't try again to do what you did in New Haven, will you?" Now one may have done many things in a city where he has lived for a score of years, and it is not surprising that I failed to catch the meaning of the doctor's question. It was only after months of secret puzzling that I at last did discover his reference to my attempted suicide. But now the burning candle in the hands of the attendant, and a certain similarity between the doctor's name and the name of a man whose trial for arson I once attended out of idle curiosity, led me to imagine that in some way I had been connected with that crime. For months I firmly believed I stood charged as an accomplice.

The putting on of the muff was the most humiliating incident of my life. The shaving of my legs and the wearing of the court-plaster brand of infamy had been humiliating, but those experiences had not overwhelmed my very heart as did this bitter ordeal. I resisted weakly, and, after the muff was adjusted and locked, for the first time since my mental collapse I wept. And I remember distinctly why I wept. The key that locked the muff unlocked in imagination the door of the home in New Haven which I believed I had disgraced—and seemed for a time to unlock my heart. Anguish beat my mind into a momentary sanity, and with a wholly sane emotion I keenly felt my imagined disgrace. My thoughts centred on my mother. Her (and other members of the family) I could plainly see at home in a state of dejection and despair over her imprisoned and heartless son. I wore the muff each night for several weeks, and for the first few nights the unhappy glimpses of a ruined home recurred and increased my sufferings.

It was not always as an instrument of restraint that the muff was employed. Frequently it was used as a means of discipline on account of supposed stubborn disobedience. Many times was I roughly overpowered by two attendants who locked my hands and coerced me to do whatever I had refused to do. My arms and hands were my only weapons of defence. My feet were still in plaster casts, and my back had been so severely injured as to necessitate my lying flat upon it most of the time. It was thus that these unequal fights were fought. And I had not even the satisfaction of tongue-lashing my oppressors, for I was practically speechless.

My attendants, like most others in such institutions, were incapable of understanding the operations of my mind, and what they could not understand they would seldom tolerate. Yet they were not entirely to blame. They were simply carrying out to the letter orders received from the doctors.

To ask a patient in my condition to take a little medicated sugar seemed reasonable. But from my point of view my refusal was justifiable. That innocuous sugar disc to me seemed saturated with the blood of loved ones; and so much as to touch it was to shed their blood—perhaps on the very scaffold on which I was destined to die. For myself I cared little. I was anxious to die, and eagerly would I have taken the sugar disc had I had any reason to believe that it was deadly poison. The sooner I could die and be forgotten, the better for all with whom I had ever come in contact. To continue to live was simply to be the treacherous tool of unscrupulous detectives, eager to exterminate my innocent relatives and friends, if so their fame could be made secure in the annals of their craft.

But the thoughts associated with the taking of the medicine were seldom twice alike. If before taking it something happened to remind me of mother, father, some other relative, or a friend, I imagined that compliance would compromise, if not eventually destroy, that particular person. Who would not resist when meek acceptance would be a confession which would doom his own mother or father to prison, or ignominy, or death? It was for this that I was reviled, for this, subjected to cruel restraint.

They thought I was stubborn. In the strict sense of the word there is no such thing as a stubborn insane person. The truly stubborn men and women in the world are sane; and the fortunate prevalence of sanity may be approximately estimated by the preponderance of stubbornness in society at large. When one possessed of the power of recognizing his own errors continues to hold an unreasonable belief—that is stubbornness. But for a man bereft of reason to adhere to an idea which to him seems absolutely correct and true because he has been deprived of the means of detecting his error—that is not stubbornness. It is a symptom of his disease, and merits the indulgence of forbearance, if not genuine sympathy. Certainly the afflicted one deserves no punishment. As well punish with a blow the cheek that is disfigured by the mumps. . . .

It was about the second week that my reformative turn of mind became acute. The ward in which I was confined was well furnished and as homelike as such a place could be, though in justice to my own home I must observe that the resemblance was not great. About the so-called violent ward I had far less favorable ideas. Though I had not been subjected to physical abuse during the first fourteen months of my stay here, I had seen unnecessary and often brutal force used by the attendants in managing several so-called violent patients, who, upon their arrival, had been placed in the ward where I was. I had also heard convincing rumors of rough treatment of irresponsible patients in the violent ward.

At once I determined to conduct a thorough investigation of the institution. In order that I might have proof that my intended action was deliberate, my first move was to tell one or two fellow-patients that I should soon transgress some rule in such a way as to necessitate my removal to the violent ward. At first I thought of breaking a few panes of glass; but my purpose was accomplished in another way—and, indeed, sooner than I had anticipated. My conservator, in my presence, had told the assistant physician that the doctors could permit me to telephone him whenever they should see fit. It was rather with the wish to test the unfriendly physician than to satisfy any desire to speak with my conservator that one morning I asked permission to call up the latter. That very morning I had received a letter from him. This the doctor knew, for I showed him the letter—but not its contents. It was on the letter that I based my demand, though in it my brother did not even intimate that he wished to speak to me. The doctor, however, had no way of knowing that my statement was not true. To deny my request was simply one of his ill-advised whims, and his refusal was given with customary curtness and contempt. I met his refusal in kind, and presented him with a trenchant critique of his character.

He said, "Unless you stop talking in that way I shall have you transferred to the Fourth Ward." (This was the violent ward.)

"Put me where you please," was my reply. "I'll put you in the gutter before I get through with you."

With that the doctor made good his threat, and the attendant escorted me to the violent ward—a willing, in fact, eager prisoner.

The ward in which I was now placed (September 13th, 1902) was furnished in the plainest manner. The floors were of hard wood and the walls were bare. Except when at meals or out of doors taking their accustomed exercise, the patients usually lounged about in one large room, in which heavy benches were used, it being thought that in the hands of violent patients, chairs might become a menace to others. In the dining room, however, there were chairs of a substantial type, for patients seldom run amuck at meal time. Nevertheless, one of these dining-room chairs soon acquired a history.

As my banishment had come on short notice, I had failed to provide myself with many things I now desired. My first request was that I be supplied with stationery. The attendants, acting no doubt on the doctor's orders, refused to grant my request; nor would they give me a lead pencil—which, luckily, I did not need, for I happened to have one. Despite their refusal I managed to get some scraps of paper, on which I was soon busily engaged in writing notes to those in authority. Some of these (as I learned later) were delivered, but no attention was paid to them. No doctor came near me until evening, when the one who had banished me made his regular round of inspection. When he appeared, the interrupted conversation of the morning was resumed—that is, by me—and in a similar vein. I again asked leave to telephone my conservator. The doctor again refused, and, of course, again I told him what I thought of him.

My imprisonment pleased me. I was where I most wished to be, and I busied myself investigating conditions and making mental notes. As the assistant physician could grant favors to the attendants, and had authority to discharge them, they did his bidding and continued to refuse most of my requests. In spite of their unfriendly attitude, however, I did manage to persuade the supervisor, a kindly man, well along in years, to deliver a note to the steward. In it I asked him to come at once, as I wished to talk with him. The steward, whom I looked upon as a friend, returned no answer and made no visit. I supposed he, too, had purposely ignored me. As I learned afterwards, both he and the superintendent were absent, else perhaps I should have been treated in a less high-handed manner by the assistant physician, who was not absent. . . .

On [one] occasion the element of personal spite entered into the assistant physician's treatment of me. The man's personality was apparently dual. His "Jekyll" personality was the one most in evidence, but it was the "Hyde" personality that seemed to control his actions when a crisis arose. It was "Doctor Jekyll" who approached my room that night, accompanied by the attendants. The moment he entered my room he became "Mr. Hyde." He was, indeed, no longer a doctor, or the semblance of one. His first move was to take the strait-jacket in his own hands and order me to stand. Knowing that those in authority really believed I had that day attempted to kill myself, I found no fault with their wish to put me in restraint; but I did object to having this done by Jekyll-Hyde. Though a strait-jacket should always be adjusted by the physician in charge, I knew that as a matter of fact the disagreeable duty was invariably assigned to the attendants. Consequently

Jekyll-Hyde's eagerness to assume an obligation he usually shirked gave me the feeling that his motives were spiteful. For that reason I preferred to entrust myself to the uncertain mercies of a regular attendant; and I said so, but in vain. "If you will keep your mouth shut, I'll be able to do this job quicker," said Jekyll-Hyde.

"I'll shut my mouth as soon as you get out of this room and not before," I remarked. Nor did I. My abusive language was, of course, interlarded with the inevitable epithets. The more I talked, the more vindictive he became. He said nothing, but, unhappily for me, he expressed his pent-up feelings in something more effectual than words. After he had laced the jacket, and drawn my arms across my chest so snugly that I could not move them a fraction of an inch, I asked him to loosen the strait-jacket enough to enable me at least to take a full breath. I also requested him to give me a chance to adjust my fingers, which had been caught in an unnatural and uncomfortable position.

"If you will keep still a minute, I will," said Jekyll-Hyde. I obeyed, and willingly too, for I did not care to suffer more than was necessary. Instead of loosening the appliance as agreed, this doctor, now livid with rage, drew the cords in such a way that I found myself more securely and cruelly held than before. This breach of faith threw me into a frenzy. Though it was because his continued presence served to increase my excitement that Jekyll-Hyde at last withdrew, it will be observed that he did not do so until he had satisfied an unmanly desire which an apparently lurking hatred had engendered. The attendants soon withdrew and locked me up for the night.

No incidents of my life have ever impressed themselves more indelibly on my memory than those of my first night in a strait-jacket. Within one hour of the time I was placed in it I was suffering pain as intense as any I ever endured, and before the night had passed it had become almost unbearable. My right hand was so held that the tip of one of my fingers was all but cut by the nail of another, and soon knifelike pains began to shoot through my right arm as far as the shoulder. After four or five hours the excess of pain rendered me partially insensible to it. But for fifteen consecutive hours I remained in that instrument of torture; and not until the twelfth hour, about breakfast time the next morning, did an attendant so much as loosen a cord.

During the first seven or eight hours, excruciating pains racked not only my arms, but half of my body. Though I cried and moaned, in fact, screamed so loudly that the attendants must have heard me, little attention was paid to me—possibly because of orders from Mr. Hyde after he had again assumed the rôle of Doctor Jekyll. I even begged the attendants to loosen the jacket enough to ease me a little. This they refused to do, and they even seemed to enjoy being in a position to add their considerable mite to my torture.

Before midnight I really believed that I should be unable to endure the torture and retain my reason. A peculiar pricking sensation which I now felt in my brain, a sensation exactly like that of June 1900, led me to believe that I might again be thrown out of touch with the world I had so lately regained. Realizing the awfulness of that fate, I redoubled my efforts to effect my rescue. Shortly after midnight I did succeed in gaining the attention of the night watch. Upon entering my room he found me flat on the floor. I had fallen from the bed and perforce remained absolutely helpless where I lay. I could not so much as lift my head. This, however, was not the fault of the strait-jacket. It was because I could not control the muscles of my neck which that day had been so mauled. I could scarcely swallow the water the night watch was good enough to give me. He was not a bad sort; yet even he refused to let out the cords of the strait-jacket. As he seemed sympathetic, I can attribute his refusal to nothing but strict orders issued by the doctor.

It will be recalled that I placed a piece of glass in my mouth before the strait-jacket was adjusted. At midnight the glass was still there. After the refusal of the night watch, I said to him: "Then I want you to go to Doctor Jekyll" (I, of course, called him by his right name; but to do so now would be to prove myself as brutal as Mr. Hyde himself). "Tell him to come here at once and loosen this jacket. I can't endure the torture much longer. After fighting two years to regain my reason, I believe I'll lose it again. You have always treated me kindly. For God's sake, get the doctor!"

"I can't leave the main building at this time," the night watch said. (Jekyll-Hyde lived in a house about one-eighth of a mile distant, but within the hospital grounds.)

"Then will you take a message to the assistant physician who stays here?" (A colleague of Jekyll-Hyde had apartments in the main building.)

"I'll do that," he replied.

"Tell him how I'm suffering. Ask him to please come here at once and ease this strait-jacket. If he doesn't, I'll be as crazy by morning as I ever was. Also tell him I'll kill myself unless he comes, and I can do it, too. I have a piece of glass in this room and I know just what I'll do with it."

The night watch was as good as his word. He afterwards told me that he had delivered my message. The doctor ignored it. He did not come near me that night, nor the next day, nor did Jekyll-Hyde appear until his usual round of inspection about eleven o'clock the next morning.

"I understand that you have a piece of glass which you threatened to use for a suicidal purpose last night," he said, when he appeared.

"Yes, I have, and it's not your fault or the other doctor's that I am not dead. Had I gone mad, in my frenzy I might have swallowed that glass."

"Where is it?" asked the doctor, incredulously.

As my strait-jacket rendered me armless, I presented the glass to Jekyll-Hyde on the tip of a tongue he had often heard, but never before seen.

III

After fifteen interminable hours the strait-jacket was removed. Whereas just prior to its putting on I had been in a vigorous enough condition to offer stout resistance when wantonly assaulted, now, on coming out of it, I was helpless. When my arms were released from their constricted position, the pain was intense. Every joint had been racked. I had no control over the fingers of either hand, and could not have dressed myself had I been promised my freedom for doing so.

For more than the following week I suffered as already described, though of course with gradually decreasing intensity as my racked body became accustomed to the unnatural positions it was forced to take. This first experience occurred on the night of October 18th, 1902. I was subjected to the same unfair, unnecessary, and unscientific ordeal for twenty-one consecutive nights and parts of each of the corresponding twenty-one days. On more than one occasion, indeed, the attendant placed me in the strait-jacket during the day for refusing to obey some trivial command. This, too, without an explicit order from the doctor in charge, though perhaps he acted under a general order.

During most of this time I was held also in seclusion in a padded cell. A padded cell is a vile hole. The side walls are padded as high as a man can reach, as is also the inside of the door. One of the worst features of such cells is the lack of ventilation, which deficiency of course aggravates their general unsanitary condition. The cell which I was forced to occupy was practically without heat, and as winter was coming on, I suffered intensely from the cold. Frequently it was so cold I could see my breath. Though my canvas jacket served to protect part of that body which it was at the same time racking, I was seldom comfortably warm; for, once uncovered, my arms being pinioned, I had no way of rearranging the blankets. What little sleep I managed to get I took lying on a hard mattress placed on the bare floor. The condition of the mattress I found in the cell was such that I objected to its further use, and the fact that another was supplied, at a time when few of my requests were being granted, proves its disgusting condition.

For this period of three weeks—from October 18th until November 8th, 1902, when I left this institution and was transferred to a state hospital—I was continuously either under lock and key (in the padded cell or some other room) or under the eye of an attendant. Over half the time I was in the snug, but cruel embrace of a strait-jacket—about three hundred hours in all.

While being subjected to this terrific abuse I was held in exile. I was cut off from all direct and all *honest* indirect communication with my legally appointed conservator—my own brother—and also with all other relatives and friends. I was even cut off from satisfactory communication with the superintendent. I saw him but twice, and then for so short a time that I was unable to give him any convincing idea of my plight. These interviews occurred on two Sundays that fell within my period of exile, for it was on Sunday that the superintendent usually made his weekly round of inspection.

What chance had I of successfully pleading my case, while my pulpit was a padded cell, and the congregation—with the exception of the superintendent—the very ones who had been abusing me? At such times my pent-up indignation poured itself forth in such a disconnected way that my protests were robbed of their right ring of truth. I was not incoherent in speech. I was simply voluble and digressive—a natural incident of elation. Such notes as I managed to write on scraps of paper were presumably confiscated by Jekyll-Hyde. At all events, it was not until some months later that the superintendent was informed of my treatment, when, at my request (though I was then elsewhere), the Governor of the State discussed the subject with him. How I brought about that discussion while still virtually a prisoner in another place will be narrated in due time. And not until several days after I had left this institution and had been placed in another, when for the first time in six weeks I saw my conservator, did *he* learn of the treatment to which I had been subjected. From his office in New Haven he had telephoned several times to the assistant physician and inquired about my condition. Though Jekyll-Hyde did tell him that I was highly excited and difficult to control, he did not even hint that I was being subjected to any unusual restraint. Doctor Jekyll deceived everyone, and—as things turned out—deceived himself; for had he realized then that I should one day be able to do what I have since done, his brutality would surely have been held in check by his discretion.

How helpless, how at the mercy of his keepers, a patient may be is further illustrated by the conduct of this same man. Once, during the third week of my nights in a strait-jacket, I refused to take certain medicine which an attendant offered me. For some time I had been regularly taking this innocuous concoction without protest; but I now decided that, as the attendant refused most of my requests, I should no longer comply with all of his. He did not argue the point with me. He simply reported my refusal to Doctor Jekyll. A few minutes later Doctor Jekyll—or rather Mr. Hyde— accompanied by three attendants, entered the padded cell. I was robed for the night—in a strait-jacket. Mr. Hyde held in his hand a rubber tube. An attendant stood near with the medicine. For over two years, the common threat had been made that the "tube" would be resorted to if I refused medicine or food. I had begun to look upon it as a myth; but its presence in the hands of an oppressor now convinced me of its reality. I saw that the doctor and his bravos meant business; and as I had already endured torture enough, I determined to make every concession this time and escape what seemed to be in store for me.

"What are you going to do with that?" I asked, eyeing the tube.

"The attendant says you refuse to take your medicine. We are going to make you take it."

"I'll take your old medicine," was my reply.

"You have had your chance."

"All right," I said. "Put that medicine into me any way you think best. But the time will come when you'll wish you hadn't. When that time does come it won't be easy to prove that you had the right to force a patient to take medicine he had offered to take. I know something about the ethics of your profession. You have no right to do anything to a patient except what's good for him. You know that. All you are trying to do is to punish me, and I give you fair warning I'm going to camp on your trail till you are not only discharged from this institution, but expelled from the State Medical Society as well. You are a disgrace to your profession, and that society will attend to your case fast enough when certain members of it, who are friends of mine, hear about this. Furthermore, I shall report your conduct to the Governor of the State. He can take some action even if this is *not* a state institution. Now, damn you, do your worst!"

Coming from one in my condition, this was rather straight talk. The doctor was visibly disconcerted. Had he not feared to lose caste with the attendants who stood by, I think he would have given me another chance. But he had too much pride and too little manhood to recede from a false position already taken. I no longer resisted, even verbally, for I no longer wanted the doctor to desist. Though I did not anticipate the operation with pleasure, I was eager to take the man's measure. He and the attendants knew that I usually kept a trick or two even up the sleeve of a strait-jacket, so they took added precautions. I was flat on my back, with simply a mattress between me and the floor. One attendant held me. Another stood by with the medicine and with a funnel through which, as soon as Mr. Hyde should insert the tube in one of my nostrils, the dose was to be poured. The third attendant stood near as a reserve force. Though the insertion of the tube, when skilfully done, need not cause suffering, the operation as conducted by Mr. Hyde was painful. Try as he would, he was unable to insert the tube properly, though in no way did I attempt to balk him. His embarrassment seemed to rob his hand of whatever cunning it may have possessed. After what seemed ten minutes of bungling, though it was probably not half that, he gave up the attempt, but not until my nose had begun to bleed. He was plainly chagrined when he and his bravos retired. Intuitively I felt that they would soon return. That they did, armed with a new implement of war. This time the doctor inserted between my teeth a large wooden peg—to keep open a mouth which he usually wanted shut. He then forced down my throat a rubber tube, the attendant adjusted the funnel, and the medicine, or rather liquid—for its medicinal properties were without effect upon me—was poured in.

As the scant reports sent to my conservator during these three weeks indicated that I was not improving as he had hoped, he made a special trip to the institution to investigate in person. On his arrival he was met by none other than Doctor Jekyll, who told him that I was in a highly excited condition, which, he intimated, would be aggravated by a personal interview. Now for a man to see his brother in such a plight as mine would be a distressing ordeal, and, though my conservator came within a few hundred feet of my prison cell, it naturally took but a suggestion to dissuade him from coming nearer. Doctor Jekyll did tell him that it had been found necessary to place me in "restraint" and "seclusion" (the professional euphemisms for "strait-jacket," "padded cell," etc.), but no hint was given that I had been roughly handled. Doctor Jekyll's politic dissuasion was no doubt inspired by the knowledge that if ever I got within speaking distance of my conservator, nothing could prevent my giving him a circumstantial account of my sufferings—which account would have been corroborated by the blackened eye I happened to have at the time. Indeed, in dealing with my conservator the assistant physician showed a degree of tact which, had it been directed toward myself, would have sufficed to keep me tolerably comfortable.

My conservator, though temporarily stayed, was not convinced. He felt that I was not improving where I was, and he wisely decided that the best course would be to have me transferred to a public institution—the State Hospital. A few days later the judge who had originally committed me ordered my transfer. Nothing was said to me about the proposed change until the moment of departure, and then I could scarcely believe my ears. In fact I did not believe my informant; for three weeks of abuse, together with my continued inability to get in touch with my conservator, had so shaken my reason that there was a partial recurrence of old delusions. I imagined myself on the way to the State Prison, a few miles distant; and not until the train had passed the prison station did I believe that I was really on my way to the State Hospital. . . .

On the night of November 25th, 1902, the head attendant and one of his assistants passed my door. They were returning from one of the dances which, at intervals during the winter, the management provides for the nurses and attendants. While they were within hearing, I asked for a drink of water. It was a carefully worded request. But they were in a hurry to get to bed, and refused me with curses. Then I replied in kind.

"If I come there I'll kill you," one of them said.

"Well, you won't get in if I can help it," I replied, as I braced my iron bedstead against the door.

My defiance and defences gave the attendants the excuse for which they had said they were waiting; and my success in keeping them out for two or three minutes only served to enrage them. By the time they had gained entrance they had become furies. One was a young man of twenty-seven. Physically he was a fine specimen of manhood; morally he was deficient—thanks to the dehumanizing effect of several years in the employ of different institutions whose officials countenanced improper methods of care and treatment. It was he who now attacked me in the dark of my prison room. The head attendant stood by, holding a lantern which shed a dim light.

The door once open, I offered no further resistance. First I was knocked down. Then for several minutes I was kicked about the room—struck, kneed and choked. My assailant even attempted to grind his heel into my cheek. In this he failed, for I was there protected by a heavy beard which I wore at that time. But my shins, elbows, and back were cut by his heavy shoes; and had I not instinctively drawn up my knees to my elbows for the protection of my body, I might have been seriously, perhaps fatally, injured. As it was, I was severely cut and bruised. When my strength was nearly gone, I feigned unconsciousness. This ruse alone saved me from further punishment, for usually a premeditated assault is not ended until the patient is mute and helpless. When they had accomplished their purpose, they left me huddled in a corner to wear out the night as best I might—to live or die for all they cared.

Strange as it may seem, I slept well. But not at once. Within five minutes I was busily engaged writing an account of the assault. A trained war correspondent could not have pulled himself together in less time. As usual I had recourse to my bit of contraband lead pencil, this time a pencil which had been smuggled to me the very first day of my confinement in the Bull Pen by a sympathetic fellow-patient. When he had pushed under my cell door that little implement of war, it had loomed as large in my mind as a battering-ram. Paper I had none; but I had previously found walls to be a fair substitute. I therefore now selected and wrote upon a rectangular spot—about three feet by two—which marked the reflection of a light in the corridor just outside my transom.

The next morning, when the assistant physician appeared, he was accompanied as usual by the guilty head attendant who, on the previous night, had held the lantern.

"Doctor," I said "I have something to tell you"—and I glanced significantly at the attendant. "Last night I had a most unusual experience. I have had many imaginary experiences during the past two years and a half, and it may be that last night's was not real. Perhaps the whole thing was phantasmagoric—like what I used to see during the first months of my illness. Whether it was so or not I shall leave you to judge. It just happens to be my impression that I was brutally assaulted last night. If it was a dream, it is the first thing of the kind that ever left visible evidence on my body."

With that I uncovered to the doctor a score of bruises and lacerations. I knew these would be more impressive than any words of mine. The doctor put on a knowing look, but said nothing and soon left the room. His guilty subordinate tried to appear unconcerned, and I really believe he thought me not absolutely sure of the events of the previous night, or at least unaware of his share in them. . . .

IV

Like fires and railroad disasters, assaults seemed to come in groups. Days would pass without a single outbreak. Then would come a veritable carnival of abuse—due almost invariably to the attendants' state of mind, not to an unwonted aggressiveness on the part of the patients. I can recall as especially noteworthy several instances of atrocious abuse. Five patients were chronic victims. Three of them, peculiarly irresponsible, suffered with especial regularity, scarcely a day passing without bringing to them its quota of punishment. One of these, almost an idiot, and quite too inarticulate to tell a convincing story even under the most favorable conditions, became so cowed that, whenever an attendant passed, he would circle his oppressor as a whipped cur circles a cruel master. If this avoidance became too marked, the attendant would then and there chastise him for the implied, but unconscious insult.

There was a young man, occupying a cell next to mine in the Bull Pen, who was so far out of his mind as to be absolutely irresponsible. His offence was that he could not comprehend and obey. Day after day I could hear the blows and kicks as they fell upon his body, and his incoherent cries for mercy were as painful to hear as they are impossible to forget. That he survived is surprising. What wonder that this man, who was "violent," or who was made violent, would not permit the attendants to dress him! But he had a half-witted friend, a ward-mate, who could coax him into his clothes when his oppressors found him most intractable.

Of all the patients known to me, the one who was assaulted with the greatest frequency was an incoherent and irresponsible man of sixty years. This patient was restless and forever talking or shouting, as any man might if oppressed by such delusions as his. He was profoundly convinced that one of the patients had stolen his stomach—an idea inspired perhaps by the remarkable corpulency of the person he accused. His loss he would woefully voice even while eating. Of course, argument to the contrary had no effect; and his monotonous recital of his imaginary troubles made him unpopular with those whose business it was to care for him. They showed him no mercy. Each day—including the hours of the night, when the night watch took a hand—he was belabored with fists, broom handles, and frequently with the heavy bunch of keys which attendants usually carry on a long chain. He was also kicked and choked, and his suffering was aggravated by his almost continuous confinement in the Bull Pen. An exception to the general rule (for such continued abuse often causes death), this man lived a long time—five years, as I learned later.

Another victim, forty-five years of age, was one who had formerly been a successful man of affairs. His was a forceful personality, and the traits of his sane days influenced his conduct when he broke down mentally. He was in the expansive phase of paresis, a phase distinguished by an exaggerated sense of well-being, and by delusions of grandeur which are symptoms of this form as well as of several other forms of mental disease. Paresis, as everyone knows, is considered incurable and victims of it seldom live more than three or four years. In this instance, instead of trying to make the patient's last days comfortable, the attendants subjected him to a course of treatment severe enough to have sent even a sound man to an early grave. I endured privations and severe abuse for one month at the State Hospital. This man suffered in all ways worse treatment for many months.

I became well acquainted with two jovial and witty Irishmen. They were common laborers. One was a hodcarrier, and a strapping fellow. When he arrived at the institution, he was at once placed in the violent ward, though his "violence" consisted of nothing more than an annoying sort of irresponsibility. He irritated the attendants by persistently doing certain trivial things after they had been forbidden. The attendants made no allowance for his condition of mind. His repetition of a forbidden act was interpreted as deliberate disobedience. He was physically powerful, and they determined to cow him. Of the master assault by which they attempted to do this I was not an eyewitness. But I was an ear witness. It was committed behind a closed door; and I heard the dull thuds of the blows, and I heard the cries for mercy until there was no breath left in the man with which he could beg even for his life. For days, that wrecked Hercules dragged himself about the ward moaning pitifully. He complained of pain in his side and had difficulty in breathing, which would seem to indicate that some of his ribs had been fractured. This man was often punished, frequently for complaining of the torture already inflicted. . . .

3. ANTONIN ARTAUD:
Electroshock (Fragments)*

And so, on the surface of daily life, consciousness forms beings and bodies that one can see gathering and colliding in the atmosphere, to distinguish their personalities. And these bodies form hideous cabals where every eventuality comes into the world to argue against what is beyond appeal.

I am not André Breton and I did not go to Baltimore but this is what I saw on the banks of the Hudson.

I died at Rodez under electroshock.

I died. Legally and medically died.

Electroshock-coma lasts fifteen minutes. A half an hour or more and then the patient breathes.

Now one hour after the shock I still had not awakened and had stopped breathing. Surprised at my abnormal rigidity, an attendant had gone to get the physician in charge, who after examining me with a stethoscope found no more signs of life in me.

I have personal memories of my death at that moment, but it is not on these that I base my testimony as to the fact.

I limit myself strictly to the details furnished me by Dr. Jean Dequeker, a young intern at the Rodez asylum, who had them from the lips of Dr. Ferdière himself.

And the latter asserts that he thought me dead that day, and that he had already sent for two asylum attendants to instruct them on the removal of my corpse to the morgue, since an hour and a half after shock I had still not come to myself.

* SOURCE: Jack Hirschman, ed., *Artaud Anthology* (San Francisco: City Lights, 1965), pp. 183–185, 188–193. Copyright © 1965 by City Lights Books. Reprinted by permission of the publisher.

And it seems that just at the moment that these attendants arrived to take my body out, it gave a slight shudder, after which I was suddenly wide awake. ⌉

Personally I have a different recollection of the affair.

But I kept this recollection to myself, and secret, until the day when Dr. Jean Dequeker on the outside confirmed it to me.

And this recollection is that ⌈everything⌉which Dr. Jean Dequeker told me⌊I had seen, but not from this side of the world but from the other, and quite simply from the cell where the shock took place and under its ceiling; although for moments there was neither cell nor ceiling for me, but rather a rod above my body, floating in the air like a sort of fluidified balloon suspended between my body and the ceiling.

And I shall indeed never forget in any possible life the horrible passage of this sphincter of *revulsion* and asphyxia, through which the criminal mob of beings forces the patient in extremis before letting go of him. At the bedside of a dying man there are more than 10,000 beings, and I took note of this at that moment.

There is a conscious unanimity among all these beings, who are unwilling to let the dead man come back to life before he has paid them by giving up his corpse totally and absolutely; for existence will not give even his inert body back to him, in fact especially his body.

And what do you expect a dead man to do with his body in the grave?

At such a time, "I am you and your consciousness is me," is what all the beings say: salesmen, druggists, grocers, subway conductors, sextons, knifegrinders, railroad gatekeepers, shopkeepers, bankers, priests, factory managers, educators, scientists, doctors, not one of them missing at the crucial moment.

Pity that no other dead person outside myself should have returned to confirm the matter, for generally speaking the dead do not return.

The electroshock accomplished, this one didn't run its course, as had the first two.

I felt that it wasn't going away.

And my whole inward electric body, the whole lie of this inward electric body which for a certain number of centuries has been the burden of every human being, turned inside out, became in me like an immense turning outward in flames, monads of nothingness bristling to the limits of an existence held prisoner in my lead body, which could neither get out of its lead coating nor stand up like a lead soldier.

I could no longer be my body, I didn't want to be this breath turning to death all around it, until its extreme dissolution.

Thus wrung out and twisted, fiber on fiber, I felt myself to be the hideous corridor of an impossible revulsion. And I know not what suspension of the void invaded me with its groping blind spots,
but I was that void,
and in suspension,
and as for my soul, I was nothing more than a spasm among several chokings.

Where to go and how to get out was the one and only thought leaping in my throat blocked and secured on all sides.
Every wall of charred meat assured me
it would be neither through the soul nor the mind,
all that is of a former world,
this is what each heartbeat told me.

It is the body that will remain

without the mind,

the mind, i.e., the patient.

*   *   *   *   *

When consciousness overflows a body, there is also a body detaching itself from consciousness,
no,
there is a body overflowing the body this consciousness came from,
and the whole of this new body is consciousness:
Think hard and long about someone you . . .

1) the vampire with its arms folded in my left ball

2) the woman with the supported nape

3) the grey devil

4) the black father
   a laying-on of black crablice

5) and finally last night
   at the New Athens
   the great revelation concerning the whole system of forming
   god in the slimey eggwhite of my left ball
   after the revelation of the antichrist abyss.

The life we lead is a front for all which the frightful criminal filthymindedness of some of us has left us.

A grotesque masquerade of acts and sentiments.

Our ideas are only the leftovers of a breath,
    breath of our choked and trussed lungs.

Which is to say for example that if the arterial tension of man is 12,

it could be 12 times 12 if it were not constrained and squashed down some place so as not to surpass this sordid level.

And damned if some physician doesn't come telling me that this is called hypertension and it is not good to be in a state of hypertension.

As for me, I answer that we are all in a state of frightful hypertension,

we can't lose an atom without the risk of immediately becoming a skeleton again; while life is an incredible proliferation,

the atom, once hatched, proceeds to lay another, which in fact immediately explodes another.

The human body is a battlefield where we would do well to return.

Now there is nothingness, now death, now putrefaction, now resurrection: to wait for I don't know what apocalypse beyond that, what explosion of what beyond in order to get straightened out
    with things,
    is a dirty joke.

Have to grab life by the balls right now.

Who is the man who decided to live with the notion he was not being fitted for the coffin?

Who, on the other hand, is the man who thinks he still may profit by his own death?

Try as they may to make us believe it, we gain no profit from the notion that we will be dead men, going back to the dead, taking our places in the legion of the dead, letting our limbs separate from our selves, and falling down in a heap in the serical charnal houses (liquids).

One doesn't die because one has to die,
one dies because it is a wrinkle forced on the
> consciousness
> one day
> not so long ago.

For one doesn't die in order to come back and remake one's life, but only in order to give up life and get rid of whatever life one had.

And whoever dies, dies because he wanted the coffin.

He accepted one day this spasm of being put through the coffin— a forced acceptance perhaps, but effective nonetheless,

and no man dies without consenting to it.

Consciousness lives before birth. It lives somewhere, if only for an hour.

All living consciousnesses have existed, I don't know in what sphere or what abyss.

And these abysms, consciousness rediscovers here.

What good in fact would the unconscious be if it were not to contain, in the very depths of itself, this pre-world, which is not one anyway, but merely the old burden, rejected (by others than ourselves), of everything which the consciousness could not or would not allow, cannot or will not admit, not under our own control but under the control within us of this other who is not the double or counterpart of the self, who is not the immanent derma of all that the conscious self envelops, and who is not the being that it is not and will become or will not become, but really and palpably an other, a sort of false spy-glove that keeps it under surveillance from morning to night in the hope that consciousness will put it on.

And this other is no more than what all the others are who have always wanted a finger in every person's consciousness.

Psychoanalysis has written a book on the failure of the old Baudelaire, whose life did not precede him by 100 years but rather by this sort of secular infinity, this secular infinity of time which came back to him when he lost his speech and learned and tried to say it, but who believed him, and who believes the affirmations of great poets who have become sick trying to dominate life? For Baudelaire did not die of syphilis, as has been said, he died from the absolute lack of belief attached to the incredible discoveries he had made in his syphilis and repeated in his aphasia.

When he learned it, then, he tried saying it,

that he had lost one of his selves in Thebes, 4,000 years before Jesus Christ.

And that this self was that of an old king.

When he discovered and tried saying that he was not and never had been Mumbledepeg,

But on the contrary that poet in a paradise alley where they were mending poetry, in Brittany, long before the Druids ever settled there.

And the skeleton of the human cock, against all onomatopoeia and reason, in order to rediscover life, found

a sound without echo or cry,

without shadow or double in life,

without the old yoke of the organ that accounts for the five senses, one day, much later, when the time came for the consciousness of the masses, and the sound of his poetry was the inert weight of planks, the horrible squishing of those six planks they could never fit his corpse into.

For to cure Charles Baudelaire, it would have been necessary to surround him with only a few organisms

enough

never to be afraid of facing a delirium in order to rediscover truth.

Therefore psychoanalysis was unable not to fear reality, however monstrous it might seem, and not to reject—in the dream-symbols representing it—the whole sadistic machinery of crime, the weaver of a vital stuff which Charles Baudelaire wished to mend, and for the sake of which I ask that, for who knows how much time to come, the few men who are its victims continue, as they are condemned prisoners born to be its *fated* scapegoats.

Translated by David Rattray

The Patients and the Doctors

Sickness is one state,
health is only another,

but lousier,
I mean meaner and pettier.
        There's no patient who hasn't grown,
as there's no one in good health who hasn't lied one day in order not
to have the desire to be sick, like some doctors I have gone through.
I have been sick all my life and I ask only that it continue,
room motto, i.e.,
for the states of privation in life have always told me a great deal
more about the plethora of my powers than the middleclass drawing-
        AS LONG AS YOU'VE GOT YOUR HEALTH.
For my existence is beautiful but hideous. And it isn't beautiful only
because it is hideous.
Hideous, dreadful, constructed of hideousness.
Curing a sickness is a crime.
It's to squash the head of a kid who is much less nasty than life.
Ugliness is con-sonance. Beauty rots.
But, *sick,* one doesn't get high by opium, by cocaine,
or by morphine.
It's the dread of the fevers you got to *love,*
the jaundice and the perfidy,
much more than all euphoria.
Then the fever, the glowing fever in my head,
—for I've been in a state of glowing fever for the
fifty years that I've been alive—
will give me
my opium,
—this existence—
by which
I will be a head aglow,
    opium from head to toe.
For
cocaine is a bone,
and heroin a superman in the bones,

Ca itra la sara cafena
Ca itra la sara cafa

and opium is this vault
this mummification of blood vault
this scraping of sperm in the vault

this excrementation of an old kid
this disintegration of an old hole
this excrementation of a kid
little kid of the buried asshole
whose name is:
shit, pi-pi,
Con-science of sickness.
And, opium of the father and shame,
shame on you for going from father to son—
now you must get dust thrown back at you
and after suffering without a bed for so long.
So it is that I consider
that it's up to the everlastingly sick me
to cure all doctors
—born doctors by lack of sickness—
and not up to doctors ignorant of my dreadful
states of sickness
to impose their insulintherapy on me,
their health for a worn out world.

Translated by Jack Hirschman

II. THE PRESENT: PATIENTS

Introduction

This section speaks for itself. People tell of their experiences in mental hospitals. Some have felt their minds and bodies were disturbed, altered; others have felt totally imprisoned and brutalized. They prepare a composite portrait of what it's like in mental institutions these days. They tell of the beatings and callous treatment, of the loneliness and isolation, of the effect of the staff, of the helpful reachings-out from other patients. Each of them has a story to tell. Listen to them.

Almost all the writers in this section are women. This is no accident. Women have been especially oppressed by psychotherapy. They were the ones who responded most to my call for personal accounts and manuscripts. Their descriptions are eloquent and to the point.

4. D.A.Y.:
Two Statements

I

I was committed to M—— State Hospital August 22 by Dr. H——, County Mental Health Officer, for a period of fifteen days.

At the end of my fifteen days, September 6, I was issued a two-physician sixty-day retainment, which I objected to, but was overmedicated and unable to think clearly.

When near the end of my sixty days, I was served with a six-month retainment, I requested a court hearing. When I went for my court appearance, I was told by Mr. S—— of the Mental Health Information Bureau, that he had spoken to Dr. H—— in Administration, who said that I did not have to go through court proceedings because my father, my petitioner, could write a letter of request for my release. Therefore I appeared in court, but was *not* assigned a lawyer as Mr. S—— explained my father could write a request for my release.

My father wrote the letter and the following Monday I went to my release meeting where Dr. H—— presided the meeting. Also in attendance was Mrs. S——, social worker, Mrs. E——, psychologist-in-training, and Dr. N——, who is not my doctor and whom I had never spoken to.

Dr. H—— then informed me that I could not be released because my psychological test revealed that I was sensitive, impulsive, that I brooded, and was depressed. (I was overmedicated when I took the psychological and consequently depressed.)

Dr. H—— proceeded to say I could not go home because I needed twenty-four-hour supervision "because I might do something to myself." (I did not try to commit suicide when I was committed, nor ever wished to take my life.)

I was upset because I thought I would be released; he told me if I withdrew my court request that my "treatment" would not necessarily be six months, and that I could take another psychological. Being upset, with due cause, I did withdraw, but had afterthoughts when I calmed down [and was] able to think more clearly. I put in another request, which was within the five-day period. (Incidentally, I was never given another psychological.)

Mr. S—— returned to the hospital and told me the judge had said I was "fickle" and could not appear in court. October 19, I received a notice of a six-month court retention.

To my knowledge, I was never appointed a lawyer and a lawyer definitely did not come to the hospital to talk to me.

Since I have been forcefully repressed in M——, I have had two job offers—one at the O—— Day Care Center where I would be assistant nursery school teacher, and an office job at U—— College which would enable me to take a few courses. This is the second offer from U—— College I have gotten and I am still on active file. I could reside with my grandmother in U——.

I have not had any definite answer from Dr. P——, the building doctor, as to when I might be released, though he feels I am "ready" for O.U.R. I definitely feel I would be able to function on the outside and fervently feel repressed, robbed of my individual rights, not at all liking to be extruded from my friends, family, and community.

I wholeheartedly object to the inhumaneness of a mental institution, the confinement, and the various labeling.

D. A. Y.

P.S. I have also been accepted to work at St. E——'s Hospital, also located in U——.

II

Being a victim of repressing forces, extruded from my community, friends, and family; unable to exercise my individual rights, I would like to express some events (experiences) before and after my commitment to M—— State.

I graduated from C—— High School with a Regents Diploma in 1969. In order to further my education I worked, procured a N.Y.S. Higher Education Loan, National Defense Loan, Economic Opportunity Grant, small scholarships, thus completing two years of Liberal Arts at R—— College.

During my last year at college, I encountered various problems (acute tonsillitis, mild concussion from a fall on ice, possible pregnancy, and personal conflicts with my stepmother) which led to a struggle with finals, term papers—sleepless nights until I chose to rest in a General Community Hospital located in F——, for a period of twelve days. I had previously made a very feeble undesired suicidal attempt, which was virtually a cry for help, rest, and the opportunity to place problems in perspective, view them from a distance, etc. I was released from the hospital by a psychiatrist, Dr. S——, who transferred my medical history to the M—— Mental Health Center. The only medication I received was Tofranil, an antidepressant. Therapy was discontinued at the end of summer 1971.

I then got a job working domestically for R——, caring for the members of his family, who numbered eight. The experience of living with a Jewish family was very rewarding, and I gradually grew in self-confidence, having adjusted quite well during the course of seven months.

In April of 1972, I moved out of the R—— household to live with my grandmother in U——, and secured a job as assistant nursery school teacher at the neighborhood center.

After a month, I rented my own apartment, was happy, adjusted, and felt I exercised a very full, rewarding life. However, the desire to grow led me "back to school" whereby I applied to work at U—— College, hoping to work and obtain free courses.

August 2, my twenty-first birthday, I moved out of my apartment into a gardener's cottage I rented from E. M——. Viewing this as a long overdue summer vacation, I prepared the cottage to reside in for one month until I heard definitely from U—— College.

Having paid $50.00 from an in-between job, it was decided that for the rest of my month's rent, I could finish the cabinets in the cottage.

Being unable to sleep during the hot spell I decided to camp out in my backyard and to remove the furniture from the cottage so that I might paint as well as varnish the cabinets. Not being sleepy I had gone across the street to "fool around" with Mr. M——'s housekeeper, J——, whom I had become particularly fond of. Obviously, she became "suspicious" of my behavior (I was happy, carefree and perhaps to a very orthodox, structured person, behaving in a bizarre fashion). I had been studying a lot, reading, and the one particular book I was reading was the Bible. Unable to sleep, feeling the need to experience, and worrying about the results of a summer affair, I ate extraordinarily little. Also, I lose my appetite in the summer heat.

August 22 at about 8:00 A.M., the state police drove up to investigate reasons why I had furniture out, why I was sleeping outdoors, as the housekeeper had called the police.

I recall relating the conception of Christ and related experiences—confused with my possible pregnancy. As I appeared to be exhausted, which I was, the policeman asked me if I would mind being examined by a doctor. I said no and was taken to Dr. H——, County Health Officer, who committed me to M——, though I didn't know until Sgt. D—— drove onto M—— grounds, whereby I protested but went in calmly.

I was then taken upstairs to Ward——, went through admission procedures, was led into the dayroom, and because of the sweltering heat went out onto the porch. When the full realization of being locked up for an indeterminate amount of time hit me, I began screaming and was given a shot of Thorazine which totally crippled me. From then on for a period of one and one-half months I was overmedicated and became depressed. During this period I was given a psychological test. . . .

I wish very much to live, but do not consider the confining life of a mental institution living, as I am separated from loved ones and the opportunity to live where I choose, which would be with my aging grandmother in U——, who lives alone at present.

I am missing life's beauty and experiences, those experiences needed for human growth and development. Having intense feelings, I feel cheated.

I remember that night so clearly—I was so afraid of this mental institution and most everyone inside of it. It was so strange—I felt alienated from the world. I propositioned a visitor to take me out for I felt desperate. It was my second night and I was sick from a lot of medication. The visitor refused to take responsibility, of course, and realizing I had no way out, I became extremely panicky.

I do not know what possessed me, but I grabbed a red crayon and drew two crosses on the wall, for I felt this place void of God. As soon as I did it, I felt embarrassed, foolish, and stupid, and the attendants gave me a brush and a bucket of water. I tried scrubbing it off but couldn't. Then I asked the attendants what would happen if I couldn't get it off. They thought I was testing them but I wasn't. I was asking an honest question, because I really could not get the crayon off. I repeated that I couldn't get it off and was grabbed and slammed against the wall. Naturally I fought in self-defense, was grabbed around the neck, my respiration was cut off as three attendants (one male, two female) put me in a half-sheet. I was then knocked on the floor while the male attendant sat on my back and injected a needle in my left hip.

I was then allowed to stand up and was given another shot in the right hip. Then I was locked in seclusion, which had only a mattress in it.

I walked around trying to wriggle out of the camisole, but instead, it moved up around my neck and gave me the sensation of strangling. I had to use the lavatory, but was not let out and was forced to urinate on the floor out of necessity.

I was not kept in seclusion all night, but the effects of the shots lasted nearly all the next day and I felt very drugged—a most horrible state.

5. VERNZAL DAVIS:
Life in Wes Seneca

My name is Vernzal Davis. I spent half a year in South Buffalo's Mental Hospital, Wes Seneca. I went for my interview November 17, 1971. I was not scared for the simple fact I was used to going away from home. The people at first were nice. One staff and I were walking down the corridor, and one of its residents was being carried down the hall laughing shrilly. Her name was Di-Di. She had just thrown water on one of the teachers working there. The next day I was admitted. Di-Di was there for passing bad checks. I was there for a series of runaways. The first day was all right except for the food, which I found out later it would always be nasty. It had long hallways and it was made up of wards. Di-Di was on the same ward as I. When I said in the beginning the staff were all right [it was] just in the beginning. They always reminded you that you were in a mental hospital. I got used to their talk and the food. As the time went by Di-Di and I got into more trouble. One time me and Di-Di had to stay after school in Mr. V——'s room. D——, another girl I knew, was already in trouble, so I wanted to get into the act. I put my foot on one of the tables. Mr. V—— told me to get my feet off the table. When I didn't he threw me out of my chair. I fell on the floor stomach first. While I was waiting for the wind to get back in me, Mr. V—— jumped on [my] back and started twisting both of my arms. He sat on my back, but not my legs. I raised both my feet and kicked him as hard as I could. He jumped up and folded my legs to my back. After a while he got tired and asked me would I behave. I said yeah. As soon as he got up off me I grabbed a chair and hit him with [it]. [The] same thing happened, but only a little harsher. Then finally Di-Di stabbed him in the back with a piece of glass. Some of the policemen on the grounds were notified. They carried me to my ward but I got a chance to kick one man in the head as hard as I could. They locked me in the quiet room. It had nothing on the floor, no window except for in the door. Two nurses came to the room and some of the staff came too. I guessed I was going to get a tranquilizer shot to calm me down. We wrestled for a half hour; they won in the fight. Time passed and Christmas came. I thought I would not be going home for the holidays because I ran away during Thanksgiving holiday. They told me that I could go home for a visit but Di-Di was not so lucky. She tried to run away during Thanksgiving too. Her parents didn't want her any more. I shared Di-Di's grief; together we tore up the ward. We knocked down the Christmas tree, tore up the decorations, went in kids' rooms and stole stuff, beat up the kids, and fought the staff. The same day we had a new boy on, we had three times as much fun. This boy was named Phillip. Me and Di-Di and Kevin could not stand [him]. We played some dirty records (which were Di-Di's, naturally), turned the volume up high as we could, and beat up Phillip. We had some matches (we couldn't smoke there) and everybody tried to make us give them to them. We hid them in the clothes room. Mr. S—— twisted Di-Di's arm and me and Kevin beat him up. Phillip tried to find the matches. He almost found them but we beat him up again. We took the matches in the quiet room when they locked all three of us in it. We took off all our clothes except our underwear and set them on fire. They came and put the fire out and stared at us while we laughed. When Di-Di found out that she couldn't see her best-loved sister she tried to kill herself. She took fifty tranquilizers she had been saving up. When the staff saw her they actually had the gall to laugh at her. How Di-Di lived is a mystery to me. Now Di-Di is in H—— where she will have to stay till her eighteenth birthday which is five years away (she's only thirteen).

Kevin is still there. Phillip died from an o.d. of heroin.

I'm now in H—— State Training School for Girls.

I just hope all mental hospitals aren't like Wes Seneca. If they are, God pity the residents. This is all of the story I would like to remember. P.S. This is my first story about any place I have been to. I am fifteen.

6. SUSAN DWORKING LEVERING:
She Must Be Some Kind of Nut*

"Crazy" is when a woman doesn't want to live with her husband any more. "Sane" is when she decides to wear a skirt and apply for a job at Bell Telephone. You don't agree? You must not be a judge or a psychiatrist, then. (Of course, there aren't many female judges or psychiatrists.) In Pennsylvania, the criterion for a court's decision to involuntarily commit a person is if she or he is "mentally disabled and in need of care or treatment." But such a vague standard is naturally interpreted according to white, male, middle-class, conventional values.

Beginning with the college date who tries to convince you that you must be crazy because you won't sleep with him, a woman has to deal with the likelihood that she will be labeled mentally ill or disturbed when she refuses to conform to standard roles. Lesbians are sick, women who are depressed after the birth of a child are ill, old maids must have something wrong up there. Unfortunately, there are more sanctions attached to female nonconformity than mere name-calling. Women can be committed involuntarily to psychiatric institutions for these manifestations of insanity. Here are some examples of real women who at one time during the past few years were imprisoned at Haverford State Hospital, Haverford, Pa. Names have been changed.

Madeline is in her late thirties. The first time she was hospitalized her husband had her committed because she was neglecting her appearance and refused to have sexual relations with him. Of course, she had been seriously depressed following the birth of each of her three children and didn't want to become pregnant again.

* SOURCE: *The Radical Therapist*, vol. 3, no. 1 (September 1972).

Cathy is in her early twenties. Her parents had her committed when she wrote to them saying that she was going to find her own life with her own values. The admission records give as reasons for her hospitalization: hippie-type appearance, masculine attire (jeans and boots), sexual acting-out (sleeping with men she wasn't married to) and being unable to find her place in life despite finishing college.

Linda is in her late thirties. Her husband had her committed after she left him and filed for divorce. At her commitment hearing, he testified that she was having a "fantasy love affair" or hallucinating. She had in fact fallen in love with another man, with whom she had not had sexual relations.

Each of these women was committed after a court hearing at which a theoretically impartial "master" (!) or judge was free to dismiss the petition for insufficient evidence. This was not done. Once court-committed it is up to the discretion of the hospital psychiatrist to release her when care and treatment are no longer necessary. Madeline escaped. Cathy was released when she made a tactical decision to start wearing a skirt and lie to the doctor that she wanted to work at Bell Telephone. Linda is still imprisoned; her therapist does not consider her ready to leave. Her husband promises that he will help her get out when she is well—but the only evidence of her recovery that he will accept is her willingness to live with him again.

Not only the commitment process but the so-called "treatment" of women rewards conformity to traditional sex roles and punishes rebellion. The treatment program in the women's half of Building 14 at Haverford is called the "token system." It is a type of behavior modification "therapy" (sic) used on older women, many of whom have been hospitalized for long periods of time. No one has been able to explain to us why this desirable program is used only on women. However, some of the behavior which is rewarded would not be appropriate for men—for example, wearing lipstick and girdles. A patient in this ward gets nothing free; she has to earn red, white or blue tokens to pay for meals, her bed, admission to the dayroom, or any other "privileges." To earn tokens, she can change her underwear, make the beds in the men's ward, cut up rags for rag rugs, perform janitorial tasks or wear a girdle. Her girdle has to be new, however; an old one won't entitle her to a token. Sometimes patients are given the special reward of a visit to the ward beauty parlor.

It is significant that treatment in Building 14 consists of changing a woman's behavior. That seems to say that what is important is how she acts, whether she behaves herself. Forget about how she feels—if she conforms successfully, she's sane. The way to beat the system is to hide your feelings, rely on appearances, and "function." Vivian, a youngish black woman, refused to do janitorial work when she was instructed to, saying she had never swept floors for people in her life and she wasn't going to start now. Vivian is crazy; she will stay in Building 14 for a long time.

Perhaps the most hopeful sign is that there is one striking difference between the women's ward at Building 14 and most other wards. Patients in this ward are conscious that the token system is unjust and oppressive, and at times will join together to help a sister who has been unable or unwilling to earn her tokens. When women patients begin to organize with an awareness of their oppression as women, hospitals will no longer be able to run these pacification programs. When sisters work to eliminate the stigma of mental illness and the writing-off of independence as "craziness," our ideas will no longer be dismissed with the phrase, "She must be some kind of nut!"

7. JANE SWIGART:
Pages from an Unpublished Manuscript

The streets of Pleasant Vale were lined with broad-leafed trees and the prim red-brick exteriors of expensive shops. Everywhere you looked there were quaint green shutters and neat shiny black lettering and everything was immaculately clean. As we drove past the town and out into the countryside surrounding it, we seemed to enter an area sacred and immune to the vulgarity of America. After driving four or five miles we came to the Foundation, where I was placed and kept for about seven months.

The roads which lead to the Foundation are narrow and picturesque. They seemed very strange to me for I was not used to seeing houses quite so far from the road. In the suburbs of Detroit, large homes tend to be built closer to the main thoroughfares, for everyone to see. The money is new and fast there and the profit motive dominates all other considerations—utilitarian, humanitarian, aesthetic. It is never surprising to see a gas station with French Provincial garages crop up next to an expensive residential area, or a Dairy Queen disguised as a Tudor cottage. But here the profit motive seemed to be held at arm's length or rather, kept out of sight. There was no danger of it crowding too near where the rich live in the form of a ten-acre shopping plaza or flashy new drive-in restaurant. Perhaps things have changed now or perhaps my vision was blurred by my exquisite elation. But it seemed as though we were entering a magical land where people knew how to live and cared about beauty and taste.

I remember traveling down a narrow winding road flanked with patches of forest and the leaves were all brilliant colors. Every now and then I would see an immense home at the end of a long driveway. More often I saw just a driveway which disappeared into luxuriant vegetation. We turned a curve and there, on top of a hill, surrounded by a magnificent forest, was a large rambling white frame mansion. This was the Foundation and its land spread far and wide on both sides of the road. Small "guest houses" were discreetly placed around the premises. There was nothing about the place that remotely resembled a mental institution. It seemed as though we were driving into a resort, an elegant resort where only very "special" people were allowed.

This is why I was very surprised when the psychiatrist I saw shortly after I arrived asked me, "Do you know that you are sick?" I thought at first he must be joking. How could anyone be sick at a place like this? Outside there was a rich fall smell of leaves burning. The sun was out, the air warm, and the trees all red, orange, gold, and tawny beige. I thought, how could everything be so beautiful that it almost hurts? My mother and I had passed by an elegant dining room and had seen a long table with delicious-smelling food beautifully arranged on it. And there were people around so elegantly dressed you wanted to reach out and touch them to see if they were real. One woman in particular—you noticed her right away—my mother was certain she was a movie star. Her hair, the color of gold and silver, seemed to light up the room. We stared at her until the nurse, who didn't look like a nurse because she wore a tweed skirt and cashmere pullover with pearls around the neck, took us over to the stone cottage where the doctors had their offices.

"Oh no, of course I'm not sick. You see, I'm loving life desperately." I smiled joyously. I wanted to tell him that everything was all right now, he had nothing to worry about, but he continued to look very serious and I became slightly confused. "But you were depressed?" he said. "Well yes, but not now." "We don't want that to happen again." "Oh no," I answered, "I never want that to ever happen again." There was something glorious about the way this man was focusing all of his attentions on me. I felt grateful and wanted to give him a hug, for his kindness, his concern. It seemed as though he had singled me out from all the people in the world just to let me know how concerned he was that I had been depressed. He mentioned something about how the depression would return if I did not take care of myself and do what they suggested. I could not think of one reason why I shouldn't do absolutely everything they told me to. After all they were going to take care of me now. I put myself in their hands full of confidence and trust.

We had a delicious lunch, my mother and I. I stuffed myself full of food and every bite was a pleasure. Then we were shown my room, off in one of the guest houses. But it wasn't a room, it was a gorgeous suite. I had dreamed about such a room—the mahogany desk, the soft chairs, golden lamps, paintings all over the walls of mountain streams and speckled trout, and a large double bed. It seemed natural that I should walk into such a room and fill it, take it over, have it be my very own. There was a spacious white tile bathroom connected to it and enough closet space for an entire wardrobe. It was cozy, yet sumptuous and refined. Sometime during that first day my mother left and I could not understand why she was crying.

I was introduced to one of my nurses, who was to stay with me from 8:00 in the morning until 4:00 in the afternoon when the shift changed and another nurse came. But they seemed more like companions than nurses. One was young, in her twenties, and until I realized she was paid an enormous sum to watch and record my every movement and to keep me from running away, I considered her a friend, like a sister or guardian angel. My other nurse was older, closer to my mother's age, infinitely kind and gentle, yet lively too. Both of them gave me back massages whenever I asked, which was usually at naptime and just before going to bed in the evening.

I can't remember if they started giving me drugs that day. I know I was very tired that night and had little trouble falling asleep. It was the first good sleep I had had in weeks and the last that was not a heavy, drugged sleep. Perhaps it was the next morning, they began giving me pills three or four times a day. And in the evening, before going to bed, we were all given the "nightcap" or "midnight cocktail," a bitter tasting liquid which was to send us harmlessly to sleep.

It did not take me long to get used to the daily routine. We were awakened at 7:00 and were supposed to take a long hot bath, after which we were to rub our arms, legs and torso strenuously with a towel. This was to stimulate the blood. Breakfast was at 8:00, a huge steaming meal of eggs and bacon, ham, or sausage, sometimes pancakes or waffles or blueberry muffins along with fresh juices and milk and coffee. During breakfast a nurse would come around to each of us, individually, and whisper what time our appointments were that day. (We saw our psychiatrists at different times each day). After breakfast there was a carefully allotted time for our bowel movements, though this was called "time to read the newspaper." We each got a copy of the *New York Times* every morning.

When I first arrived, Dr. T., the founder, gave lectures in the mornings a few times a week, from around 10:00 to 11:00. I do not remember these lectures very well for I would have to get up to urinate at least three times during his talks. The only thing I recall him saying was that Freud had it all wrong. It was not sex hang-ups that made us miserable, it was . . . but here my memory fails me, unless he said it was "bad habits" that had done us in. He soon told my nurse that I did not have to attend these lectures due to my unruly bladder.

If Dr. T. did not give his morning lecture (and I believe he stopped altogether a few months after I arrived), half of the patients would work in the shop while the other half took their morning stroll. After an hour or so, the latter half would work in the shop while the former walked. There were alternatives. Some were allowed to play golf and there was a paddle-tennis court in back of the main house.

There were two walks: the three-miler and the five-miler. Both of the walks were beautiful. Old rustic timber fences and stone walls marked the boundaries of some of the hidden mansions. There was an abundance of pine, maple, cedar, and oak. There were lawns and parks with a pond or creek running through, and usually a quaint dam or waterfall holding back the gentle waters. I remember exquisite rock gardens designed to look wild, as though nature would do anything for the rich, even curb and direct her growth. There were farms and summer homes and old cottages built a hundred years ago. My nurses, of course, would walk every step of the way with me. Otherwise I probably would have kept on walking.

At 1:00 lunch was served, rather, placed on a large table. Every manner of cheese and lunch meats, soup and fresh fruit. There were always fresh vegetables, salads, and deviled eggs. We helped ourselves to this meal though the crisp, tidy maids stood nearby, making themselves available if any of us wanted anything "special." After lunch we were all to lie down and try to sleep. Thereafter, we would work in the shop again and take another walk until "tea" was served in the lodge, a large room with a beautiful stone fireplace with blazing logs. From 5:00 to 7:00 we were to take another bath and to "dress." This was to be a ritual, devoted to cleaning and grooming and primping until we looked our very best.

Meals were very important here, each one an occasion, served punctually four times a day by Anglo-Saxon maids, imported from England, dressed in tidy black dresses with white collars and aprons. Whether breakfast, lunch, tea, or dinner, the food was served graciously, and it was the best food I had ever tasted. I could not get enough of it, even though I often had second, third, and sometimes fourth helpings. The vegetables were always fresh, never overcooked, and the meat, except for pork, was always medium rare. You never had lamb without mint jelly or pork without some delicate tasting preserves to enhance the flavor. Dinner was always at least three courses and we ate by candlelight. When I say we "dressed," I mean the men wore coats and ties and the women charming dresses in the latest fashion. Some of the women wore long flowing outfits which rustled and swished the floor when they walked. Of course there were patients who came to dinner looking slovenly. They were considered "bad off." I learned quickly that here, as in the "outside world," people tended to judge you by your appearance more than how you really felt. To buy and wear expensive clothing and have your hair and nails done, to make a stunning impression on the world—this was a sign of health at the Foundation.

After dinner was "play" time. Games were brought out and people played Scrabble, chess, bridge, ping-pong, and other games until 9:30, when we were given our "night-cap"—the bitter potion which many of the patients longed and waited for throughout the day.

Everyone saw his doctor five, six, sometimes seven times a week. There were supervised trips to town daily. Once in a while we were taken to movies. In the winter, my young nurse took me ice skating on the pond at the outskirts of the town.

When I awoke from that first long night of sleep, my nurse was there to give me pills, make sure I took a bath, and take me to breakfast. I noticed three young men at breakfast, sat next to them, and made it known immediately that I would go out drinking and fucking with them the first chance we got. They appeared shocked at first, then delighted. We began discussing windows to climb out of, where to meet and go once we had escaped. I flirted with them openly, violently, full of laughter and enjoying every minute of it. When we set that night as *the night,* I noticed my nurse becoming anxious. I think my dosage was increased that day for during the later afternoon I discovered my limbs had become heavy and cumbersome. My legs and arms felt like they were being held down by weights. Though I had carefully worked out plans for escape, by evening the most I could do was sit up in a chair. For days I was so incapacitated I could hardly move. One afternoon I asked my nurse to take me into town to have my hair done. We went to the swank beauty salon many of the patients patronized. But when I sank into the chair and my hair was being washed and curled, I realized I could not move, not even lift my head. I told my nurse, who was sitting nearby with an issue of *Vogue,* that I was immobile. They had to carry me out, the curlers still in my hair, my hair brittle as glass from all the sprays and goop they put on it. Back at the Foundation I was put to bed and I remember laying there, my mind awake and alert, yet unable to open my eyelids. My doctor came in and said, "I never thought I'd see her this quiet." I tried to say something but couldn't move my lips or tongue. My dosage was decreased after this episode but I had been slowed way down and found it difficult to move around as fast as I wanted to. I was not angry about this for I felt it was a game, like cops and robbers. I was going to try to escape and they were going to try to keep me there. I had my wits and irrepressible high spirits. They had drugs and nurses who followed me like detectives. Those first few months, everything was a "gas"—all fun and games and jokes and laughter. I didn't know it then, but I was the only one laughing.

They called it "mania." It has never happened since. Though the drugs slowed me down, I still felt like a comet or meteor, racing through space, never able to slow down unless I collided, head on, into something or someone unpleasant, upon which I would fly into an uncontrollable rage or else cry hysterically for hours. I felt so exhilarated, so desperately happy, so speeded up and energetic, I could have not slept for weeks on end without the slightest feeling of fatigue. My nurse told me later that my concentration span at that time was only a few seconds. I would dash from one topic of conversation to another, from one activity to the next. Despite the drugs, I would awake early and jump up like a shot, dashing around as though bombs were exploding in my head. I wrote dozens of letters a day and many poems. Everything I wrote I was certain would go down in posterity. It seems very strange to me now that they mailed all of my letters—which I wrote to people I knew and didn't know. When these letters began to circulate, my parents were horrified and embarrassed for, they said, I had "stigmatized" myself. But nothing could have stopped me. These letters were fragments of great beauty and made perfect sense; this is what I thought at the time. I talked incessantly to everyone, and was loud and obnoxious. I was convinced I was a genius and told everyone. Several months after I arrived my doctor told me I was to take some tests. I shouted, "Whoopee! Today you'll find out what a genius I am!" I literally skipped down to the testing center, crashed into the room and told the elderly woman who was to administer the test that I vas a raving genius. I was given blocks to sort out, asked questions like, "Who is the President of the United States?" and was then told to make up stories about the pictures I was shown. She wrote down every word I uttered, because, I thought, it was all so brilliant and intelligent.

The same happened as I took the Rorschach. A few days later, when the results had been analyzed, my psychiatrist said, "These tests, I'm afraid, show that you are not a genius. In fact, your I.Q. is below average. One thing they do suggest is that you are very sick." For a few minutes, I became very confused; a wave of shame came over me. I suddenly felt glad and relieved that I fell into the "sick" category, for this excused me for the low I.Q. From then on, I began more and more to identify myself as a "very sick person" rather than as a gifted and brilliant one. This crutch I was to lean heavily on for many years, excusing myself for every failure and weakness. For hadn't I been in a mental hospital, diagnosed as seriously "ill"? I believe this happens to many mental patients who've been institutionalized. When they are not feeling overwhelmed by guilt and shame, they brag about their "disturbances," take pride and comfort in the fact that they've been bad off enough to be "put away." Often there is a competition between ex-inpatients as to who has been the sickest. Your weak, fragile, tentative sense of identity becomes interfused with the idea that you are "sick," and for want of anything better, you begin to take pride in this. You have to puff yourself up some way, so you use your deficiencies to try to maintain a feeling of superiority.

Despite my frenzied energy, I must have been slowed way down for in a matter of months I went from 130 pounds to 167 pounds. I ate like a pig, but then I have always been a glutton for food. Never did the fat cling in rolls of puckered flabby flesh as it did while I was at the Foundation. I began to resemble a giant, obese Amazon. At the time, however, I thought I was a ravishing beauty.

I honestly believe Dr. T., the founder, and all the doctors there meant well. Everything at the Foundation was made as pleasant for the patients as possible. The staff had been carefully chosen for their ability to soothe, soften, pamper, and caress the patients' troubled minds. The daily regimen, the surroundings, the food, everything was calculated to make us "happy," relaxed, as comfortable as possible. I did not remain for long in my spacious suite which, I learned later, they saved for the richest and most famous patients, or, as in my case, those whose relatives felt the guiltiest. I was moved several times to smaller rooms in different guest houses. But I never had to lift a finger. You never had to lift a finger at the Foundation unless it was to eat or work in the shop—painting, weaving, sewing, or working in wood. Even your nylons were washed for you, by hand, never showing a ladder unless you put it there. As soon as clothes became soiled, they disappeared to be carefully washed and ironed or dry-cleaned, after which they would appear again, folded neatly in your drawer.

Everything was carefully designed to hide the fact that it was a looney bin. It was "open"—not fenced in or locked up tight. It seemed as though everyone except me could leave at any time they wished but were kept there by their own free will. For a long time I fooled myself into thinking it was a place where people came to rest a while during their journey through life. In fact, many of the patients called it a "rest home." During my stay I saw many patients leave only to return a few months later. Some, I was told, came back year after year, as though it were a spa. One friend who came to visit asked, "What do I have to do to get into this place?" It took me a while to realize there were some clearly defined prerequisites. Except for two patients who were not well off financially, and who did not stay long, most people seemed very rich and very sleek. Many of the women there were so well groomed and elegantly dressed they could have stepped out of a fashion magazine. There was only one Jew, a sad, lonely woman. Someone said she was the heiress of a large department store chain.

Perhaps I knew all along that Dr. T. favored only the rich, that if you didn't have money or someone to foot the bills, you couldn't have stepped through the door, except to work as a servant or nurse. I never saw a black person there—not even in the capacity of maid or gardener. Dr. T. was from the South as well as many of the patients. Perhaps the presence of black people would have stirred up too much anxiety and it was not a simple case of race prejudice. I can't pretend any of these matters bothered me then. I was elated. Someone could have told me an atomic bomb was going to blow us all to hell in the next minute and I probably would have burst out laughing. My social conscience is a recent acquisition, except for when I was depressed. But then it was a matter of finding people who seemed as miserable as I was in order to prove I wasn't entirely alone. It never occurred to me, at least not consciously, that if I had been poor, no one would have had anything to do with me.

I believe now that the Foundation had been created to ease the rich through the crises of life and to try to protect them from the pain and horror of living. It was as though life had been reduced to a few simple physical pleasures. Good food was one. A sound night's sleep another. The motto was "Work, Rest, Exercise, Play," and our daily routine included all of these things. The Foundation was a refuge, a retreat, and the use of drugs and shock were magical means of ridding the privileged of all discomfort and needless, distasteful, psychic disturbance. Three assumptions gradually emerged. If you were rich enough: (1) you didn't have to suffer, (2) you shouldn't allow yourself to suffer, (3) you shouldn't be allowed to suffer. If you persisted in feeling tormented or acting strange, you were to be drugged or shocked out of it. But while you were there you should pretend that nothing was wrong. There was an unspoken agreement that if someone acted looney or tried to commit suicide, you were to act as though nothing out of the ordinary had happened. You were to continue taking your walks, working in the shop, sipping tea by the fireside, and dressing for dinner as though everything always turned out well in the end, and that it was only a matter of time and "Work, Rest, Exercise, Play" before you—everyone—would be able to go back to the high positions, expensive schools, clubs, servants, and elegant social life awaiting us in the outside world.

It was very expensive at the Foundation. Each doctor's appointment was $50; it was at least that much a day for room and board, though this depended on which room you had. There were additional luxuries, like laundry, taxi service, birthday cakes, and special attendants, like my nurses. But I did not find out the high cost of everything for a long time. . . .

Many of the young people there were sophomores and juniors at Yale, Harvard, Vassar, and Smith. These were the universities everyone at the private girls' school I attended had tried desperately to get into and only a select few had made it. Just the names of these famous prestige schools filled us with awe and reverence. Girls had been accepted for two reasons: either they were the brightest in their class, student council president, and had won awards for outstanding scholarship, or they came from "good families," which often meant not only wealth but that their parents had attended these universities as well. I had long since noticed this made both the parents and offspring "different." They made fewer mistakes, never said anything gauche or silly, were very careful and reserved both in their clothing and behavior. All of these things had been very important when I was growing up. So I tended to make those young people at the Foundation who had attended the famous Ivy League schools into fantasy people, much like the Great Gatsby did to Daisy and Tom Buchanan. Like Jay Gatsby, I felt there was a world just beyond my reach where people always did and said just the right thing because their money had given them power and absolute control as well as beauty, taste, refinement.

You might say that when I was elated, "manic," I saw things the way a snob or social climber sees them. Yet this was complicated by another tendency, equally strong, to mock, shock, ridicule as well as try to win everyone's affection and approval. So when I was around anyone who seemed to belong to some exclusive elite, I oscillated between acting blatantly snobbish—turning up my nose and saying things like, "Let them eat cake!" or "How terribly Non-U!"—and then being as loud, brash, and vulgar as I could. It was as though I had to see certain people as snobs, then be as spiteful and defiant as I was impressed and envious. I had to be "taken in" and then "see through" them, pretend I was as good as they pretended to be and then show them what was underneath it all.

There was only one girl there who came close to intimidating me. She had silver blonde hair and a gold ring engraved with what looked like a family crest. She went to Vassar and seemed infinitely refined, aristocratic. We shared the same doctor, which may have contributed to our mutual hostility. Once I heard her mocking me in a group of young people, mimicking my loud, raucous voice, my silly gestures, designed to get as much attention as I could. When I heard her imitation, listened to what I must sound like, the things I did and said to draw everyone's attention to myself, I became overwhelmed with shame and embarrassment and began to cry. Later I learned she hated Vassar. Everyone hated the school they went to regardless which one it was. Her boyfriend, a slick-looking lad from Yale whom I also imagined as a snobbish aristocrat, attempted suicide one night and had to be rushed off for shock treatments. Once I heard her talking to her mother on the phone and it became clear her mother was a horrible bitch. Later she confided in me: "Dr. K. says I have two choices: stay here until I am cured or remain a screaming neurotic the rest of my life." I noticed there were times she acted dizzy and times she stared vacantly into space, one eye wandering slightly to the left of center.

Four years later I was committed to another institution, a closed ward where the patients seemed much more overtly or severely ill. I was shocked at the small cramped hideous rooms, the damp gray walls and barred windows, and the dirty, shabby, desperate patients who were brutally treated by the staff. I was depressed when I saw horror, despair, hopelessness, oppression. But I wondered if money had made so many of the Foundation patients more discreet and refined in their symptoms and behavior or whether it was my elation and Great Gatsby fantasies—some need to see certain people as members of a privileged elite from which I was excluded because of some inherent inferiority. Perhaps it was the huge dosages of drugs which made the majority of Foundation patients seem so genteel. Or perhaps the fact that when disorders became more violent and uncontrollable, people were immediately sent off for shock treatments or to closed wards. Not all the patients at the Foundation were so refined of course. But none resembled those I saw four years later, in the closed ward, who had neither wealth nor status, privilege nor refinement to hide behind or fall back upon. . . .

Perhaps Dr. K. meant well. Perhaps he felt he was truly helping humanity by his work at the Foundation. He must have been enormously rich like all the shrinks there. He saw many patients a day, each appointment costing $50. That means eight patients a day, $400 a day. This so astounds me now, yet at the time it seemed perfectly natural. Many patients feel their shrinks deserve every penny they get and I think this has to do with the guilt and self-hatred every mental patient feels. Inherent in every "emotional disturbance"—the way you have been made to feel stupid and unworthy, ignominious or guilt-ridden—is the feeling that no amount of money is quite enough to pay someone to be kind to you or simply to devote fifty minutes of their time to your tedious, filthy, murderous psyche.

I believe many psychiatrists and analysts unwittingly use their patients' deep-rooted self-hatred to make them pay through the nose. They have very noble justifications here too. "If you don't make a patient feel he's made a big investment, he won't try very hard and he might stop treatment just when the going gets tough." Perhaps this is true in certain cases, but it's also the way we are enticed, in our culture, to keep making payments on shiny cars and plastic prefab houses, the latest washing machines, skimobiles, motorcycles. There is something about psychiatry which smacks of capitalism; you begin thinking about returns and investments, as though mental health, "normality," was something you could buy on time, own, and turn into a profit. . . .

A part of me was shocked and appalled the moment I entered this famous psychiatric ward. The place was drab and hideous, the walls a damp gray, the rooms small, stinking, and overcrowded. But then, I was used to the Foundation when it came to looney bins. It is no wonder my nose wrinkled in distaste.

Though I thought I would feel safe, my shame and fear and panic followed me and would not go away. I spent that first day hiding my face in my hands, crying continuously, until late afternoon, I fell into a light uneasy sleep. I felt that I had descended to a new low, in part because the patients I saw there were what people call "looney," "nuts," "off their rocker." Unlike the refined, elegant patients at the Foundation, they were poor and shabby and destitute and their symptoms were terrifying and severe. You could not carry on a normal conversation with them (except for William, my savior, whom I met a few days later). I believe my initial reaction to these patients was ferociously snobbish. I am ashamed now when I think of it.

But I did not spend much time feeling superior. I hated myself and suddenly grew suicidal. I banged on the screen and would have flung myself down the three stories if it hadn't been one of those nuthouse screens that don't break. I remember trying to walk out. I couldn't believe it was a "closed ward" and that bouncers had been hired expressly to keep you from trying to escape. A strong young orderly told me I couldn't leave and when I kept on walking, he took me back to my room.

Sometime that afternoon I fell into a light sleep. I remember hearing or sensing someone sitting very close by, rocking back and forth in a chair. I heard a harsh voice say, "Come away from there. She's asleep. Now leave her alone." A young girl's voice pleaded, "Oh please let me stay. I'm not bothering her. She's so nice." I opened my eyes to find a small, dark-haired girl staring at me, rocking violently back and forth in a chair beside the bed. I felt irritated, turned my back on the child, faced the sweating wall, and went back to sleep.

I was awakened in the evening by a nurse who crossly said, "Come to dinner. You've got to eat something." I told her I wasn't hungry, but she said I had to. Rules were rigidly enforced there. I got up and walked to the small, cramped dining room down the hall, which smelled of urine, antiseptic, and vomit. At first I thought there was a riot going on. Food was slopped everywhere. People were talking in loud, hollow voices and walked around senselessly in an agitated manner. The nurse helped me to a plate of wilted, colorless food. There were strange buzzing and hissing noises going off in my ears and I felt totally confused. Yet I gradually made out a male voice, talking louder than the rest. "You see the hydrochloric acid builds up in your stomach, but if you eat enough of it, you can fly up to the moon in a big fart." I suddenly began laughing hysterically. Then I got up quickly and ran out. The buzzing and hissing grew louder, then deafening, and

I saw fluffs of gray cotton entwined with a heavy black wire which all melted into spinning flags or wheels. The last sound I remember was the crack of my skull on the hard, brittle floor.

When I came to, a voice was saying, "If she cracked her skull she could sue this hospital and then where would we be? In deep trouble, I can tell you that."

I opened my eyes to see a circle of women surrounding my limp, sprawling body. I got up slowly and told them I was all right, I just needed sleep, and was helped back to my room.

The rough, insensitive treatment of the patients was appalling. I could not believe it. I thought there must be some mistake. Perhaps I wasn't perceiving reality correctly? People just don't treat mental patients this way because, after all, like me, they are "sick" and in such desperate need of kindness, compassion, attention. This is what all that pampering which had been "bought" for me at the Foundation had done. I was totally blind to the way the vast majority of mental patients are brutally mistreated. I honestly thought the Foundation was the "rule," that everywhere patients are pampered and waited on and catered to. This could not be further from the truth. Most people feel contempt for the weak and disfigured, the way children do, openly, when they make fun of cripples and harelips and retards and anyone who seems odd or "different."

There was no kindness in this ward, except among the patients, who aligned themselves against the cold, contemptuous attitude of the aides and nurses and orderlies. Yet the therapists were like a thin vein of gold running through the cold, hard granite of the staff. Dr. R. was no exception. He saw me every day, even on Sunday, and he was incredibly kind. I was surprised to find he had a real elegant office, above the ward, and a private secretary. The patients told me he was some high official of this ward and were impressed that he was my doctor. Yet later, I could not help but think about his fine office, the elegant cut of his clothes, his shiny Mercedes, and then compare it to the dreary, hideous ward and shabby patients over whom he had such power, like a feudal lord.

8. JANE EPSTEIN:
Vinton Cottage*

Vinton Cottage is home for twenty women on the grounds of Pontiac State Hospital. Each woman is classified as an inpatient although not subject to regulation by most of the larger hospital's administrative machinery (piggery). These women are restored most of their rights as human beings and given the responsibility of determining the course of their own lives. They administer their own medication, keys, cooking, cleaning, passes, money, and so on. There are no seclusion rooms here, no attendants to lock up our sisters when they express anger and pain. In fact there is a "Crazy Room" painted in psychedelic subway scrawl by the women and volunteers, where craziness—that is, acting out feelings, no holds barred—is not only sanctioned but encouraged. Write on the walls, beat the punching bag, yell yourself hoarse, just do what comes naturally. Don't fight the feeling.

The Vinton Cottage program started two years ago. Sel Fidelman, Dan McIvor, and Carole Sheppard, all professional staff at Pontiac State Hospital, decided to try an experimental alternative to traditional ward care using a model inspired by the work of Fairweather and Sanders. The original orientation was one of behavioral modification and proved unworkable if the program was to have relevance to the real live women involved. The experimental model was modified in order to accommodate the residents. In simplistic terms Vinton Cottage is now a place where each sister can manage and care for herself in an atmosphere of mutual caring.

Each woman is expected to take the lead in initiating her own

* SOURCE: *The Radical Therapist,* vol. 3, no. 1 (September 1972).

program that will ultimately end in her release and freedom. Vinton women have the opportunity to look for work in the community so that they will have some independent means on which to live on the outside. This summer the cottage program, which operates on funds from an NIMH grant, is branching out with satellite apartments in Pontiac. It is hoped these apartments will provide another link between the cottage and the city of Pontiac, helping to cushion the return to an insensitive and some-times hostile community. When a sister finds employment she can move into one of the apartments, pay rent to an apartment fund, and have the benefits of contact with the cottage community while making it on the outside. After a year in a satellite apartment, the woman has the option of taking over the lease or finding a place of her own.

The three professional staff volunteer their time. They must wangle the twelve and more hours they spend at Vinton each week from their main hospital duties. They come for group therapy which meets four times per week and meetings with nonprofes-sional staff and student assistants. The two student assistants (I am one) are the only paid staff. We spend our time talking to our sisters, sharing the work load, participating in group therapy, and taking trips in state cars. No attendants or guards monitor the comings and goings of Vinton residents and no staff sleep in the cottage.

The most obstinate impediment to success in the program is institutionalization. The average history of hospitalization shared by these sisters is six years. The internalization of the dependency/ oppression fostered in the hospital is practically inevitable. It is horrifying to contemplate the violence done to people in state hospitals. The destructiveness of the internalization of the role of "patient" is untold. These sisters have been oppressed so long and so relentlessly that they now equate identity with "illness." The dependency engendered by the state/hospital/father establishes itself in a tragically vicious circle.

What is it we are saying to a woman newly referred from the main hospital to Vinton when we tell her she can reclaim responsi-bility for herself and her situation? What self is left to be reclaimed? A self, mutilated by the world and at her own hands? A secret female self that has escaped effacement by the forces of male-dominated institutions? An embryonic self denied sentience who knows how long? It is little wonder many Vinton women view their renewed "freedom of responsibility" with distrust and incredulity.

Sadly, the sisters at Vinton Cottage are not aware that their personal struggles relate to the struggles of their sisters and brothers at Pontiac State Hospital and the larger struggles of all oppressed peoples. That these women have been taught/socialized not to see beyond their individual problems is no accident. The political necessity of limiting the consciousness of the oppressed is well understood. At the very least Vinton Cottage provides sanctuary from the programmed atrocities in the main hospital. At best it will be a place where recognition of a shared humanity will give rise to the consciousness of our unity in struggle.

9. CYNTHIA CEKALA:
If This Be Insanity*

I was a mental patient for three months in the fall-winter of
1969–70. I got out by a lie and only now after I have seen my
records do I know why I was sent up. I asked for help in the
beginning. My life was in confusion—I had given up the only thing
I knew in life, academics, and was powerless to make the transition to any other. I wished to reach some state of sensitive nonin-
tellectual relation to the world. I had lost all my friends through
graduation and thus all my territory. I had lost my lover through
God knows what mistake or misunderstanding on his or my part.
Graduate school had been a hell of cross purposes. I could no
longer feel happy about analyzing poems (Pablo Neruda's "Resi-
dencia En La Tierra") because I felt they were ego lamentations
and if the poet had been full within himself he wouldn't have
written them. My credo at the time consisted of Dylan's "Love
Minus Zero—No Limit" and "She Belongs to Me." I wanted to
remain secure with the memory of my lover for a while but found
myself hassled by all the straight males on campus who wanted to
sleep with me, including two faculty members. And worst of all I
had to speak Spanish all the time in preparation for Madrid; I was
alienated from my own language. God knows I tried to make it
through. I tried to continue my chosen life style in the face of
lowering professionalism. The contradictions were too much and I
dropped out and sought psychiatric aid.

The shrink was very nice, white, male, about sixty-five. He asked
me about my life, what I believed in, whether I had a sex life, what
were the details of it, whether I took drugs, and what I wanted to

* SOURCE: *The Radical Therapist,* vol. 3, no. 1 (September 1972).

accomplish. I saw him four times. His advice to me consisted of going to dances at Penn and meeting young law students and staying away from black men. On the fourth time he told me and my mother that I had schizophrenic reactions due to drugs and two months to two years in a hospital would fix me all up. On the strength of his status in the psychiatric world (I later found out that he had been the first to introduce electroshock to the United States) he convinced the second shrink who interviewed me at the hospital, and who was unwilling to admit me upon interviewing me alone, to sign a "404 commitment." The petitioner was my father and the evidence was a letter I had written home from college about finding myself and my own life style. My admitting diagnosis was "Sexual acting-out—if not hospitalized might get pregnant or get VD."

I was admitted the 18th of October to a locked ward. My clothes were taken away and I was given a set of hospital pajamas and a robe. When I arrived on the third floor and looked out from the window toward the beautiful landscape of the outer world and was admonished to come back into the dayroom, patients are not allowed to wander in the hall, I knew where I was and what was going to happen. Days were unique only in what I could do with myself in a confined place. I did not set foot in the open air for two weeks and had no form of communication other than the TV. Some days I analyzed the values of toy commercials. Other days I tried to see how long I could play solitaire in perfect silence. I pondered the metaphysical implications of having seven apples and whether it was good to give them all away to those who had none. I pondered what my lover had been to me, what he had taught me, what was the ethos I must now create for myself. I was interviewed by the shrinks. One asked me to talk to him in Spanish. I suppose I talked about books. He wrote down that I was a pseudointellectual. Another asked me if I believed in the Bible; I told him I believed in a higher plane of existence. He wrote down that conventional psychotherapy would be useless for me since I did not listen to what the psychiatrists told me. Once I was asked to draw pictures about people and houses and an object I disliked. For the picture of dislike I drew a huge open mouth. I explained that I hated people who were always endlessly talking without thought. I took personality tests. Those indicated that I was normal. I went to staff and talked to them. I was sent down to an open building.

The open building differed from the locked wards in that each patient had his or her own room and nothing was locked during the day. There was the same lack of stimulation and the same impersonal contact with the nurses and the aides. The psychiatrist I had there conducted group therapy once a week; that was usually the most I got to see him, although I had maybe three private sessions in three months, the third being the last. He would ask us all (us mostly being housewives; there were two men out of about ten people, as I recall) if we had any problems or questions. And then if we didn't have anything to say the talk would be general. One of his sure-fire openings was, "And what is your favorite kind of dog?" I said I liked cats but he didn't pick up on that. Another time I told him of a vision I had had the summer before but he wasn't interested; "There are no such things as visions." My Lai happened at that time, so one day I asked him about that. He said that he had been in the Korean War (which I could well believe, since at forty or so he still wore a crewcut) and he knew American boys did not kill unarmed women and children, so there was nothing to talk about. Sometimes, in deference to the married women, the discussion would go on to the lovely innocence of childhood and how nice it was to take the children to places like Disneyland. Finally I just began a war of attrition against such a stupid waste of my time and would braid my hair or play with my lighter while all the student nurses sat in fascinated attention, believing that here they were really learning to help these poor people.

I had a few friends of my age there but most of them were in the adolescents' building. In the beginning I and another friend would go over there and play records in their lobby, but that activity was stopped by official order. Either they would corrupt me or I would corrupt them. We also would go to the music building and into the little rooms and play records, but they finally made a ruling that only one person could be in there at a time since God knows what we were all doing in there together. The one girl of my building I was friends with usually went to bed at six o'clock since she was on very heavy medication. Sometimes I would go to her room or she to mine and we would talk. My doctor accused me of having a lesbian relationship with her. Throughout my stay there I wore what I had worn at school—boots and jeans and sweaters. The shrink told me that if I didn't give up being a hippie and wear skirts I could not be considered to be cured. In my records I was "masculine." It was at this session that he asked me if I was a lesbian. My friend was also warned that if she hung around me it was sure to be a bad influence. (She is still there, three years later.) Another friend of mine was put into the hospital by her husband who was a shrink. He took her kids away to his mother and had the courts deny her custody. We used to listen to Dylan's "Subterranean Homesick Blues." It was rather less consolation than an expression of solidarity against the system we were in.

Although there is occupational therapy for every patient in the hospital, there is a limit to how many ashtrays and clay things and water-color pictures you can finish without feeling a little bored. I got very bored; I wouldn't even get up for breakfast, though at this point I was consistently overeating and had gained about ten pounds. Anyway breakfast wasn't much. Once they served us creamed hamburger on toast. Not even the least picky of us could eat that at 7:30 in the morning. So I just slept all day. I nagged my parents to get me out. I wore skirts with a wrathful submission. Finally I was sent to my doctor. He asked me what I was going to do when I got out. I said I was going to get a job at Bell Telephone and go back to graduate school in the fall. I felt that peculiar tightening of the throat one feels when lying outright, and though I kept my eyes unblinking, fastened on his face throughout, I felt he knew I was lying. He didn't. "Patient is better motivated toward life." I got released a week later.

It's three years later. I still wear boots and jeans. I still haven't got a job nor have I gone back to grad school. And for that matter I still smoke occasionally. I have followed a queer resolve born of that time to leave the privileged class of professionals I could have been a part of, and live in the underbelly of the Beast. It's not easy; sometimes I still think I am crazy in the way I was and in a way they could never perceive. But I have some comfort in knowing that the better part is not to rest your life on the largesse of institutions and the pleasant truths put down by this society. If this be insanity, make the most of it!

10. DANIEL SCHOFIELD:
A Manic-Depressive Case History

My first sensation in a psychiatric ward was that things took on a mystical quality. I felt completely different than from being in the hospital lobby. A television program had a special meaning and a message meant only for me. I found it difficult to think straight. Also, I had an unusual preoccupation with the Bible. A sports columnist from a Detroit paper supposedly made a reference to me in an article about Joe Namath. I signed myself out several times. I was sure that I didn't need any help and wanted to be outside for a while. All the time I was making less and less sense. In a consultation with the attending psychiatrist, he asked me what was causing my peculiar behavior. In my confused state (which the doctor should have recognized as such), I was not aware that a biochemical disorder was the source of my trouble. I felt I should have something to tell him. I made up a completely false story of being on an LSD trip. The doctor believed it as if I had been Timothy Leary. Obviously this inept professional wanted to believe this story or else was too lazy to check it out. Probably both were true. He neither conducted a blood test nor even checked with my roommate. Without one bit of follow-up, he accepted the "fact" that I was an LSD user. If I had told him that I was God, which was just as possible, would he have bowed down and worshipped me? Not only was this falsehood put on my record as fact, it was detrimental in future drug therapy. Other doctors, seeing this on my record, accepted as the truth that my manic behavior was induced by hallucinogenic drugs and treated it as such. Because they accepted it with the same gross naivete as the incompetent who put it there in the first place, I was to take a very potent dose of a strong tranquilizer (Thorazine). Not until two years later was I ever questioned about drug use, nor were my close friends ever questioned. For two years I suffered needlessly because someone in Jackson thought it would be too much effort to take a blood test or ask a few questions. Why do a little extra work if you can avoid it?

After I signed myself out of the hospital, my roommate called my parents to inform them of my actions. They immediately traveled five hundred miles to take care of me. With much discussion and persuasion, I again returned to the hospital. Although I had repeatedly signed myself out of the hospital, I had always done so in a peaceful and orderly manner. I showed no indications of violent behavior. The only reason I kept leaving the ward was that I couldn't stand to be confined to the floor. So when I reluctantly returned with my parents, I was not only confined to the ward, but was locked, like an animal, into a bare room with a barred window, metal door, bed, and four walls. (Obviously the logic of the aforementioned doctor.) When in doubt, lock 'em up! Being resentful for having to return to a place where I felt that I didn't belong, then being forced into a locked cage, I had to take my anger out on the only things around. Being caged like an animal had an adverse effect on me. I completely destroyed the bed, ripped open the pillow, and scattered feathers throughout the cell and over the window screen, to make a difficult mess to clean up. I mistakenly thought I would make the attendant feel sorry for locking me up by rubbing my knuckles against the screen causing them to bleed. (I was unaware of their acute insensitivity.)

The so-called doctor was soon to prove himself a genuine, first-rate incompetent. My father had to argue and demand at length, as only he can do, to have me transferred to the Plainwell Sanitarium where my cousin worked and which is within easy visiting distance of about ten relatives. The doctor wanted to transfer me to Ypsilanti State Hospital which was closer to Jackson but over sixty miles from the nearest relative. This is the way he had always done it, and it involved less paper work for him! Consideration for me as an individual was light years away from his mind.

Although violent while in the locked cell, when the door was opened I became calm and in no way tried ever to hurt a person.

Two policemen were to transfer me to Plainwell. I offered no resistance to them at any time. Even the handcuffs I was forced to wear didn't bother me as long as I could get out of that cage. It was an hour's trip to Plainwell. I talked and joked with the policeman riding in the back seat with me. When we got to the sanitarium he even let me wear his cap into the admissions office. (Would he give his hat to a violent patient?)

Immediately I learned that Jackson did not have a monopoly on ignorant doctors. Although I had been completely calm while being admitted and for the entire hour-long trip from Jackson, and had never been violent previously except when treated like a violent animal, the attending psychiatrist made the worst possible decision and locked me into a stronger, yet similar, cage. Because the bed was built better, I could not destroy it, and I had to settle for tearing up the bed sheets. After a week I burned myself out and got accustomed to life in a cage. Therefore when I could stand close confinement, I was released to a larger area, that being the sanitarium itself. Later, there were times when I felt agitated and uncomfortable at being confined to the sanitarium; so their logical treatment was to put me back in the cage again. (Apparently so I would realize what a good thing I had going when I was let out.) When in doubt, lock 'em up! This, of course, worsened the agitation, causing more destruction again till I wore myself out. Then I would be freed to the ward. Seeing that being treated like an animal wasn't helping, the next step was to send an electric current through my brain. I was given ECT or electric shock treatment without ever being consulted. . . .

Jack, my cousin, arranged for a court order that committed me to the Kalamazoo State Hospital (which, I was to find out later, made the Black Hole of Calcutta look like a resort hotel). They had the mistaken idea that the doctors there had to be an improvement from Jackson and Plainwell. Oh, how wrong they were!

When I was finished with the admissions procedure at Kalamazoo, all done in an orderly fashion, I was taken to the third floor ward. Here I was to get my first taste of mental patient abuse at its worst. I was taken to a bare room, and was ordered by one of eight husky, mean-looking attendants to remove my clothes. When after two seconds I had not made sufficient progress, all eight of the attendants began simultaneously to attack me. One had a choke hold that a professional wrestler would be proud of. It almost suffocated me. The others twisted legs and arms or punched me, according to their particular preference. It seemed to me that they enjoyed such unnecessary and cruel tactics and viewed them as a fringe benefit that went with the job. For a while I was extremely cautious, to say the least, fearing for my life. (Maybe next time they would forget to release the choke hold!) This opinion was strengthened when I saw what happened to a harmless (but unresponsive, because of LSD use) black youth. In full view of the other patients (maybe to let them see what happened if you didn't jump when the master spoke), an attendant put his arm around the black boy's head and rammed it into a wall. The attendant might have been racially prejudiced, but I think he just enjoyed doing this sort of thing. Even after my own experience and the young black man's torture, I still retained my faith in human nature and thought there was a possibility that the attendants had some humane characteristics. (This thought in itself should have been proof that I was indeed sick!) These thoughts were soon proven false. One morning I was routinely awakened by an ape-like (physically and mentally) attendant. He mustered up the sum total of his wit and intelligence to bark out, "Time to get up." For some unknown reason I was in good spirits and thought I'd be cute and say something funny. Little did I know this would be wasted on a person with no sense of humor when dealing with his lowly patients. I made the fatal mistake of jokingly saying, "How come?" He showed his appreciation by locking the door behind him. This was done after he took my blankets and half-inch mattress off my so-called bed. The door was not opened for the next twenty-four hours except to deliver "meals." Combined with the eight hours previously spent in my room, this meant a total of thirty-two hours of confinement. I wasn't allowed the luxury of leaving my cell to go to the bathroom either. After I was forced to answer nature's call in a corner of my cell, I was severely reprimanded for urinating on the floor. (As if sleeping in the room that night wasn't enough punishment.)

We were allowed the privilege of changing our clothes twice a week. This took place when we took our showers and shaved. Evidently the water and shaving cream were too valuable to be used more than twice in one week. When we were lucky enough to be able to shower and change clothes, all fifty of the male patients on our ward were herded like cattle and lined up to receive our allotment of clean clothes. We then were directed to a dressing room where we undressed and put the dirty clothes onto a pile, then waited for our turn at the showers.

Long hair, beards, and extreme mustaches were all forbidden. The "food" was the worst-looking and -tasting stuff that I have ever had the misfortune of experiencing. There was separation of the sexes for the patients. This made it that much further removed from a normal situation.

Each patient received an audience with a doctor for a maximum of five minutes per week. This was done not in the privacy of an office but on the ward with others standing around waiting their turn to speak with the man who controlled their fate. During these brief consultations (at which time the doctor invariably reminded you how valuable his time was, assuming that yours wasn't), it was rare to receive anything remotely resembling therapeutic counseling. The main purpose was for the doctor to judge your improvement or condition. How I or anyone was expected to improve enough to be released while in that hell-hole and while receiving no therapy from the doctors except for drugs, is amazing. It's a wonder that more patients aren't mentally scarred permanently from their experiences in places like Kalamazoo State Hospital. Very little was done to speed my recovery and absolutely nothing was ever done to inform me as to what might have caused my erratic behavior.

Therapy consisted of two things. One was to sedate me to the extent that I was in a zombielike state. I was ordered and forced to take 800 mg per day of the extremely strong tranquilizer, Thorazine. This is commonly used to treat LSD users and I probably have the doctor in Jackson to thank for being on that drug. Never having been under the effects of drugs before, I thought there must be something wrong with me that I couldn't perform in a normal way. I couldn't understand that it was actually the powerful drug that was depressing me. The other form of therapy was the one high point of my commitment. This was the one thing I looked forward to, besides looking forward to my release. This was the occupational therapy program. In the program I made pottery, paintings, wallets, and so on. The therapist happened to be the wife of a fraternity brother. Therefore we had something to talk about from the start. It was so wonderful to be able to talk to someone intelligent who was also a female. She showed concern and compassion, rare commodities at this institution. I will always be grateful for that one ray of sunshine amid the darkness and gloom.

A patient, who was my best friend at the hospital, had an interesting and tragic tale to tell. One of the reasons I liked him was that he showed no unusual behavior, and I could carry on an intelligent conversation with him. He was from New York City, and I enjoyed hearing about things from that city. At first I wondered what he was in a place like this for. Then I learned of his pathetic story. He was vacationing in a northern Michigan town. A rash and pimples had appeared on his backside and he wanted to clear this up. His cottage was surrounded by high bushes on all sides. He decided to expose the troubled area of his body to the sun. Since a bathing suit covers up the area he wanted the sun to get at, he sunbathed in the nude. To people on ground level he was impossible to see. But with some considerable effort an unbalanced, puritanical woman spotted him and took considerable offense to his bare bottom (as if everyone didn't have one!). Unfortunately for my friend, this nut just happened to be married to the police chief. Then, probably through sexual blackmail, the chief was forced to give this innocent and completely normal young man a choice of imprisonment in jail or imprisonment in Kalamazoo State Hospital. Because he was unaware that the name hospital was a misnomer and that there existed such brutal and inhumane treatment at KSH, he mistakenly chose the worst of two bad institutions.

While I was on my potent dosage of Thorazine, I had to prove to the staff that I could perform all normal activities in a prescribed manner. (Could the staff do their jobs under this handicap?) Therefore I had to do work (at no pay) that should have been done by hospital employees. This was supposed to indicate that I was fit to leave and was rehabilitated. In actuality its purpose was to provide a work force at no cost to the hospital. In this way the administrators could afford to hire more goons to torture and beat up patients.

The final humiliation before release was to be put on the stage of an auditorium filled with more staff than I had seen the whole time I was there. There were psychiatrists, psychologists, social workers, and a whole class of student nurses. In front of these peering eyes, I was forced to prove that I was in fact ready for the outside world. After doing time there, I was ready for anything!

Upon release I was strongly persuaded to report to a social worker at KSH for outpatient therapy. This outpatient therapy was an improvement over the therapy while a patient, but not by much. The Thorazine was cut to 200 mg a day. (This still causes most people to resemble a zombie.) Under the handicap of this drug program I was expected to seek employment. But, when I applied for work, I was continually told that although my work record and academic record were excellent, I appeared too lethargic and listless. With the Thorazine it was impossible to appear otherwise. They thought I was still sick, when in reality the medicine was causing this effect. Already sedated and depressed from the tranquilizer, I was now being driven further into depression by my lack of success in finding a job. The social worker compounded my depression and lack of self-confidence by trying to tell me that I couldn't handle a job of the caliber I had previous to my commitment and that I should get work as a factory worker or janitor. I was naïve enough to think there might be a grain of truth in what he was saying, and this depleted what little self-confidence I had. So, just as I lost my job because of a mistake on the part of the staff at the Plainwell Sanitarium, I was prevented from getting a new job by the misjudgment of the staff of Kalamazoo State Hospital. Again, being naïve as I was, I never considered that my medication was doing any harm. I thought I must be to blame. Thus I convinced myself that I was sicker than I really was.

I had not yet learned of the tremendous discrimination on the part of employers against former mental patients so I told the truth about my illness. It didn't take me long to realize that honesty was not the best policy in this case. A former mental patient who tells the truth will not get the job. If he lies, he might get the job. Of course if the employer later finds out the truth he might get fired, but at least he will have worked for a little while. Then there is the possibility that if he finds out he will not fire you because you have proven yourself or that he will never find out the truth. Judge for yourself, the odds are in favor of lying to the employer.

After four months of discrimination by employers and lack of success due to apparent lethargy and listlessness, I was forced to leave the Kalamazoo area for Calumet, Michigan, in the upper peninsula of the state. I went there to live with my parents. The employment possibilities were even less up there, but I was having no success around Kalamazoo and the lower peninsula, and besides I didn't want to impose any more on my aunt whom I was staying with near Kalamazoo. This turned out to be a very good move. I felt much more comfortable in my own home with my family and I got away from the jurisdiction of KSH. I began seeing a psychologist at the Copper County Mental Health Clinic in nearby Houghton. She immediately realized that I was on too much medication. Therefore she switched me to a less potent tranquilizer and began a gradual reduction. In a few months on her program, I progressed to the point where I was feeling good again, and I was doing volunteer work for the local Head Start program.

11. BETTE MAHER:
Personal Account

Telling only of my experiences in mental hospitals is like telling an astrology class that the twelve planets of the zodiac are the only planets in the universe. There are perhaps billions of planets which make up our universe, just as there are myriad experiences that make up our lives.

What happened to me that finally made me end up in a mental hospital is just as important as what happened in the hospital. But since I must concentrate on my hospital experiences, I'll only say that the things that happened before were just as oppressive as the hospital experiences themselves, maybe even more so.

At about the age of twenty-two I found myself not being able to stand my life as it was and had been, and for the next year I gradually but very definitely began to withdraw from everything that was a part of my life at that time. I wanted and knew that my life had to change drastically then. Anything would have been better than that life without love, affection, and human closeness. Even death would have been better than that robot existence. I never knowingly demanded attention. I know at the time I felt I didn't have the right, that I didn't deserve love or recognition from anyone. But I so desperately craved it.

I think that somewhere deep inside of me I must have believed I deserved something because finally I made people pay attention to me. I lived with a family in whose house I was the only boarder. They were a very close-knit, loving family, but strangely enough my observations of their lovingness for each other made me face my own terrible aloneness and isolation. They were very nice to me and tried to include me, but the more they tried, the more I felt and realized that, as in all family situations I had been in, I wasn't and never could be one of them. No mother had ever held me close when I was scared or hurt, no father had ever held me on his knee and made me feel safe and protected. No father or mother had ever done, over a period of time, those million and one little things that make a child know she's loved and safe. My needs were too great. The realization of all I never had finally caught up with me. I couldn't stand it anymore. I had to know love at any price, even at the price of death if need be. I knew that something drastic had to happen to change me and therefore my life. As I said then, anything was better than this, *anything!* I began to think very seriously of suicide. The pain and agony I was feeling, feelings I couldn't define really, became too much to bear. I had gone through so much alone I began to think I didn't want to go through that terrible despair I was in with no end in sight but death. I was seeing a shrink as an outpatient at Massachusetts Mental Health Center at the time. I had only been seeing him for a short time and had in fact missed the past two appointments with him. I didn't like him and the only way I could describe what I thought was happening in therapy was that he was just going through the motions, so I did too.

A neighbor, who I was babysitting for, began to show some concern when I refused to come over to visit. She also knew I wasn't going to my job. She finally called me and told me that her little boy was very upset because I had been away so long and didn't want to go to bed that evening until I came over to see him. So I went over and said goodnight to him, but when I tried to leave her house she threatened to call the shrink unless I told her what I was thinking. At first I was reticent, but finally broke down in tears and told her I didn't want to live anymore. She told me if I tried to leave her house she would call the police. Since I knew a lot of the policemen personally (I'd gone to school with them) I didn't want any of them to know what was going on in my personal life. She called the doctor and he told her to keep me there until they found room for me at the hospital. That night I couldn't stand the agony or the vulnerable situation I was in, so I took eleven Seconal capsules. Although I later vomited them, my friend knew I had taken something. I hadn't wanted to do this in her house but the agony I felt transcended all other considerations. She called the shrink the next morning and told him. He came to her house that day and found me pretty heavily drugged but not in danger. He felt I should be hospitalized as soon as possible, so he arranged for a social worker from the Brookline Family Service to take me to Glenside Hospital until there was a bed at Massachusetts Mental Health Center. When I got in the car, the social worker asked me to promise I wouldn't try to jump out of the car while it was moving. I nodded my head in agreement as I was thinking I didn't have the energy to do that or even to tell her that I didn't. When we got to Glenside I was so depressed that I didn't care what happened. I cared so little that I don't even remember being admitted. I remember being brought to a ward with all women and the ward was very small and seemed overcrowded to me, but that didn't matter. Somewhere in the back of my mind I hoped that some patient would go berserk and kill me because I knew we were all being watched very carefully, so I couldn't do it myself. If I was afraid at all it was of the staff and not of the patients, which in retrospect surprises me considering all the stupid things I'd always heard about mental patients.

The patients were kind and let me know the rules of the ward to make it easier for me. I felt somewhat vulnerable about the staff because of their power over me, but I kept very much to myself. I felt that it was senseless to talk, so I didn't say more than five words in the week I was there.

After a week I was taken to Massachusetts Mental Health Center.[1] When I got to MMHC I was brought right into the admission office. A lot of people were in the office—the therapist I was to have, the social worker I was assigned to, the social worker I came with, the admissions officer, and a nurse from the ward. For a few minutes I felt overwhelmed by all the attention focused on me. For the first time in my life I felt truly visible. Then I heard

1. Although I wasn't aware of it at the time, I was transferred from Glenside Hospital because it was a private psychiatric hospital and I had no money to afford such a "luxury." MMHC is a state hospital and is run by Harvard Medical School for "teaching" purposes.

someone say that MMHC was a teaching hospital. Although I couldn't define why at the time, I instinctively realized the implications of this and felt myself recede back to invisibility again. I knew I was only a specimen and not a person to them. I guess without knowing it at the time, I hated them because they just wanted to use me, so I decided not to talk from that point on. I guess I felt it was my only defense. For about the first three months I communicated by nodding my head or shrugging my shoulders. I also thought to myself, "What's the sense of talking?" No one ever seemed really to care to know the real me, the hurting, agonizing me. I remember at different times in my life that I had to remind myself that I was a human being and couldn't help but have feelings. I remember also daring to think somewhere in the back of my mind that I had rights just by the very fact of my being. I was afraid to think these things because they stirred up so many feelings in me, feelings I later discovered were anger.

I was put on a ward with both men and women. The ratio of staff to patients was much greater than at Glenside. There were no locked doors, but there were so many rules and restrictions there might as well have been. At first I couldn't distinguish the other patients from the staff or visitors, but I knew right away who the doctors were. They walked around with such an air of importance and untouchableness that you'd have to be almost dead not to know who they were. I don't think it was ever actually put into words, but all the patients learned that these shrinks came from the elite Harvard Medical School and their word was not to be questioned. If you dared to question what they did, said, or decided concerning you, you were put down by being told your questions were hostile and a symptom of your illness, therefore invalid and negated.

When they allowed themselves to be human, there were some staff members I liked, such as nurses, attendants, and an occupational therapist, but when they got caught up in the power struggle bit, they really turned me off. I knew of course that the doctors were human but they put up so many walls of professionalism and authority, it truly made me wonder if they were automatons made to appear human.

One of the most degrading experiences at MMHC was the Patient Presentation Interview, otherwise referred to by the staff as a Stress Interview and by the patients as the Inquisition. I found these interviews excruciating, because one doctor would ask me very intimate, personal questions in front of a whole group of people who were strangers to me. I'm sure none of those people would have allowed themselves to be asked these same questions by some of their closest friends, much less strangers. They didn't even ask the patients if we in fact would be willing to go to these interviews. It was understood by all the patients that they were mandatory. I finally reached a point, perhaps because of self-respect along with anger, when I decided I no longer wanted to be a teaching-material guinea pig. This was when I was informed that I had to go to my sixth or seventh Inquisition. They tried to force me down to the conference room by pushing me into a wheelchair, which I kept jumping out of. Then they tried some strong-arm stuff, like twisting my arm behind my back and trying to drag me down, but finally the head attendant rushed over, yelled at the guy who was twisting my arm, and said they couldn't force me to go and left it at that. Within the next couple of days I was informed that I would be transferred to a big state hospital called Metropolitan State. I knew it was a punitive action taken by the shrinks for they realized that I no longer would cooperate and play the game their way. I was glad, but still pissed—for obvious reasons—but I got nothing out of their so-called therapy and outside of missing friends I had made among the patients, I had nothing to lose. I was at MMHC for six months and the only real help I got was from the other patients and some friends outside. I can honestly say that I received no positive help from the doctors there. I felt they were all cut from the same mold and related to me on a strictly authoritarian, intellectual level. I never could get near their personness—that was taboo. I felt they compounded my feelings of worthlessness and made me all too aware of my class position. They certainly didn't improve my self-image any!

When I was first brought to Metropolitan State, I remember being frightened by the size of the place. There are many old buildings, all of which look alike. They looked like what I thought mausoleums or prisons must look like. There were two buildings that looked more modern, the administration building and the admission building.

I was taken to the admission building. The admission procedure was much simpler than at MMHC. For one thing, the nurses wore white uniforms, whereas at MMHC the staff wore their regular street clothing. They went through all my possessions, gave me a physical, asked a few questions, and had me sign a few papers, none of which I bothered to read. As I was being brought to the ward I remember thinking for the first time that once a person enters the doors of a mental hospital he or she becomes a puppet whose moves are determined by other people. Your life is not your own; you cannot, like the people outside, come and go as you please.

I couldn't define why at the time, but I know I felt much less intimidated by the staff members. There are probably many reasons for this, not all of which I can define now. But I did know that they weren't going to use me for teaching purposes and that they didn't come on like gods with all the answers. I guess it was less confusing because I came closer to knowing where I stood. I was a patient and they were the ones who ran the ward. They didn't come on like heavy professionals. There was no mystery in what they did. There wasn't that awful pretentiousness that there had been at MMHC. There was distance between the staff and patients but they never did anything that made me question whether or not they were human. I must make a point of saying that I realized after a very short time that I was treated with a little more kindness than the other patients. I honestly believe it was because I was (to them) perhaps more physically appealing and more quiet. I made very few waves.

Although I may be wrong, I don't remember hearing of too many patients having to go to patient presentations. Although I know a few did, I never did at Met State.

I was in and out of Met State for a period of three years, two and a half of those years in and six months out. At those times when I tried to make it on the outside I'd very shortly get to the point where I felt as lonely and isolated as I had ever felt before. Jobs weren't easy to come by, I had lost most of my friends, but the worst part was trying to make the transition from inside to outside.

At least inside there were other people who had very similar experiences. Also, the pace in mental hospitals is much slower than outside. Making the adjustment on the outside is a tremendous strain physically, emotionally, and intellectually. Just getting used to such little things like the noise, the traffic, and public transportation is like experiencing a cultural shock. Also when an employer knows you've been in a mental hospital you're treated like half a person. They don't think you can take the pressure and responsibility that the other employees take. They don't even give you a chance to find out. It gets to the point where you begin to think they're right and you start playing the role they expect of you.

I believe it was about a year after being at Met State that the staff decided I should have a battery of psychological and I.Q. tests. After these tests were completed and evaluated, the staff determined that I had a fairly high I.Q. and I was diagnosed "psychoneurotic." They also determined from the tests that I would probably do well in individual psychotherapy. I knew that to be given psychotherapy was rare because in the whole time I was there there were perhaps only three other patients who had individual psychotherapy. In all honesty I realize that this is because the ratio of doctors to patients was very small and also because they only gave therapy to those patients whom *they* thought had the most potential and greatest possibility of "success" through therapy. Each time I had therapy another patient would say, "You just came back from therapy, didn't you?" I felt awful about this because I knew that they too wanted the same consideration and, even more, the individual attention.

The therapist I had was a Filipino woman. At first she came on as a strict professional but even during those times I never once thought of her as other than human. She was a very warm person and had very little problem with spontaneity. I knew then and still know that she cared very much about me and wanted me to get as much out of therapy with her as I could. In the two and a half years I had therapy with her, she only pulled the professional bit a few times but even then I knew she did it because she cared about me and thought she was doing the right thing. I guess the greatest thing I got out of therapy with her was a change in self-image. I began to feel that I wasn't such a bad and worthless person after all. I wasn't ready yet to deal with really heavy feelings like hate and rage with her. That's just not where my head was at the time. In her humanness and caring for me she gave me a strong base from which to explore other, more heavy emotions when I was ready.

When I had a pass, I could walk the grounds of the hospital. When I first saw the patients from the back wards I felt such terrible rage. These were human beings, most of whom had no one to care about them on the outside. I remember thinking what an incredible waste of life and human resources. They got so little attention. I knew they only saw a doctor about once every two or three months and only for a few minutes at a time. I knew that so many of them could leave the hospital if only their families and others cared enough, but no one did. I would cry at night, thinking about those people. I also felt guilty for getting the attention I was getting. I was also afraid that if I stayed in the admission building long enough I too would be sent to the back wards and be forgotten.

When I finally left Met State for the last time I went to live in a halfway house for ex-mental patients in Cambridge. The halfway house is a story in itself, which I can't go into here. I will say that it kept me from going back to the hospital and that the support I got, especially from the housemother, helped me tremendously.

It was five years before I had another hospital experience, one which was completely uncalled for and unnecessary, and the most frustrating and brutal of all. This was at Westboro State Hospital. In order to explain why I felt this hospitalization was unnecessary, I must tell what led up to it.

I have been subject to migraine headaches for years, but for the past three years they'd been much more frequent and intense. I also had two lumps on my right hip that caused me terrible pain. These lumps had been diagnosed as swollen lymph nodes by an intern at Cambridge City Hospital. The diagnosis of swollen lymph nodes had been made six months previously,[2] so I had this terrible pain in my hip and leg for all that time. Along with this

---

2. A year after this diagnosis of "swollen lymph nodes" was made I was operated on for those two lumps which turned out to be occlusion cysts encasing the sciatic nerve and causing tremendous pressure.

pain, I had a migraine that lasted five days. I couldn't sleep because of the pain. I went to Cambridge City Hospital to get medication that was stronger than what I was taking. But the couple of times I went there in that five-day period they informed me that the pain was psychological. They made me feel like a hypochondriac and a nuisance. I felt so angry and frustrated about all this, but even worse, so much at a loss to know what to do about it. Finally on the fifth day, after not having gotten any sleep and in continual pain, I decided to take one pill every hour, a barbiturate, until I finally fell asleep so I could escape the pain, even if only for a few hours. Finally, after about fourteen hours and just as many pills, I went to sleep. The next morning a friend of mine who knew how much I was going through called me. She realized I was pretty groggy and asked me how many pills I had taken. I remember, as groggy as I was, that her voice sounded kind of frantic. She told me to hang up and a short time later the fire department rescue squad came to my house and told me they were going to take me to the hospital. I told them to take me to Mt. Auburn Hospital because of what I had experienced at Cambridge City. My friend arrived at Mt. Auburn and was asked to speak with the doctor. During the time I was there, the doctor asked *me* no questions about why I had taken the pills. I think my friend told the doctor I had made serious suicide attempts previous to this, because after talking to her, he came over to me and said that because I had made an attempt at suicide I had to go to Westboro State Hospital. I tried to tell him that it had not been a suicide attempt but that all I wanted to do was get away from the terrible pain and thought I could do this by getting some sleep. He didn't listen to me; instead he harped on the fact that I had made previous attempts on my life. He didn't listen to me—he'd already decided he'd send me to Westboro.

I feel that if this doctor hadn't known about my previous history of suicide attempts he would have had a completely different approach to my case. I feel he used my history against me.

Westboro—*oh, God—Westboro!* My experience there was so *awful*. I was admitted by a physician who also didn't listen to my reason for taking the pills. I realized he simply didn't care and was so indifferent and going through the motions only because he had to.

I was put on a ward with all women. It was so small! At one end there were three rooms, each having four beds. At the other end were the seclusion rooms. In between were the two dayrooms and the nurses' station. This was all except for a corridor going the length of the ward. The nurses were very abrupt and, unless really pressed for an answer, would not say a word. In fact, they deliberately ignored you when at all possible. For the five days I was there they would all shut themselves in the nurses' station and would have as little to do with the patients as possible. When you had to ask them a question they would get really pissed at you and make it very clear that you were a pest and interrupting their conversation. You had to knock on the door of the nurses' station a number of times to ask them for anything, even though there was a glass partition and they could see you standing there.

The first night I was there, they put me in a seclusion room that had a heavy grate on the window and a corklike grate on the tiny door window, through which you could only look straight ahead. I told the nurse very calmly that I didn't feel it was necessary to put me in a seclusion room and that I didn't see why they couldn't at least put me in one of the four-bed wards, as it was a locked ward anyway. She told me not to give her any trouble and pushed me into the seclusion room, slammed the door, and locked it. I was so angry at the treatment I was getting! After I was in the seclusion room for a short while I had to go to the bathroom. I kept knocking on the door and asking if I could please use the bathroom. I knew they could hear me for they were no more than twenty feet away, but they completely ignored me. They even walked by my door a number of times and still wouldn't answer me. This went on for more than a few hours when I became so angry I couldn't stand it anymore. I started screaming at them but still they ignored me. Finally, I decided to take the cot and ram it against the door until either the door broke down or they responded. After I did this for about a half hour, two female and two male attendants came to the door and unlocked it. They shoved the cot aside and the two male attendants grabbed me. One of them grabbed me by the arms and lifted me off the floor, pulling my elbows in back of me till they almost touched. The pain in my shoulders was so great I thought he had broken them. The other male attendant grabbed my leg—with one hand he grabbed my shin and with the other was pressing in on my knee. I thought any second it would snap. I said to him, "Go ahead and break it! Then I'll have something to show a lawyer!" At this point they both let go and I crashed to the floor. For more than two weeks I could hardly raise my arms to wash my face or comb my hair and there was such a lump on my leg—the size of a baseball—I thought it was a blood clot. There were other bruises all over my body.

The next morning I was told I had to go to staff presentation. I had to wait in a small crowded corridor with about twenty other new patients. I waited for more than two hours for my turn. I watched each patient come out from the Inquisition—each one looking as if he'd been demolished. I knew I had to play it cool when my turn came. When I walked in, I was as composed as possible. I saw the clinical director of the hospital, Dr. Benjamin Simon, sitting by himself at the end of a long table. Surrounding him, crushed together, were about fifty staff members. I sat down at the table without being invited to do so. Dr. Simon's first question was, "Why isn't an attractive girl like you married yet?" I said, "I haven't found it necessary." Then he said, "Have you had many boyfriends?" I said, "I guess I've had my share." He then said, "Are you still friends with them?" I said, "Yes, with some of them." To which he said, "Maybe that's your problem—you're too friendly." And I said I didn't think friendliness was a problem.

Then he asked me what kind of pills I had taken. I responded, "They were Fiurinal." He asked me, "What is Fiurinal?" And I said that the doctor who had prescribed them for me said they were a barbiturate. At that point he turned and raised his arm like a conductor and said to about ten female attendants sitting near him, "What is Fiurinal?" They all yelled in chorus, "Nothing but bona fide aspirin." It all looked so rehearsed that if I hadn't felt so intimidated, I would have seen it as very comical. I knew he wanted an angry response from me, but I didn't give him one—I just nodded my head and didn't say a word. Then he said to me,

"Do you have any questions?" And I said, "Just one. When can I leave the hospital?" He responded by saying, "Well, I'm no biblical scholar. Maybe ten years and a day." And I said, "Does that mean ten days?" And again he said, "Like I said, I'm no biblical scholar." I stood up and said, "This is ridiculous." And I walked out of the conference room.

Two days later I asked for medication for a migraine, having heard from an afternoon nurse that the ward doctor had ordered it for me. This nurse was not on duty when I asked for the medication. The nurse that I did ask said no, I could not have it yet. I tried to tell her that unless I took the medication when the migraine started, it wouldn't be effective. But she told me not to bother her and to go away. A couple of hours later I asked again. And again she said no. I was so upset at having to face more pain that I went into the day hall and just sat down and cried.

That afternoon, the doctor I was assigned to came up on the ward. I told him I had a headache and couldn't understand why the nurse had refused to give me the medication. He told me that Dr. Simon had told the ward nurse not to give me medication for migraine—that I should be made to suffer for them because I had been spoiled by too much access to medication. I was so enraged at this, and at the memories of trying to get medication at Cambridge City, that I wanted to kill someone. But I could only go off by myself and cry.

After being there for five days, I managed to get myself out. Those five days were so painful, not only for myself, but for the other patients who were even more abused than I was, that I resolved I would never again give in to that kind of dehumanization without a fight. This gave me the impetus to start a mental patients' rights group, which I have been involved with now for over a year. The group is the Mental Patients' Liberation Front. We have drawn up a statement about the physical abuses of patients and violations of their rights. We are also trying to do consciousness raising with the general public about the abuse of the power psychiatrists have and about the myth of so-called mental illness. We are now working on a handbook of rights for people currently incarcerated in Massachusetts mental hospitals.

12. ANONYMOUS:
Letter to Dr. B.

Dear Doctor,

I am so very tired afternoons, and I had been in a ward where I could lie down to rest as all of us did lie down in the afternoon. The other doctors advised me to lie down to rest two hours every day. Please have me transferred to the other ward, over to E53 where Edith Meade is. She said she is given permission to rest every day over there.

Another trouble I have is my bed is so far down the hall I have to walk so far so many, many times every night to go to the bathroom. Every two hours I have to get up to urinate. It is also very difficult to hold my urine until I get to the toilet.

I wonder what kind of false reports have been made to you about me, since I have been told I cannot have any of my refreshments out of the locked cupboard, only at one hour after meals. That makes it very disagreeable for me.

The reason I cannot eat some of the food on my tray is because I have no teeth. Also that thyroid enlargement in my throat chokes me with some food.

Another reason is because I am and always have been allergic to tomato in any form; raw or cooked, it makes me sick and nauseated, in all my past life. These cooks mix the tomato in with so many foods. When I was only ten years old I could cook better than the cooks that are here. Sometimes the potato is hard and not half cooked and we do not have a fork to eat with or to mash our vegetable with. I like potato and other vegetables and always eat them when cooked soft as they should be. Many times I have been disappointed with the carrots and potato because it was not half cooked and was hard, and no teeth for me to eat with.

I wish you would please have me go out to a family care home before Christmas this year. Please do speak to the social workers for me. It is heartbreaking here to me in this noisy, lonesome ward. It is not noisy when you are in here for your short daily calls, so I do not expect you to know how awful it is in here in E52. I never have been in as noisy a ward before. Please consider this in human kindness and conscientiously. Thanking you sincerely.

S.

13. FRAN GARBER:
Mad Familiar Shorthand on the Wall

How do I say it? How do I show you that my life is not a long line starting in one place, going wrong in another place, getting straightened out, fixed, mended, and headed toward a respectable finish? How do I show you this lined out view of time and life is *so* wrong? Can you see my life the way I see it? Whole. Round. Stretched through courtrooms and LSD, mental hospitals and hurt, bewildered, angry husbands, frantic mothers and sunny children, happy friends, heaven's music, and drawn police guns. Whole. Completing itself. Growing like a spreading net, not a measly time line.

My mother begs and pleads with me to get some help, seek professional treatment because "you are not meant to live this way, you are meant for something better." She does not think my friends are good for me. I have gone wrong. Something has got to set me straight.

Mother, can't you see? I am *here*. No better or worse than I always am or will be.

My husband argues and explains: "You have got to admit you have suffered a severe physical and emotional breakdown. You used to be a sweet and loving person. Now you are angry and hateful. You have got to be willing to get real professional help."

Can't you see? I am *me*. Loving, angry, hateful, sweet. No better or worse than I always am or will be.

I would leave you all and run, run far. Except for one quiet voice that says, don't leave me. I am afraid to go, afraid to stay, afraid to live, afraid to die. Don't leave me. To live in the full knowledge of your own fear, this is courage, this is strength. I do not leave him. I need his strength. Because of him I do not kill myself. Because of him I wish I were dead. Because of him I know I am alive.

The vice squad comes bursting in. Fifteen men in two rooms. "Never mind about her. Her daddy's a preacher. He'll pray for her." "Yeah, the bitch." Fear. Fear. Anger and hate. How can paper-thin walls contain it all?

"She's under arrest."

"For what?"

"Let's say we found seven ounces and bust them all for it."

If you love me you will live. If you love me you will die. What is love? What is death? I don't know anymore.

Downstairs, as I write, my aunt is asking, "What went wrong with that marriage?"

"Young lady, I believe you are the only one who knows the truth," the judge says.

"Guilty," the judge says.

Presentence Investigation:

"You are a young woman. You entertained young men in your apartment. Are you sure there was no hanky-panky?"

Hanky-panky indeed. One of those young men did twenty-one days in a state mental hospital for trying to kill himself after that bust. His hospital social worker had only one question to ask me about him: "Was there really a raid on your apartment?"

"No, there was no hanky-panky."

That night in jail my stubbornly red, white, and American blue head is coming apart at the seams. If I am corruption, then fifteen years for corrupting the youth of America, that I can understand. But jail for nonexistent marijuana? That night I decide I *am* crazy.

The courtroom is a nightmare. I will not cry. No one can understand my tears. I do not cry. A young black woman is up for assault on her mother's obnoxious boyfriend. Boyfriend is healthy and prosecuting, showing off a well-healed Pepsi bottle cut. The woman is head of house for her mother and two small children.

"Eight months in the state women's prison," says the judge.

My case comes back up. My history reads like out of *Who's*

Who. B.A. from a respectable college. Four years respectable school teacher. Brother doing vocational rehab work. Mother a mayor. Father a preacher. Judge is obviously confused.

"Is your father present in the court?"

"Yes, sir."

"Is your mother present in the court?"

"Yes, sir."

To my lawyer: "Do you think this young lady is capable of handling a suspended sentence?"

"Yes, sir."

"Six months. Sentence suspended. Three years probation," says the judge.

My parents save my neck. All I can think of is that black woman. Eight months.

In my probation lady's office I have more to think about. She won't let me stay where I am staying. Wrong influence, she thinks. I won't go home with my mother. Wrong jailer, I think.

My back is to the wall.

Once again my mother (she is *not* an ogre; she is frantic to help me, bewildered by my way of living for the last six months); once again my mother describes Appaloosa Hall: friendly, resort, rest setup. Good help and all that. Since I would be voluntarily committing myself (uh huh), I would have freedom of the house and grounds.

I agree to it. A new clause is written into the judgment. "She will voluntarily commit herself to Appaloosa Hall for a period of up to six months. Early discharge will be at the discretion of the probation officer."

I arrive at Appaloosa Hall. Tall, sprawling, yellow stucco and gray granite breathing carefully preserved decaying elegance.

"Someone will be free to take you to your room after lunch."

Father, Mother, and I calm each other with jokes and smiles at lunch on white tablecloths.

I load my clothes, books, and hairbrush—everything I have— onto the elevator and wave good-by. The elevator shakes up a floor. The old cage gates open. I bend to pick up my luggage.

"Honey, you can't have your things." And I hold a new joker in my hand.

I follow without comment. The hall door locks behind me.

Locks. Fear. The mark stays with me. At any door latch clicking my stomach goes tight, fear rushing.

"Honey, I'll have to have your clothes." She gets them with no comment.

I sit in my green hospital gown and consider the bars on the window. Relationships chase each other through my head: jails, jailers, clothes, patients, inmates, victims, rings, bracelets, rules, fear, guilt, sanity, trustees, and wardens.

In jail I absorb the fact that my jailers expect me to be docile, patient, and *grateful* things are not worse. My cellmates are afraid of being shouted at, terrified of being deprived of cigarettes, and the possibility of a night on the pipeline or maybe even the hole is a real threat. On the other hand, they fight each other for the privilege of being trustee on the hall and watch each opening of the door with unguarded excitement. And I am very glad for the shower, the food, and Jane's small, quiet, comforting radio.

Hour after hour, jail lights are turned too low to read, too bright to sleep. I listen gleefully to the thundering music of an angry pipeline girl pounding on the iron walls, listen, cheer, silent, wholeheartedly, and consider the relativity of freedom:

O.K. Nobody's free. The narrow scramble for power inside the jail mirrors the larger battle in the deceptively freer prison we all want out into.

The question before us all—always—even tied hand and foot in a dark cell—is:

What will I do with the freedom I have?

and equally important

Where do I draw my lines, saying:

"O.K. You can have all that—those things which are mine—but you'll have to take

This Precious Item from me by force.

I will not make you feel better by giving my consent, smiling for your ripoff.

I will not be grateful to you because things could be worse."

And you may have to take my very life for this precious item. I refuse to give it up.

On both sides of the bars the jailers hold their power and *expect* the consent of the inmates.

"Honey, we've got to have your rings and bracelet."

"Why?"

"It's the rules. Itstherules."

"O.K. You can have my school ring. You can have my diamond ring if you can get it off. But you can't have my bracelet."

"Why not?"

Waste my, uh, rationalization on them? Are you kidding? Besides. This is standard power procedure. Suddenly I am supposed to prove why I should keep a bracelet that I obviously have *some* reason to wear since I am wearing it.

"Because I like it. I want to wear it and you haven't given me enough reason to take it off."

Seven women up the line of command try to get that one poor measly strip of copper.

"What's that on your arm?" begins Number Three innocently.

"It's my copper bracelet." Me with pride.

"May I have it?"

"No."

"Why not?"

"Because I want to keep it."

Number Four and Five content themselves with soaping off my diamond.

"Don't you want to give me your bracelet?" opens Number Six.

What a question. Obviously I don't want to give them the bracelet and it is causing a minor scandal on the hall.

I feel fairly safe. Nobody can do anything more to me than has already been done sometime. Someplace. My fate—when and how I get out of here—hinges on far more than a battle over a piece of copper.

Or does it?

The main thing that puts me here is an insatiable desire to meet people on their own terms, find out what they base their ideas of "reasonableness" on, and avoid making them unhappy.

What are *my* terms of reason? I have to find that out.

It is very difficult for me to keep myself from giving in. I *am* being unreasonable from their point of view. And they *are* upset. And that really bothers me.

But they aren't as upset as I will be if they get my precious item without a fight, laboring under the delusion they have my consent and my gratitude for being so nice.

Besides, their reason for taking it is stupid.

"Honey, it'll be safer. Something might happen to it with you."

It's survived this far with me, I scream silently. What's going to happen to *me* here if my bracelet isn't safe here? But only . . .

"No," out loud.

It is hard for me to stick to my bargain with myself and avoid trying to reason with them, trying to get them to see it my way, *but*—

I have no more right to expect their consent than they have to require mine.

All that matters is that I keep the bracelet.

I know it seems ridiculous to you sitting there in your silk upholstered chair—that I risk a physical battle if necessary to avoid the ripoff.

You know, they never say,

"Give me the bracelet."

It's only, "Don't you want to?"

Tie me down and take it and you haven't hurt *me*.

Make me say I want something I *do not want* and you are handing me death.

Number Seven finally says she'll tell the doctor.

Fine.

I have this terrific problem. I am very, very angry. Anger in any form is dangerous in a mental hospital. I analyze my alternatives.

1. I am angry enough to break heads and windows, rip sheets, and crash chairs. But if I do these things I will only be tied down in

security. "Honey, you cannot be let out until you learn to control yourself." Me and my buddies cheer new patients coming in, busting faces, tearing clothes. We're behind them blow for blow.

2. I can smile and bury my anger so deep it will not show. And who will I fool? "Young lady, you have a problem. It's this terrible anger you are hiding."

3. I adopt the only possible alternative. I do not scream, break heads, or even argue or complain. I am just carefully, quietly, openly angry.

I try to decide who I am angry with. Where will I plant the bomb? Women bitch and scream at the aides. I can't. I'm not here because of them. I count over everyone I know. I'm not here because of any one of them. No, a bomb to blow up the forces that put me here has to blow the whole world. Each time I stretch my head to figure things it winds up stretched around the world and boils back down to just one problem: *me*.

It's not the walls, the hall door lock clicking that draws blood. It's the iron schedule, the constant hawkeyed supervision. Everywhere I have to go with the group, shepherded by nervous aides. We're not allowed to walk the stairs. We trundle onto the old cage elevator. I hate the elevator worse than anything. I want to go to my room for the rest of my life, but I know cooperation is the only thing that will get me out.

I refuse medication. I take care of my own head, thank you. Everyone on back hall is out of her mind to begin with, doped out of her mind, or having shock treatment, or all three. Betty can never remember the door at the end of the hall is locked. She comes in several times a day to tell me about it. She asks me to please get the key and take her down to lunch. What's worse? Me, sitting there twenty-four hours a day knowing the door is locked? Or Betty, feeling trapped again every time she tries the door?

I see how tightly I control *myself*. I have the freedom of my room and the hall? I draw my own line and will not step out of my room unbidden. I rise, eat, am herded to occupational therapy, to fenced playground, to rec room, to group therapy, to Monday night bingo, to Tuesday night dance, to Wednesday night fun and games on a careful hospital schedule? Fine. I schedule myself more strictly within those lines. I study shorthand faithfully at my appointed hours. I divide my reading and writing to completely control my time.

The OT shop is close to heaven. I wonder if my joy in picking up my picture work is worth the jolting hurt when it's "Honey, we have to go up now." But everything is O.K. when Sad Lisa comes through in nails and string. I read Cat Stevens over and over. Music to dare monsters. I don't know what schizophrenia is, but I know who Sad Lisa is.

> She hangs her head and cries in my shirt,
> she must be hurt very badly. Tell me what's
> making you sadly. Open your door, don't hide in
> the dark, you're lost in the dark, you can
> trust me, 'cause you know that's how it must be,
> Lisa Lisa, sad Lisa Lisa.
> Her eyes like windows tricklin' rain
> upon her pain, getting deeper, though my love wants
> to relieve her. She walks alone from wall to wall
> lost in a hall, she can't hear me, though
> I know she likes to be near me, Lisa Lisa, sad Lisa
> Lisa.
> She sits in a corner by the door. There
> must be more I can tell her. If she really
> wants me to help her, I'll do what I can to
> show her the way, and maybe one day I will free
> her,
> 'though I know no one can see her, Lisa Lisa,
> sad Lisa Lisa, Lisa Lisa, sad Lisa Lisa.

A man stands by the chain link fence. He is dressed in starchy white, green web scout belt. Patient, doctor, aide, ice cream man. The wind through the fence blows his light brown hair. He is looking toward the mountain. Both hands on the cross bar. I am sitting five feet away on a green wooden park bench. I am talking, talking, pleading, explaining eighty miles a minute.

"That's all right," he says. "I understand."

Hope rising wild, I look up into the flashing brown eyes of a stark mad man.

The shock of that connection brings me wide awake. I know I am much more afraid than I yet understand.

I write (to myself) an ultimatum to my doctor. What do you know about fear and anger? How long have you knocked your head against the bars of everyone's wrong best intentions? What do you know about the desperation of insanity? Have you ever walked the road of living, being to where the path narrows, dropping off into complete understanding on one hand, total insanity on the other? I give you two months to figure things out. If I'm not crazy then I'll opt out into the safe confines of jail. Safe with an out date.

I find out why the locks and bars. I'm voluntarily committing myself, right? My probation officer calls my doctor. Lock her up, she says. My doctor calls the state for permission to unlock me. Fran Garber? Who's she? My papers are being processed. Unavailable. Twenty-five days drag on. My head climbs the walls. I know why mental patients get well. He that endures and figures a way to get things together and get out resolves: I won't ever let anything put me here again.

I lie in bed, awake at dawn. The howler is howling again. Thin, wordless, wolflike moaning, background noise for days. A universal cry, ageless, sexless, helpless. But this morning in the half light the words take shape—"Fran, Fran, help!" I hear. I go rigid, complete physical spirit answer rushing. For half a minute the nameless howler assumes the realness of a voice I know and love. The voice dissolves into even harder reality and I weep hot tears of shame. How tough and callous, deaf, blind, and hardened can I be? The voice has cried and cried for days. *I never heard it* before this morning. I lack the sensitivity even to hear a voice before it is named and known. God forgive my arrogance and ignorance.

I am unlocked. Still no word from the state, but my doctor takes the responsibility to move me to the open hall.

Being unlocked is taking off for a long, long flight that can never crash.

I listen at my window in my new room to the words drifting

down from a room above. Soft, measured, commanding, toneless, pleading words.

Downstairs back yard
Will you speak to me or not
It's a matter of life and death
Will you or won't you answer me
Back yard downstairs
Come to the back yard to talk to me
All against the law
Speak before we all die
I'm on the second floor
Will someone answer
Will someone talk to me
Can you open the door
Can you look up to me
Just look up to the second floor
And talk to me
Can you do that
Can you please do that
This is my last night
Will you please
Just come to this window
Right here
And talk
Ordinary talk
Talk to me
It's very, very serious
Is anyone down there
Look up
And out
Is there someone out there
You'll be dead by morning
Hello down there
Back yard
Bury them bury them
I'm right here at the window
Looking out at the yard
Right under our nose
Never alive when we are dead.

Never alive when we are dead. An echo to my answer to a drawn police gun a year gone by.

> Walk the line
> Am I an outlaw?
> The choice is mine
> I live the line
> Life in the Shadow of Death
>   or
> Death in the Shadow of Life
> Shut my eyes
> Play so hard. But
> There is no line.
> The stakes are high.
> "We are all outlaws in the eyes of America."

I make a decision. . . .

I decide to choose again for life. Sure. We all live behind bars. But I'm ready to recognize the individuality of everybody else's case at least. I'm ready to crawl out of the corner of my cage where all I can see are the general screens of the police cage, the law pen, the hospital stockade, the locked staff lounge, the patient security room. I'll look into every person's cave. See the personally carved bars, the carefully home-decorated feel, mad familiar obscene longhand shorthand on the walls, private keys that fit every lock—mashed out of shape but hanging on pegs marked Honesty and Responsibility.

Katy is still screaming. In short, take your cages people, I'm coming out. . . .

> 3:00 A.M.
> Appaloosa Hall
> Day 60   Tuesday

I have only one remark to make:
                    REALITY IS UNREAL

7:00 P.M.
Appaloosa Hall
Day 64   Saturday

Dear Beloved People,
    HA-HA. Did you ever get fooled? I've been twenty-five years crazy all along. Now I'm flipping out trying to get sane.

Love,
Fran

10:00 P.M.

But I'm gonna be!

Love,
Fran

    I find fear, anger, closedmindedness, ignorance, deceit, craziness in the world at large, government, schools, lawnorder. I find the same wrongness in husband, Mother and Father and friends. And me? Because I cannot wrap myself around it all so fast, I stay inside my own world that does not recognize the uglies.
    When time and circumstances force me to take a look whenever I peek through a crack in my wall, all I see is monsters. *Help!* I refuse to believe people I love are as ugly as that!
So I don't.
So I am crazy. . . .

    The judge says, "There's something wrong here. Young lady, I believe you're the only one who knows the truth."
    If that is true, I am sorry. . . .

    Last night I dream I am in jail again. I am trying to find something to wear to court but I can't because they've ripped off all my clothes.
I wind up in court anyway in fur boots and brown tights (and some sort of dress, I guess). The judge looks at me. "You are a threat to America. You and your actions and ideas. You will have to go to prison to keep America safe."
The scene shifts. I am back in my room at Appaloosa Hall.
I go to the cabinet and take out the bottle of leather dye—*poison*.
Katy drinks leather dye in OT and almost finally kills herself.

I keep it there for emergencies. I sit and debate awhile. The question is not do I want to die rather than get locked up. The answer to that is simple. *Yes.*

The question is: are they really going to lock me up?

I wake up.

Nightmare to bad dream. I think about the judge. Up to now I've always felt that my problem with the judge is more or less one of communication. He really doesn't know *me*—who I am, what I do, and why.

Suddenly I realize—*why am I so slow?*—even knowing more and more about me wouldn't make him feel any different. *Me*—my whys—are a threat to the America he understands.

Poor America.

But what is worse? America is so easily protected. My prison time does nothing, proves nothing.

It only hurts me. I alone count the minutes. America continues untouched.

My existence, locked or free, means nothing to America. It means everything to me.

I will not get locked up.

Yes, judge. There's something wrong here. And I know the truth. If I'm alone in that knowledge—we're all in for a bad time.

The truth is simple. The truth is as old as people. If men go crazy in socially acceptable ways, they're ignored, to live out their days with their melted bubblegum heads. If my crazy reactions send me fighting across society's security lines, I get immediate attention: treatment, punishment, different forms for different circumstances, but all attention.

Admittedly, my psychiatric studies are a little one-sided.

But I well understand the formula:

$$\text{Power/Pressure} + \text{Lies} \longrightarrow \text{Crazies}$$
$$\text{(OPPRESSION)} \quad\quad \text{(DECEPTION)} \quad\quad \text{(ALIENATION)}$$

It's in how to fight the crazies I fall off most bandwagons.

The formula contains:

$$\text{OPPRESSION} + \text{AWARENESS} \longrightarrow \text{ANGER}$$
$$\text{LIBERATION} \longleftrightarrow \text{AWARENESS} + \text{CONTACT}$$

That's where I fall off. If my freedom depends on my understanding, I am doomed. If I feel, aha *now* I see *everything completely* —that's a sure sign I'm fast painting myself into a corner delusion. Oh, but it's *contact,* group solidarity somewhere along the line that's going to save me from my anger at my newly understood oppression.

Yeah? Show me a solid together group holding tight onto each other and I'll show you people one by one who are demanding that each member buy reality as defined by this group.

If I turn to contact one by one—which is all contact ever *really* is—I'm O.K. until I depend on that contact to buy my freedom.

Depending on AWARENESS and CONTACT for LIBERATION, I circle into crazy reactions. Desperate understanding, despairing contact—that's what insanity is. . . .

CONTACT: I answer my probation lady's running quiz program calmly, honestly, neither hiding, nor desperately trying to convince, change her, make her see.

AWARENESS: On top of open and hidden pressure to persuade me *not* to apply for permission to move to another city, my probation lady tells me, "Look, Fran, I don't want you to feel we are trying to control your life." And I am aware that this time it's the lady who is out of touch.

RESPONSIBILITY: My lady says over and over, "It's your life we're planning for. You're the one who's got to live it. Look, if you are pulling the wool over our eyes, you are only hurting yourself." She repeats herself in order to convince herself. But I *know* it's true. The decisions are mine. I bear the responsibility for my life.

"Young lady," the police captain speaks over his gun, "if you take responsibility for anyone, you're asking for trouble."

Perceptive man. . . .

> Sad Lisa crawls out of her cage.
> Nobody loves her to set her free.
> She is free because she loves.
> The measure of her love will grow
>   as she recognizes Death
>   and chooses Life.

14. JANE JILL WATERMAN:
Personal Account

I arrived at Taylor Manor (a private psychiatric hospital near Baltimore) in a haze of drugs resulting from an attempted suicide. I was informed later (to my dismay) that, in my drugged stupor, I had signed a paper committing myself to the hospital. No doubt my signature was persuasively solicited by the doctors who admitted me.

My first few days at the hospital were spent in fear and confusion, vainly attempting to come to grips with the situation. I was confined to the admissions building along with other new patients, chronically ill and retarded patients, and "unmanageable" adolescents. Though the hospital states in its advertising brochure that it does not possess adequate facilities for treatment of retarded patients, it still has the cruel and unethical policy of accepting them (probably for mercenary reasons). Mental, physical, and sexual abuse (including rape) of patients, especially retarded patients, was common. Many of these ugly incidents included staff members.

The admissions building was austere and prisonlike. No privacy was allowed patients. We were forced to leave our doors open and were watched continually by nurses and aides. My constant requests for phone calls were refused. All my mail was opened and read. I was appalled to find that I could not see visitors for more than two weeks after my admission to the hospital. All these things, I was told, were standard hospital procedure.

One night, in terror and anger at my predicament, I became hysterical and was promptly injected with Thorazine. At about this same time I was experiencing frightening hallucinations and asked repeatedly to talk to a doctor. Finally, after several days a therapist was sent to see me. For some reason, he took a personal interest in me and arranged for me to be moved to a more comfortable part of the building, where I could have some privacy.

Patients were routinely tranquilized, seemingly without regard to individual problems. Many could not get up in the morning because of heavy sleeping medications and were punished for this "infraction." Even before the effects of my almost suicidal overdose had subsided, I was regularly given a foul-tasting chemical immersed in apple sauce, which made it impossible for me to remain awake, speak, or think. This, I believe, was the reason drugs were given to most of us. I begged my therapist to remove the order for the drug, but he would not, saying that if I refused to take it orally, I would be given injections. After this, I managed somehow to dispose of the drug in cups of coffee, pretending I was swallowing it with the coffee. This was risky, since the nurse usually watched fairly closely as I took the medication. Soon after, I became rather sick for two days from withdrawal from the drug, which luckily was unnoticed by the staff.

The admissions building was infested with roaches. There were often insects in the food. One day while sitting alone in a hall, a ceiling tile dropped to the couch beside me, after which fell a large rat.

After about two weeks I was transferred to a different part of the hospital. The attractive stucco architecture was quite misleading. The security was just as tight in this section of the hospital as in the admissions building. The rest of my time at the hospital was spent in an area with other adolescent girls. I lived in a rather small room with two other girls. Considering the exorbitant prices ($75 a day, excluding private and group therapy, which were $25 and $15 respectively), the living space provided was hardly adequate.

Patients were supposed to see their private therapists twice weekly. Many rarely saw their therapists even once a week. The lack of sincerity that many of my patient-friends exhibited during group therapy sessions was understandable; all of them had been involuntarily committed, usually because they had been labeled "uncontrollable" by their parents. One girl had been committed by her parents because they wanted to prevent her from seeing her boyfriends. The hospital appeared not to question such absurd reasons for commitment.

About twice a week electroshock treatments were given. As a rule only adult patients received shock treatments, though unfortunately there were several adolescents who got them. (Since my discharge from Taylor Manor, the use of shock treatment has been extended to include many adolescents.) Shock treatment transformed people into zombies. Patients in shock treatment suffered from amnesia and a general disorientation. Of course there was a tremendous amount of fear generated by this horrible practice, but patients' apprehensions were assuaged with the lie that shock treatments shortened a patient's stay at the hospital. One woman would try to hide to avoid shock treatments, only to be found and dragged screaming away to the treatment room. A patient told me that a nurse had threatened her with shock treatment unless she wore a bra. Shock-treatment patients usually received no therapy whatsoever. I learned from my therapist that (to my horror) I had narrowly missed getting shock treatments because, upon my admission to the hospital, my behavior due to the overdose had been misdiagnosed as psychosis. Only my therapist realized the real reason for my behavior, and consequently prevented me from getting electroshock.

After I was transferred to the adolescent section of Taylor Manor, it was about three weeks until I actually went outdoors (with a nurse).

We were told that the hospital functioned principally by the "milieu therapy" method. In other words, patients were supposed to get well through forced interaction with one another during the insulting little activities included in the daily schedule. All activities and meals were compulsory (under threat of revoked privileges) because the staff was determined that we would mingle and have "fun" no matter what.

Recent books and periodicals were nonexistent; thus the possibilities for intellectual stimulation were few. The boredom was emotionally draining. I remember particularly the night a girl in tears told me that she was certain her brain was dying.

The hospital controlled its patients through a complicated system of reward and punishment. Appropriate "progress" merited the "privileges" of being allowed to see the people that one loved (in carefully measured amounts of course), walking around outdoors, and perhaps spending time away from the hospital. These "privileges" were condescendingly bestowed upon patients by the unspeakable amalgam of hypocrites who called themselves "doctors" and "therapists." A lack of progress caused one to be deprived of these things. The anxiety and paranoia that this system created succeeded very well in coercing several hundred miserable people into obedience.

One day, out of the blue, I was told that I was to be given a different therapist. This upset me badly because my therapist was the only person on the staff at Taylor Manor that I had really trusted. By this time I was allowed to go outdoors at specified times, so I managed to escape in a delivery truck that was leaving the hospital grounds. Unfortunate circumstances forced my return to the hospital the next day, and I was immediately put in "seclusion," where I remained for two days. Seclusion was a punishment which the staff utilized for many different crimes. Seclusion consisted of being locked in a tiny, stark room, in underclothes, with a mattress and blanket (if the patient was lucky), and nothing to occupy one's mind for sometimes undetermined periods of time. The only relief was that of tranquilization (given upon request) and the privilege of seeing one's therapist (mine was "too busy"). Seclusion was used effectively as a threat against adolescent misbehavior and sexual "acting out."

I inquired of several staff people the extent of my legal rights. I was given vague, evasive answers. Supposedly, I had the right to phone a lawyer, which I was of course not allowed to do. My therapist told me that the only legal possibility of extricating myself from the hospital was through a sanity trial, which would certainly be lost. Subsequently I learned this was untrue.

I remained at the hospital for about five months. This (I was told) was an exceedingly short stay for an adolescent (the average is one year). I was only discharged because I was accepted at a college which would provide the "structured environment" (repression) which the staff felt I needed. Shortly before my supposed discharge date, an alcoholic therapist on the staff took me to his office to give me a battery of pychological tests. He said (as he blew cigar smoke in my face) that if the tests were unsatisfactory, I would have to remain at the hospital well beyond the discharge date I had been given. At any rate, the results would be sent to the college which I was to attend after my discharge from the hospital. Needless to say, this statement induced a sufficient amount of anxiety to completely destroy any fleeting concentration that I might have maintained throughout the tests. However, it was of no consequence, because the tests were given so as to add a couple of hundred more dollars to my already astronomical hospital bill, and two days later I was discharged from Taylor Manor.

III. POETRY

Introduction

This section contains some poems written by people who have been mental patients. The poems are excellent in their own right—but art and literature should never be seen "in their own right," for this would separate them from the class struggle and from the reality in which they were created. They present a picture with emotional impact of what it is like to be in a mental hospital.

15. ANONYMOUS:
Alone

From childhood's hour I have not been
As others saw I have not seen
As others brought I could not bring
My passions from a common spring.

Then in a most stormy life was dealt
All the emotions that could be felt

125

Feelings that became unbarricaded
Too soon to be kept incarcerated.

It makes no difference from whence you came
These walls treat you all the same
They absorb all your identity
Once they put you under lock and key.

16. MARGARET HUTCHINGS:
Poor Old Soul

Poor old soul, she's old and gray, but why feel sorry for her today.
She sits and thinks with a smiling face, and the day goes on and she
  reminisces far far back to her bridal kisses.
The gown of white and the dear sweet words of which all her life she
  had never heard.
So why feel sorry for her today. Poor old soul, she's old and gray.

17. F.:

Four Poems

I

i dont know why.
been using those words a lot lately
you with your stoned head
how many times do you have to repeat something?
whats wrong with you?
just took some tranquilizers
need them
youre the cause
of you
you dont even know what
what?
what youre doing to me
i wish i could feel sorry
for you
you you with your
empty blind heart
he sometimes gives me
blind eyes
nothing is worse
than an imperceptive heart.
no no no no
nothing.

II

you you—
of my soul
my hand turns
beautiful language
into . . .
NO ONE
you make me write
of suicide and death
while i think of making love
and soft warmbodies
pressing against each other tenderly.
see what ill do.
ill simply . . .
well?

III

Uphill

The sight of blood and gore
and everything else that goes along with it.
I wanted the hurting
and I wanted the pain.
It was midnight
and I wanted to cry.
She had told me
that everything is uphill—
uphill the whole goddamn way.
what a way to go.
SometimesSometimesSometimes
I really wanted
TO DIE.

IV

A Good Look

I took a look—
a good look
at the scars all over my body.
All coming from self-inflicted pain.
But that was the way that I had wanted it,
and he had told me to do it.
And so I had obeyed that voice—
inside my brain.
And look—
take a good look
at me
and where I stand
TODAY.

18. ANONYMOUS:
Poem

In this mental institution looking out through these iron bars
How could he put me in here, how could he go this far
Yes, I need help but not this kind. He didn't love me from the start
   but it's not my mind that's broken, it's my heart.
When he said he loved another, I was crazy with jealousy
But that's because I was crazy over him and I couldn't stand to set him
   free
He said he didn't love me and I cried and cried for days
And he said that I was crazy, but he just put me in here to get me out
   of his way.
Daddy, come and get me and take me home with you
I'm depending on you Daddy, 'cause there's nothing I can do.
You said that I could come to you if I ever was in need,
But Daddy, I can't come to you, you'll have to come to me.

19. JUDY GREENBERG:

Two Poems

To a Psychiatrist

I speak salads, mixed and seasoned, too much, madly
Peppered and sourly salted, occult herbs and verbs
Well oiled, the leaves flow swiftly
Over the edge of the tilted bowl
Like strips of old newspaper in an eddying river
Tainted with the wrath of time's spittle
Weary of traveling down to somewhere
To some open sea too far beyond.

I am the Escoffier of such salads, naïve genius
An intuitive cook, the encapsulated mind
Plotting ingredients, some bordering on the foul
But only you have the recipe
And like the river's inquisitive sailor
Swifter than the hours' twisted stagnant river
Can gather those pulpy ancient journal's sheets
Bad advice to the lovelorn, yesterday's news
And with them to that distant sea, sooner voyage.

In the Asylum

The tired windows sag there
Panes caught in dove-tails
Half-defoliated, lagging
Behind the winds
So bland and brittle
Heart-whistle desiccated
Groaning the fulminations
Of arteries gone dead.

Here the black beacon circles
Heads in a vise, but expanded
To dwarf even the cold stars
So great and blanched, pallid
Reflected in eyes too many
To count, each, garbled stares
Wet death-kisses pursing at them
To suck—but not yet—into a void.

It is white as winter sleep
In a manger for lesser
Men in gray pajamas, panting nicotine
Over the empty card-tables
With royalty: kings, queens, all deceased
But other games persist, encapsulated
Below these chilly rafter-gallows
Brazen even in their own dusk.

The black beacon circles on
Smacking every face
In turn, gawk-eared and eyed
At a silence that drools
Thumbs set in rotations
Run slow of dire sadness—
This sleep could sharply wake
The sleeping if they saw.

They do not see
And the men are chalky shadows
On an unteaching blackboard
Soldered to the unreachable sky
Dreaming of infanticides they never had
Dusty rats in their houses, parched nostrils
Goodnight to the paltry
Stars, old holes, give no wishes.

20. JULIE JOSLYN-BROWN:
Three Poems

Hotel

> She'll turn that dial
> to a dead stop and
> freeze the sun there
> on the screen so it
> don't move a scant
> hair for weeks . . .
> —Ken Kesey

12

Don't need no
socks here:
slippers will suffice.
and the floor
waxed so clean
the stains the
shocks don't show.
We are waiting
for the cure
to work, that
second coming down.

I am stringing
paper clips like
days. This magic
string my abacus.

Please label your pajamas

all the while
a flesh lump
wad of bubble
gum, thin and
greening
hangs from
a strap in
the rush.

For Helen on Her Return

You're going
back to
crazyland?

Father
(confessor)
your words
ring of
care-not.

Corduroy shirt
worn daily.
Back to jeans
a size too small
each week. 500
Rummy hits the
million mark, arm
muscle tired: all
that shuffling
that overdosed
posture. A home-
made catatonic.

Father
(oppressor)
your genes
have sprung
a jail break.
Fly! Out the
nest, you.

Candy land
of puce and plum
of puke and piss
and everyone
is happy.

Reunion

three cats, stoned
marble statues stare.
guard a fortress ready
to jump the next guy.
The red one, she's king
cop. I take this as an
omen, pearl eyes.

two women
draped in goddess
mink and muslin
and melancholic
smiles. They guard
they watch for
images quite unholy
voices calling die.
I take this as my
warning, brown eyes.

when I went to
crazyland I found
much smile spilt
and cut with all
sorts of weeds with
fancy names: elite
addiction. doctors
prescription.

two ladies,
stoned marble statues,
stare at each other
one eye mine, one
yours. double vision
strains for resolution,
strains to see the
mugger, the brain monger.

We have this in common,
this fatal secret.

21. ELLEN LINK:
Ten Poems

I

You cannot stop me now,
not grave,
nor night,
nor rage
can still my song.
Sweet singer of Zion am I
this year in Jerusalem
of my heart
I treble bass my words.
Skipping over the mountains,
leaping over hills,
I bound,
determined,
dauntless,
free in flight.
Far below
chasms leer
madness of
Shakespearean regality.
Neither Hamlet's doubt,
nor Richard's loneliness,
no,
not even
raging Nuncle King's
insanity
can check my strength.
I am the Cordelia
of love

the Deborah
of power,
woman
am I
enduring,
persevering,
accepting all.

You have tried me,
I emerge from the womb
cocoon
of my first death
to soar on high,
victorious.
I lift my eyes unto the hills,
from whence I came,
from whence I hope.

II

I'm just vegetating along
here in the hospital garden patch.
I've met some friendly carrots
and talked to a turnip or two.
We're just one happy salad bowl
filled with unwashed wilted greens
doused in therapeutic oil
and vinegar of doctor dressing.
There's always one rotten tomato
who resists the knife and the fork;
they say she scorns authority
and will not give in to the plate.
I just munch contentedly
devouring the squash in my brain,
eating my pills as they come.
Now why is that onion crying?

III

The dark destroyers of the moment,
mind mucked meddlers of the might,
dumb deniers of the light;
in the woods they blast your courage
to tell you you are not a tree,
that the gray rock and the soft sky
and the green grass and the wild wind
are not your cousins,
though their atoms be like yours.
They wash your brain,
they wring it damp,
they hang it on the line to dry
to shrivel to a wrinkled pulp,
that you will nod at proper moments,
laugh not loud or long,
weep not deep or strong;
that you will find tranquillity
in roundly righteous small blue pills
whose acid core will gnaw its way
into the red rage of your head.
True, there is a bomb inside me,
true its flames can kill,
but you cannot destroy it
unless you should one day explode
the bomb that is in you.

IV

When my heart was paralyzed
my head held whiteness of a sheet
spread against a darkening sky.
Behind the shadow players
danced their misty rituals.
My hand reached to grasp
another hand outstretched,
but in the black night's haze
my body faded and was nought.

Human touch thereby denied,
I smothered in the whiteness
of the sheet turned shroud.

V

Because it hurts too much to hurt,
Because I cannot stop the pain,
Give me a chance to live for awhile,
and perhaps I will love you again.

VI

Is it over then?
Will there never be
another flower or
another spring?
Relentless calendar
of winter days
blanking out living
with pallor of snow:
I do not know,
I do not know,
why I wake,
where I go.

VII

Borrowing Superman's cape
I am flying over Amerika
to see what I can see:
graveyards and snow,
missiles for killing,
factories for death.
(They say it's warm in California—
can't make it here, baby)
I'm crazy or sick
or something like that.

Home is where the heart is
(heart is hard, Pharaoh Nixon).
Let my people go
away to where the music is,
a place for us somewhere.
Some have tried razors,
others pills; one drank Drano
to drain her brain.
Madness is brief,
despair is slow:
I am flying over Amerika
looking for the port
of last resort
where decaying engines go.
I pledge allegiance
to the home where the
buffalo roam—
but they are all dead now,
aren't they?

VIII

Nothing portends so much
as the leaving of a place
which one has known as home.
It matters not whether one
has danced or cried
inside those walls
which have been shields.
They stand substantial,
unmoved by hate or love;
walls remain as I depart.

IX

There is a certain distance
beyond which is no passage.
Red flags warn against the risk
of steep inclines and dead end

inclinations we may not fulfill.
Here at the foot of the hill,
we gather our gear for the climb
to see if the sight from the top
of the earth will be broader
or deeper or more filled with truth.
But if in the walking we laugh aloud,
if our eyes should meet and share the sun,
be ready, I warn, to leap from the edge
of the splintering earth.

X

Silently I greet you:
My silence is
the scream in a dream
awakening me
by its absence
of voice
when terror
rises and
I most
would call
for hell,
    hell,
    hell,
HELP!
It would not
come, though
the faces
seemed real
they were
plastic,
cardboard,
tin
(o gods,
    my sin,
    my sin)
Blame me not;

I am voiceless;
no one stands
to speak for
me.
I
am
alone.
Listen,
Use your
eyes to hear.
I call upon
you, friend;
bear witness
to my
presence.

IV. THE PRESENT: STAFF

Introduction

Not only patients live in mental hospitals. The staff is there, day after day, carrying out the administrative tasks. But the staff is a mixed group of people, a hierarchy. At the lowest levels are working people, working for a living, taking care of the patients. At the upper levels are the professionals and bureaucrats who run the show. It's important to understand who is the real enemy.

At times, attendants have been cruel and abusive. As a rule, though, they are not. Some attendants and ex-attendants have written about their experiences for this book. Some other mental health professionals have also written about their experiences.

By and large, the professional administrators carry out the inhuman policies. They are the ones most in league with the ruling class—the bosses, the judges, the police—and best able to prescribe the required "treatment." They have not written self-critical articles for this anthology. Instead, they write laudatory articles for one another, in the professional journals, and they plan even more effective ways of doing their antipeople work.

Brutality by mental health workers, in all forms, must be opposed. So must the brutal ideology which stands behind the locked doors, electroshock beds, "quiet rooms," forced commitment, intramuscular medications, and so on. So must the ideology of "mental illness" which puts all the burden on the individual and none on the society, and which makes "treatment" a "neutral" activity of a trained elite instead of a clearly political activity of the people themselves.

22. RICHARD KUNNES AND STEVEN SIMRING:

Paper Psychiatry

"Titicut Follies" is a documentary film exposé of the antitherapeutic conditions at Bridgewater (Mass.) State Hospital for the criminally insane. While the New York state hospital system is not designed for criminals, its therapeutic approach is nonetheless somewhat punitive. This, at least, is the opinion of the writers, based on two months' observation as psychiatric residents at one of these institutions.

For example, 20 to 30 percent of patients often go without supper, or at least have no meat for supper because substantial quantities of meat are taken by hospital employees for their private use. A majority of the residents are foreign reared and trained, and many speak English poorly—a disaster since communication skills are often crucial to therapy. Observations of and knowledge about patients are so limited that the staff cannot prevent the smuggling of alcohol and drugs onto the wards. Much of this abuse and neglect occurs outside the control, or even the awareness, of the physicians in charge.

With some regularity, articles appear in professional journals or the lay press attempting to define and solve the basic problems of the state hospital system. Almost all see the difficulties from one of two points of view: "economic" or "humanitarian." The basic argument of the "economists" usually takes the form: if there were more buildings, or more nurses or doctors, or "better" facilities, the state psychiatric hospitals might truly become treatment centers. That is, more money must be spent; and, to the extent that more funds are available, patient care will improve. The "economic" point of view is always, therefore, quantitative. Implicit in it is a basic agreement with the institutions' philosophy and overall organization. To paraphrase it: there is nothing wrong with what is being done, only with how much. Those who argue from this point of view declare that their state ranks low in *per capita* mental patient expenditure, or that their state hospitals are not recruiting enough trained psychiatrists. They recommend increasing salaries to outbid private hospitals for staff, or cutting patient loads to increase individual treatment time, or expanding the physical plant to provide more ancillary treatment facilities. The assumption that all solutions lie in money and numbers is so firm they never consider that the expansion of a basically unreasonable system may have no relation to improved patient care.

The second group of reformers who would apply "humanitarian" remedies to the state hospitals also fails to solve the basic problems. Those who argue from this point of view see the problem in terms of inhumane care of psychiatric patients. Their arguments vividly, often gruesomely, depict patients being underfed, or locked up, or neglected, or even physically abused. Hospital staff are shown as callous or sadistically cruel, and physicians as quasi-wardens. Such descriptions are often true, and have great emotional appeal. They have the advantage of periodically bringing public pressure to bear, shaking up the institutions and producing minor reforms. Those few individuals who are unfit to treat sick people may even be rooted out. In the wake of the scandal, however, whatever morale exists may be damaged, and this may lead to staff losses or difficulty in recruiting good personnel. All of these consequences of the "humanitarian" approach, good and bad, are relatively minor. As with the "economic" approach, the basic system of the state hospitals is still fully accepted, and all attention is directed toward expanding it or patching it up. Again, the question is never asked: if every building were cleaned and repaired, if every incompetent were replaced, if every deficit in terms of numbers of personnel and facilities were filled, would the treatment of mental disease be significantly altered? Would it then be possible to offer patients in state institutions the full range of medical and psychiatric treatment techniques that are available to patients at large? In this article we plan to demonstrate that the answer to these questions is: No.

There's an ever increasing amount of paperwork associated with the practice of modern medicine. Although doctors bitterly complain about this growing burden, they still see it as merely a nuisance, ancillary to patient care. In both private and hospital practice, patients are treated, and long hours are then spent filling out forms. In the state hospitals, the situation is quite the opposite. Forms are filled out, and, if there is time, patients are seen. To say that the emphasis has shifted from substantive to formal treatment of patients would be to understate the case. The entire state hospital system is founded on satisfying the *formal* requirements of patient treatment; it functions on a superstructure of paperwork. The patients themselves have become secondary to the paper machine. The individual resident's rewards, in terms of recognition by the hospital administration and his or her superiors, are based on how good the case load looks on paper. Criticism is not related to therapeutic management, but to untyped summaries or incomplete statistical data sheets.

In the ordinary practice of medicine, the physician's time commitments are usually limited only by the needs of the patient. Paperwork must somehow be fit in. In the state hospital system, far from increasing one's absolute work load, the sharply delineated paperwork requirements clearly circumscribe one's responsibility to the patient. If, for instance, a clinical progress note must be written once a month, the implication is that the patient need be seen *no more than* once a month. Again, if the rules state that a personal history must be on the chart within five weeks of the patient's admission, the resident is *relieved* of the responsibility of taking a history when the patient first arrives. In both instances, rules which supposedly lay out the physician's duties actually permit his or her limiting them. When all the blanks are properly filled in, the psychiatrist's responsibility ends. The paperwork allows the resident not to treat the patient, while at the same time allowing the resident, the hospital, the state administration, and the citizens of the state to believe that the mentally ill are being treated. The paper is a rug under which are swept some of the more irritating social problems of the day.

To work in a state hospital is, therefore, to work in a world of fantasy, where one is almost totally insulated from patients requiring direct, personal services. It is not too far-fetched to imagine the system functioning smoothly on paper without the patients even being present. A state hospital administrator was once scolding the resident staff for letting their charts fall behind. The team of "medical inspectors" from Albany was due to arrive the next week, and the hospital was being readied for inspection. "But we can't possibly get all our charts up to date in one week," said one resident. "Our work load is too heavy." "No one ever asked you to write long histories," replied the administrator, "or good histories. In all the time I've been in charge of this hospital, no one has ever read a history, let alone criticized it. I don't care if you write one history, copy it, and change the patients' names. As long as it's there." This is not a fictional statement from an irresponsible administrator, nor is its type uncommon. It is a quotation from a man who was acting in a manner totally reasonable vis-à-vis the demands of the system. He knew full well that the so-called medical inspectors would never inspect anything even remotely medical. They would never get past the record room, where the charts were neatly laid out, and never touch anything more human than a pile of papers. . . .

Shortly before the inspection at this hospital, there was a "blue sheet panic"; a number of the "initial staff conference" sheets, which represented an imaginary conference held on the patient by the staff, were missing and their absence might have been conspicuous. The "medical inspectors" never set foot on a ward. They checked off the proper number of psychotherapy sessions on the proper sheets, but might have been very surprised had they tried to verify just how many such sessions ever took place. They were pleased that all the doctors' medication orders were neatly initialed and charted by the staff nurses, but would probably have been shocked to step onto a ward and discover the percentage of doses which were never delivered. And they would have been more upset to discover the most common reason for this criminal failure: the hospital pharmacy is often simply out of stock. They would have blinked in disbelief at the piles of ward requisitions of the most commonplace and essential psychiatric drugs marked "not available at this time—order from Albany has not come through." They never saw these; they are not part of the official records. These inspectors, who piously noted that the hospital listed the proper number of "teaching conferences" required for accreditation for the residents and staff, might have tried sitting in on some. Most never take place. Those which do deal with topics no more lofty than the use of the new IBM dictaphone machines, or the alarming state of incomplete summary sheets.

Why is the psychiatric community surprised that residents at the state hospitals are cynical and disillusioned? One physician reported that, upon beginning his residency at a smaller state hospital, he was shown a pile of charts and ordered to dictate physical examinations, histories, and mental status examinations on patients who had been discharged *before he was born*. Why is the commissioner of mental hygiene bewildered that the new, and by all standards, quite generous salary scale has failed to attract competent, or even English-speaking residents? A resident who spends three years in a state hospital program receives almost no psychiatric training beyond what he can infer from being near large numbers of very sick patients. Why is the public alarmed that, despite ever increasing budgets, there are still periodic scandals in the state hospital system? Despite increases in personnel and buildings, the basic system remains unchanged.

During our rotation, we were assigned to Male Reception, a service that houses over 600 of the most acutely ill patients in the state hospital. The senior staff was composed of four administrators; the junior staff comprised about a dozen residents. The patient load and the new admissions were divided among the residents, who, in theory, had primary responsibility for their medical management. In practice, all patient management was the exclusive province of the senior staff.

A patient was accepted for admission by the director of the

service, who wrote an admission note and ordered medications. From time to time during the course of hospitalization, the patient would be presented to one of the various "staff conferences" for decisions on management, privileges, a change in legal status, and ultimately on release. The "staff" consisted of a single hospital administrator. All decisions were made by this one man. The patient's resident was neither informed nor consulted; only occasionally were his notes or recommendations even read. "There is a legal requirement, under the silly new mental hygiene law, that all dispositions be approved by three qualified physicians," one such administrator stated quite openly. "There are two others who sign the papers. But make no mistake about it; it is *I* who make all the decisions." When asked how he could singlehandedly accept so much responsibility for so many patients, he replied: "When you've been in this business as long as I have, it only takes five minutes to understand a patient. It's a matter of feel. I rarely make a mistake."

Each step in this actual patient management on the part of the senior staff is reenacted in form by the residents. A mental status note must be dictated within three days of admission. If the patient dies in the interim, a mental status note must be dictated in any case, utilizing all available information in the director's admission note, to arrive at a premorbid evaluation of thought content, emotion, and sensorium. The history in the admission note is followed, within five weeks, by a more extensive resident history, one which is never read, much less supervised. By this time, the patient may have been transferred or discharged. No matter; if the resident cannot get the history, one must be fabricated, in the standard form, from existing information. The resident may or may not write a case formulation, but must use the tentative diagnosis of the "initial staff conference." All diagnoses, such as the perennially popular "schizophrenia, mixed type," come from the obsolete New York State standard psychiatric nomenclature. Clinical progress notes, dictated by the resident once per week for the first month, then once per month, then twice per year, reflect the treatment decisions made by "treatment staff conferences." Finally, the resident must dictate a "presentation for discharge." He does this two weeks after the patient has been released, without his foreknowledge or consent, by "the discharge staff conference." The resident then has several weeks to write a summary, fill in a statistical sheet, and the case is closed.

Critics often state that the size of the resident caseload is the single most important factor which precludes good psychiatric treatment. We maintain that the size of the resident caseload is irrelevant; his treatment load is nil. It is nil because residents do not treat patients, they treat paper. The irrelevance of the case-load size is suggested by the fact that we functioned as full-time residents, but carried only a half-patient load. Yet, we were able to provide no better patient care than the state hospital's own residents. Therefore, it seems apparent that increasing the number of physicians, and doing nothing else, has little to do with the quality of care.

No amount of paperwork, no increase in the number of inspections, can insure that a single patient is being treated or that a single resident is being trained, let alone insure the quality of the treatment or training. It therefore seems pointless, if not destructive, to continue the present emphasis on forms, charts, and data sheets.

A thorough revamping of the system is needed.

23. K.M.:
Statement

I worked in a mental hospital in Ohio. Electroconvulsive therapy was used, and also electrostimulation recovery therapy. Most patients were put on what we called the Thorazine Project. That is, they were started out on a dose of maybe 100 mg bid (twice a day), and each day it was increased 50 or maybe 100 mg until they got up to 600 or 700 mg a day. They were very lethargic; they were drooling at the mouth. Many of them were "Parkinsonized." [A side-effect from phenothiazine drugs. Symptoms of Parkinson's disease: rigidity, stooped gait, expressionless face, tremors—Ed.] And they often refused to take their medication, or we found out they hadn't been taking it. . . . We gave them the next highest level, which was terrible; it really knocked them for a loop. If they wouldn't drink it, they were forcibly put down on the floor, wherever we could put them, and they were given the shot intramuscularly. And sometimes, many times, in state hospitals, they use what they call the "tall 100 in a syringe." That is, if the doctor writes a prescription for 50 mg of Thorazine, and the nurse or the aide is afraid of the patient, he pulls the plunger back and gives an extra 50 mg, because he's afraid to handle the patient's acting out—or whatever it is. And also, many times, I've seen liquid Thorazine being used, besides. I've seen patients given glasses of orange juice with the medication, without orders for it, but they were told to take the orange juice, that it was ordered by the psychiatrist; they were given a dose to quiet them down and sedate them.

I worked at F—— Hospital. Restraints were used. Sometimes the attendants were not exactly physically abusive to the patients, but they would purposely excite the patients so that they could get an order from the doctor to sedate them so they wouldn't have to bother with them for the evening.

The psychiatrists: one was not board certified; he was a pediatrician practicing psychiatry for the state. The other one was board certified. I think he was the only one in the hospital. The one on the second floor was a dermatologist practicing psychiatry for the state of Ohio. But the care was simply chemical therapy; and if the patient did not respond, he was told "we're going to send you to a long-term hospital where you can get more care." And that was a bunch of bullshit. Because I visited that "long-term hospital." It was H—— State Hospital. They had one attendant for maybe a hundred patients, and he used to carry a cake of soap in a sock at night because the attendants were fearful of taking care of a hundred patients. He would lock himself up in the nurses' station at night and leave them go, let them do whatever they wanted to do in the cottages. It was a big hospital. I think it cared for 1,000, maybe 1,500 patients. And they had only one R.N. on at night. There were very few psychiatrists, very few psychologists, and the care was simply custodial. H—— State Hospital does not provide "intensive long-term care." It's a long-term custodial place. It's a garbage place.

Then I worked in a place in New Jersey called E—— Hospital. It's about a 2,000-, maybe 3,000-bed hospital on a sprawling hillside in G——, built in the Kirkbright plan; that is, when a ward was needed another one was built in back of the other ones. The care was absolutely horrid there. The attendant's authority was his keys. One ward that I worked on was for regressed schizophrenics and some retards who wore farmers' overalls. They had other clothes to wear, but they were kept locked up in the clothing room because they said the patients were so regressed that they couldn't keep their clean clothes on them because they'd defecate in them. But these patients would lie around on the benches and urinate and crawl on their hands and knees on the floor, and they only had one or two attendants taking care of them. The ward was sparkling clean, but it reeked of urine. I don't see how anyone could even possibly get well in that setting.

I remember there was one patient who was transferred to the ward because he was regressing. He was exposing himself, so they put him on that ward. To me, he seemed to be responsive, he seemed to be in better contact than the other patients. And I thought that he should be transferred back to an intensive-care ward where he could get more therapy. But the little catch was that this patient was a good worker, and the attendants didn't want to lose him. So the attendants kept him on that ward. And that seems like a crime, when a person who is regressed starts coming out of his regression and they're not going to help him.

Another thing about that ward is that they were doubling the medications. At 12:00 the patients never received any medications. The reason for this was simply that the attendant was giving all the medication for 8:00 and 12:00 at 8:00. He was doubling the medication. And all one hundred patients drank out of the same cup. (They did have medication plastic cups, but the attendant was too lazy to wash them.)

My job on the ward was to keep the patients from drinking out of the toilet. Incidentally, in most of the wards at E——, they didn't have any toilet seats, just porcelain bowls.

On the second floor, above the wards, were the dormitories, nothing but big vacant halls with beds that were five or six inches apart. The mattresses were hard, thin, broken-down plastic things, and the beds were old and low, and the place wasn't painted. They had one attendant for all five dormitories at night. The attendant sat at a little table in the hall, and left the doors of the dormitories open, and he told me he never went into the dormitories at night because he was afraid.

Most of the care on another ward was custodial care. Some of the attendants (they were black) wanted to paint the ward, but they were told they couldn't do it because it was against the union rules. They had to have the painters' union do it. On this ward the attendants often paid for things out of their own money to give to the patients. The patients sat on straw chairs on all these wards with the TV hanging from the ceiling and no reading material at all. They did have therapy in the basement of the hospital, in a complex of tunnels underground. But very few of the patients went to the therapy. Only those who the attendant thought deserved it could go.

Regressed patients were taken to the front to a visiting corridor when visitors came to see them. The visitors were not allowed on the ward; if they had been, they'd have shit their pants at what they saw. I worked there three months. It was so repulsive. There were just too many patients to take care of and not enough attendants. All they were worried about was whether you were wearing your white jacket, your white shirt, and your black bow tie.

I've seen electroshock given. I've seen people regressed with it. They were given three treatments a day until they went back to their early childhoods, so to speak. The treatments were not given consistently. The method of giving the treatments was pushing a cart down the hall, pulling the beds up to the door, telling the patient to sit up and touch his toes, and putting a pillow under his back. He lay down, the electrodes were placed beside each temple, seven and one-half grains of Amytal were given, no body relaxant was given, the patient was restrained to the bed so he wouldn't fall off. A screen was placed around the bed, and the next patient was lined up for the next treatment. The treatments were given Mondays, Wednesdays, and Fridays.

The patients at one hospital I worked in were denied their liberties. Their mail was censored. They had to smuggle letters out of the hospital. Vicious things were charted about them, things which should not be on charts. Patients would come to you with their problems. If they had any sexual problems, the attendants would run back and write them in their charts. Basically, these are permanent records and can be subpoenaed, and I don't think that this is fair to the patient.

24. STEPHEN GLEICH:
Personal Account

Having worked in three psychiatric hospitals over the past three years, I have a lot of firsthand experience of what goes on behind their locked doors. As an aide (or orderly or technician or whatever) I was in the position of being on the lowest rung of the staff ladder and at the same time being a cut above the patients (I had the keys). I often identified with the patients, was several times convinced I was crazy and ought to have been a patient, and at the same time was one of the most respected and valuable staff members. To say the least, this was a curious position to be in.

Most of this article was written during a three-month period between jobs. I was fired from one hospital for refusing to put a patient in restraints. That incident showed me once and for all what I had been hired as: a bouncer or enforcer. I could have abused the patients verbally, come late every day, or caused any number of other job foul-ups, but the thing that got me fired was refusing an order to be the heavy. During those three months I did a lot of thinking, read some history and some socialist theory, and generally took in a lot of information from left-wing sources. The result is the analysis which runs through this firsthand account. My thinking has been influenced by the reading of Laing, Szasz, Fanon, Newton, and by several patients I've gotten to know, in and out of the hospitals. My intention is to pass along information about mental hospitals and to suggest a mental model for dealing with mental institutions. My wish is that the information and the analysis be useful to those of us seeking to have an unsettling effect on that facet of our society called institutional psychiatry.

My Role: A Job Description

The duties of an aide in a mental hospital don't seem to vary much from hospital to hospital. Regular duties usually include: (1) Attend report—where information is passed on from the nursing staff leaving to the one coming on duty. This consists of a brief account of how each patient is doing, changes in doctors' orders, accounts of incidents on the ward; (2) Count the sharps— all scissors, knives, kitchen utensils, razors must be accounted for at change of shift; (3) Observe the patients—for moods, behavior, rule breaking, medical problems, suicide, escape. At one hospital this was done at regular intervals throughout the day, every thirty, fifteen, or five minutes depending on the doctor's order, for reasons I will go into later; (4) Collect the dirty laundry and empty the wastebaskets; (5) Take vital signs on some patients if they are sick or are being monitored for adverse physical effects from medication; (6) Supervise the patients in various activities on the ward or on hospital grounds or, rarely, in town with them. This consists of participating, of trying to get the patients to partici- pate, of dealing with hassles that come up and generally of being in charge. We are there to keep track of the patients, to see that they don't escape or buy razor blades, get run over by a bus or act too strange in public; (7) Talk with the patients assigned to us and find out how they are getting along. This ranges all the way from admiring something a patient has just made in occupational therapy to getting into an intimate rap about feelings and reasons and motivation; (8) At the end of the eight-hour shift of work, write notes in the patients' charts based on our observations and interactions during the day; (9) Enforce the rules. This includes checking a patient's privileges before unlocking the doors for him to go out, going after escaped patients and trying to talk them into coming back, seeing that they make their beds, attend meetings, get to their appointments on time, and go to bed at a certain time. We also had to check visitors and patients returning from passes and the patients' rooms for contraband (see section on admission). We also controlled patients who resisted and dis- rupted the proceedings or were unusually loud or excited. One example comes to mind of a young man of about thirty, whom I'll call James. He persistently called for a town meeting of everyone in the hospital to work out our differences. We, the staff, persistently told him how crazy this idea was and a few times physically restrained him, even locking him in a seclusion room. My own opinion was to let him alone, let him call his meeting. If people were interested, they would come; if not, eventually he would give up on it. But the "psychiatric" opinion was that this was a "delusion" of his and we were doing him a favor by stopping him. But because his wish for a meeting was not allowed to run its own course, it became a fixed idea in his mind and he doubted that he had ever tried hard enough and then felt like a failure. The real issue here was control. James wanted the meeting to include people who were locked up, who didn't have the right privileges. And the doctors weren't about to let anybody do any organizing in their hospital. James came on like a mix between a messiah and an organizer and as such was very threatening to those in power. His fantasy was to hold a gathering, to make decisions collectively against racism and oppression. Paranoid schiz, right? Another incident, involving a young man I will call Roger, illustrates the power struggle in the hospital. Roger liked to walk around the ward in his bathing suit, dancing gracefully. He stood by the windows with his shirt off. He said he liked the sun and wanted to feel it on his body. Exhibitionist, right? He was strongly discouraged from walking around without his shirt and was told to do his dancing in recreational therapy. He didn't "get better" and was transferred to a state hospital. And he kept complaining about the rules and how they hurt him.

The above statements describe most of the things that made up my day. Now I want to describe how the patients reacted to these duties. After all, these are all things I performed with or on or at them every day. (The numbers refer back to the "Job Description.") (1) Most patients wondered about what was written about them in the notes. Some hospitals allow the patients to read the nursing notes written about them; most don't. Some patients wrote notes of their own which were placed in their charts. (2) In general, patients resented having the sharps locked up. When someone was punished for leaving scissors lying around, for example, he or she was always amazed that we took it so seriously. And there was always the comment when the rules about sharps were explained to a patient: "What's the matter, you afraid I'm going to kill myself or something?" To which the staff member replied with a "concerned" look, "What makes you say that?" I remember a couple of examples of patients bringing razor blades onto the ward. A forty-one-year-old man wanted to keep the possibility of suicide open to him. And a sixteen-year-old boy wanted to force his way out of the ward by threatening a student nurse with the blade. Both of these men made it known that they had the blades before trying to carry out their schemes, and the blades were confiscated. (3) Every patient resented checks (the regular observations). They invariably felt their privacy was being invaded and resented having to sign in and out when leaving the ward. Two extreme examples come to mind. A young woman, Jane, had become quite upset after a phone conversation with her mother and she wanted to be alone. She was placed on five-minute checks. This meant that a staff member had to observe her directly (visually) at least every five minutes. She became explosively angry when the staff person on checks repeatedly came back to her room, opened the door and looked in on her. The staff decided to place her in the seclusion room (a lockable room with a window in the door) so we could keep an eye on her whether she wanted us to or not. This decision necessitated carrying her down the hall while she screamed and chanted and kicked. She stayed in seclusion for about two weeks and the entire ward was uptight because of it. Other patients protested that we should have let her be, to work out her feelings by herself. Instead we interfered and, perhaps, prevented her from reaching her own resolution.

In another instance, we had a twenty-seven-year-old man who was very depressed and anxious. He had been on our ward for a week or two and was on five-minute checks. On Sunday night, he hanged himself in his clothes closet between five-minute checks. In the investigation that followed, it came out that the staff member had indeed been checking on him at the prescribed intervals. Was the patient's timing off? (Was he expecting to be saved by the next check?) Or was his timing just right? (Did he simply want to die?) More on checks later. (4) Most patients laughed when they saw us emptying the wastebaskets, cleaning the kitchen, or collecting the dirty laundry. "So that's what we pay you for?" or "It's about time you did some honest labor." (5) The taking of vital signs was a neutral activity. (6) Generally the patients preferred to go about their business without a staff member along. But, there we were, accompanying them one-to-one or one-to-five, depending on how closely they were to be supervised. More on the privilege system later. (7) Patients seemed to like talking to me and other staff members. Often their motivation was to get out of the hospital by talking to us. After all, that's what they were told: "Talk to staff." So they would talk to us in order to get us to support their attempts to get privileges. Other times they wanted to use what skills we had to unravel some knot of their own or better to understand their feelings. In a few cases friendships developed which might have broken free of the staff-patient dichotomy. But they rarely did, for social relations between staff and patients, even ex-patients, were strongly discouraged. When patients kept to themselves, various means were used to get them to talk. We locked people out of their rooms, then came on to them all understanding, with: "It must get lonely staying in your room all by yourself. Wouldn't you like someone to talk to?" Or, more honestly: "If you ever want to get out of here, you'd better come out of your room and start joining the activities." Often, staff used the fact of a patient's keeping to himself or herself to justify a more disturbed diagnosis and to treat the person as "really sick" and obviously in need of "long-term treatment." (8) Patients would often ask us not to include certain things in our nursing notes. When I was most gung-ho, this was a difficult decision for me. After a while, though, I tended to write shorter and shorter notes for I felt more and more strongly that exposing the patients' thoughts and behavior in this way was an act of violence I didn't want to commit. Still it is important to understand what it must feel like to have intimate notes written about you and available to any staff member who wants to read them. (9) The patients resented us the most for enforcing the rules. In an apparent paradox, rules were often broken openly, as if to invite punishment. More, later, on peoples' desire for recognition.

I think I have given the bare bones of life in a mental hospital—the basic interactions between the nursing staff and the patients. Interactions between doctors and patients may be different from these, but remember the staff and the patients are in close contact. Doctors come and go. And among the nursing staff, the aides/orderlies/techs have the closest contact of all. The next section of this essay will be about various aspects of hospital life, from admission to discharge. The emphasis will be on the issue of power and the values which the hospital enforces.

Admission

I have seen people come into the hospital kicking, screaming, punching, and biting as four burly ambulance attendants drag them in. I have also seen people walk in off the street and ask to come into the hospital because they looked in the Yellow Pages under Mental Health. In my experience, about ten times as many people are physically forced into the hospital as come in under no force at all, physical or otherwise. And I would say that the median lies way to the right—that is, an overwhelming majority of people become mental patients with considerable reluctance. I worked under a psychiatrist in Chicago whose routine procedure with adolescents was to get them into the hospital under the pretext of seeing them for an initial interview and/or giving them a few tests. He would then admit them, put them in full restraints, and knock them out with a shot of sodium amytal. I saw this happen at least ten times in less than a year. As this doctor's reputation spread, he became more subtle, promising patients a stay of ten days and keeping them for months. Others would come to the hospital accompanied by several members of the family who never let the person out of arm's reach. The new patient would then be urged to sign the voluntary admission form. Once I saw a doctor put a pen in the hand of a semiconscious man and yell over and over at him, "Sign! Sign! Sign!" until he made a few scratchings on the paper.

She left triumphantly, for she now had the necessary authority to administer shock treatments. The last argument used to get someone to sign in is: "Now if you don't sign this paper, we'll have to take you to court and that means lawyers and doctors, and the judge has to drive all the way out here and lots of paperwork. So why don't you make it easier for everybody and just sign?" In other words, "Rescue me from my tedious responsibility. Do me a favor." This sudden switch of tactics often works wonders as it gives the patient the opportunity to believe he or she is in a position to do the hospital a favor. In fact, this game-playing maneuver is used extensively by hospital personnel in manipulating the patient to do something he or she doesn't want to do. An example: "Look, I don't want to give you this shot but I'll have to if you don't keep quiet and take your pills. Come on now, make it easier for both of us." Thus, the patient is given the illusion of having some power over the nurse and the nurse gets the patient to participate in his or her own oppression. More on coercion later.

If a person refuses to sign in, he or she can still be confined in the mental hospital. In Massachusetts, there is a forty-day paper authorizing involuntary hospitalization "for observation." The courts can issue similar orders here in Illinois. Many times I have seen patients kept under no legal authority at all.

Once inside the hospital, each new patient goes through an admission procedure that resembles, in many of its details, a police operation. A new patient is given a brief physical exam, frisked and searched for contraband. Among those items generally confiscated are wallet, driver's license, and other identification, personal valuables such as wedding ring and wrist watch, razor and razor blades, belt, tie, and money. Very few patients cooperate completely with this procedure, and often they have to be talked out of their possessions: "It's a hospital rule, sir. You can't keep your belt/watch/ring." Sometimes these items are just taken, even if it means a struggle. Since the staff are "sane" and "must know what they are doing" even the strongest patient probably entertains the thought: "Maybe there's a good reason for all this. I mean, I never thought of hanging myself with my belt but, who knows, they're the experts. Maybe it's best for me that I give them my belt."

Thus, two main messages are given to the new patient on admission. First, the hospital makes the rules and has the power to enforce them. And second, you, the patient, are sick. There is something wrong with you that you may not know about yourself. *You would do better to let us protect you from yourself.* This places the patient in a passive, irresponsible role from the beginning. Let us now look at ways people confined in mental institutions are kept in that role.

Confinement

Many psychiatric wards are locked. Some, called maximum security wards, are double or triple locked. Others are "open wards." This means that patients can leave the ward when they want to, if they have permission from their doctor and the nursing staff. But the majority of persons in mental hospitals are prisoners. And this includes so-called voluntary patients. A "voluntary" patient who wants to leave the hospital (in Illinois and Massachusetts, at least) can do so only after waiting three to five days from when he or she submits a written request to leave. During those days, the psychiatrist can initiate commitment proceedings or discharge the patient. If commitment is initiated, the patient must stay in the hospital until his or her court date. This is one of the ways the mental hospital, with the help of the state, can force its patients to purchase its services—room, board, and medication—all of which are expensive.

The amount of freedom given to a person in a mental hospital is regulated by the doctor, with varying degrees of advice from the nurses, aides, and social workers. It is determined by how well the patient is "adjusting" to life on the ward, in the eyes of the doctors and staff. People who persist in talking about suicide, confusing others with their delusions, or expressing considerable anger will all be slow to get "privileges." On admission, most patients get no privileges; in other words they are confined to the ward. Meals are brought to them, they can have no visitors, no phone calls. At the other end of the spectrum is the patient with full privileges, who can come and go at will as long as he or she keeps the staff informed of his or her whereabouts. . . . Let us not forget that the cards are stacked in favor of the doctors and staff. The whole privilege system is nothing but a system of rewards and punishments. It requires a parent and a child to play such a game, and the hospital staff has a firm grip on the parent role. In other words, the staff has overwhelming power over the patients. They have, above all, the power to confine and the power to release. This is very important in the life of the ward. New patients, especially adolescents, often spend their first few days checking out the doors and windows, watching the staff members come and go, and asking about privileges and keys and how the system operates. They see who gets to go off the ward, and who gets thrown in restraints. And that is the name of the game. For a person who is in the hospital against his or her will, to discover that there is no way to avoid playing this game is a scary experience. . . . Cooperative patients get privileges. Their acceptance of and dependence on authority is rewarded with token freedoms. Anyone who questions the distribution of power is considered sick and is described as "acting out."

People get privileges. And people take them away. When a patient breaks the rules, his or her privileges may be cut back. The interpretation made by staff of such behavior is that the patient is "asking to be pulled in" or "asking for controls." This is nothing less than staff projecting its values onto the patient, without knowing why he or she broke the rules. Simple resentment or anger at restrictions and confinement is never enough, in the staff's eyes, to justify rebellious acts. This is probably a class phenomenon. Most psychiatrists and nurses and aides don't know oppression directly, don't know the rage it generates, and can't see rebellion for what it is: the only way left to survive. Most psychiatric workers view rebellion as pathological behavior, motivated by some deep-seated, unresolved psychological conflict. But most mental patients will tell you about the oppression they experience in the hospital. They will tell you they feel like they're in prison, that they can't just go for a walk, that they are bored and wish they had something meaningful to do. And they will tell you that the rules and regulations, the confinement and the routine are not what they need. Perhaps a thousand times I have heard patients say, "I'm getting worse here. I don't belong here." In many ways, the hospital reproduces the world outside, and forces people to play by its rules.

Coercion

I have already described some of the methods of coercion used in mental hospitals. Now I want to describe how the doctor gets you to do what he wants you to do and how that feels.

Almost all persons confined in mental hospitals take medicine. The medicines prescribed affect the mind, the mood, and the energy level. They are described in medical literature with the same technical jargon that is used to describe other drugs. But whatever the merits of the drug itself, here in the hospital the medium is the message. *How* are drugs given? With a vengeance. Patients are not allowed to keep their own medication. They must come to the nurse at certain times of day, usually 9–1–5–9, stand in line, and receive medications in a little cup. The nurse pours out some juice to wash them down and that's it. Some patients get injections regularly because the nurse can't get them to take the pills. If a person decides not to take any more medicine then he or she will be forced to get an injection. I have seen this happen in 98 percent of the situations where medication was refused. One woman played it smart and announced, on admission, that she was a Christian Scientist. Since the hospital was afraid of a lawsuit, she was never forced to take her medication. Her prescribed medication was, of course, prepared at the designated times and, if she refused it, then thrown out. It went on her bill. She was an exception. Most people will find themselves on the wrong end of four orderlies and a nurse with a needle if they refuse their medication. . . .

Another demoralizing aspect of hospital confinement is the ward routine. It consists of a predictable cycle of events: medication, ward meetings, therapy meetings, activities, "free time," and meals. The main theme of it all is Boredom and Stagnation. Virtually every person who has been a patient where I have worked has complained of this boredom. To be sure, there are activities, usually called occupational or recreational therapy, and their staffs are eager to "help you get better" through supervised activity. In a mental hospital, people don't ever just have fun, or do something they like to do. Oh no. It's got to be "therapy."

These "activities" that everyone is encouraged or forced to participate in are something else again. In art workshop or OT people do kindergarten projects: "Today, we will make things with string/toothpicks/clay/rubberbands/and so on." Or make belts (which are confiscated back on the ward because they are dangerous) or candles (which also are confiscated). Other activities run the gamut of supervised play: volleyball, charades, basketball, sing-alongs, ping-pong tournaments, pool, maybe swimming and horseback riding in the more exclusive hospitals. All these "activities" have in common that they are overly regimented, leisure-time activities that are (sometimes) less boring and less regimented than the ward itself where the patients live. People must come and go to these activities as a group and be supervised by a staff member at all times. All of these factors contribute more toward reinforcing the child in a person who has everything provided and organized "for his or her benefit" of course, but who has no decision-making power.

Some hospitals have work programs. At one hospital, male patients could work up to two hours per day on the grounds crew or the maintenance crew for fifty cents an hour. This obviously exploitative program, it must be remembered, was for most people more attractive than sitting around the ward. Other hospitals require their inmates to do some work every day around the ward, usually basic housework. . . . Never have I seen an attempt by the confined group to assert the latent power they have, say, by work stoppage, activities boycott, or meetings boycott. These are tried and true methods for gaining power and raising consciousness, and should be considered as a weapon by those who want to try to force the hospital to respond positively to their real needs. Many institutional psychiatric methods are effective in keeping people blinded to these possibilities by emphasizing individual solutions. More on that in the political section.

So far, in this section on coercion, I have described the rules and regulations. But there are many unwritten rules, whose enforcement varies from one staff member to another, that have a great effect on the lives of the patients. They concern behavior— what is acceptable and what is not. In general, I've observed that acceptable behavior is that which reinforces the role structure of the hospital, while unacceptable behavior challenges it.

Persons are not allowed to commit suicide in the mental hospital. Elaborate systems of supervision are designed to keep an eye on patients thought to be suicidal. Ultimately suicide is a purposeful, deliberate act and I believe that it is just this "taking things into one's own hands" that threatens the psychiatrists. Many times have I heard such remarks as "Well, if he's going to kill himself, I hope it's not on my shift." Or, "Don't do it here, it'll make us all look bad." What I object to is the hospital's willingness to accept the responsibility for life or death. I told the story earlier of the successful suicide. The question to ask is: "Did he believe we would save him? Wasn't he given the impression, in fact the assurance, that we would protect him from himself? Did he therefore feel free of the real consequences of his act?" Of course I can't answer for his thoughts. Only that it is consistent with everything else that goes on for a patient to be made to feel like a spoiled child: "When I fall, I'll be picked up (or caught before I hit the floor!)." At another hospital, this attitude was taken even further. Most people who expressed suicidal thoughts were placed in full restraints to prevent them from acting on their thoughts. Of course some people would feel relief that they were no longer free and didn't have to face their own music. Others would continue trying to cut themselves on the restraints or anything they could get their hands on. Others were given electroshock treatments the day after a suicidal gesture. I remember a young man, Bill, diagnosed a chronic schizophrenic, who managed to sneak out a fifth story window to sit on the roof. He said, "I wanted some fresh air. I was just looking at the sky." In fact there was never fresh air in the building because the windows were always locked and in fact he was never allowed outside. Next morning he was given electro-shock treatment and no one, including Bill, had any doubts that it was punishment for this "suicide attempt." More accurately, I believe, it was punishment for acting on his own and slipping away from the doctor's control. In a crazy place, attempts at sanity are seen as crazy.

On the street or in the community, people who make known their suicidal feelings can be dealt with differently. They may need someone to help them make it through the night and they may need some encouragement to seek other ways of solving their problems. That they make it known that they are thinking of suicide means they are looking for another solution besides death. But they don't need someone to take responsibility from them and exert power over them, as is done in the hospital. The basic idea is that people have, individually and collectively, the means to solve their problems and meet their needs.

Other behavior that is met with punishment usually involves aggression and anger, especially if directed at psychiatrists or hospital personnel. I have seen maybe a dozen teenagers put in restraints for insulting their doctors. Needless to say, the doctors were nowhere to be found when it came to the actual struggle. Many psychiatrists are afraid of physical struggles, but are perfectly comfortable having others do it for them. . . . For the confined person, the survival value of such an experience is: "In order to get out of this place, play it cool, do what they tell you to do." This involves repressing anger and, if the person is hospitalized long enough, this becomes a habit. Turning off feelings is generally dangerous, leads to physical illness and growing frustration. This is one of the ways that mental hospitals train people to take the role of mental patient. When the repressive habits learned in the hospital break down (as they must because they are anti-survival) the person comes back to the hospital for "reprogramming." More, later, on this process of socialization.

I have seen some aggressive acts in the hospital that made me very angry. I remember two teenagers beating up a third and forcing him to give blow jobs. When they were caught, they were placed in restraints by order of their doctor and I felt entirely justified in carrying out this order. On thinking about this incident now, I would rather the group—of patients and staff—had reviewed the case publicly and decided the outcome. Of course that would only be real if all the people involved were in the hospital voluntarily and conditions mutually agreed upon. . . .

The first step in any program to revolutionize mental hospitals must be the discharge of all persons who want to leave and the refusal to accept, as new patients, persons who do not want to be inpatients. To me, it is self-evident that people who do not want help cannot be helped. And any attempts to help people against their will are nothing but violence.

To sum up this section, coercion in mental hospitals is carried out by those in power. They remain in power by acts of force. Persons confined in mental hospitals will find no aspect of their life free from interference. They will be forced to play along. Is this much different from what we encounter every day in relating to our various institutions? Decisions affecting the food we eat, the houses we live in, the jobs we have or the jobs we can't get come down from those in power who have a definite interest in staying in power. Our choice? To ally ourselves with them (kiss ass) and hope for a few morsels for us and ours, or to ally ourselves with others in a struggle to take control for the people.

Coping

In this section I want to talk about how folks cope with their confinement. Some people take the opportunity to "let it all hang out" and they throw tantrums, cry endlessly, play with their shit, talk nonsense, or act terrified. Sooner or later they learn that such behavior assures them of confinement and they respond in one of two ways. They keep it up or they cut it out. Those who keep it up are considered difficult patients and the staff may be tripping over one another trying to cure them. The result may be shock treatments, insulin coma treatments, high doses (like two or three grams per day) of heavy tranquilizers, restraints, seclusion, etc. In some situations, the patients and staff decide to play a prolonged game of Sickie:

Staff: "I want to get to know you so I can help you."
Patient: "You're the only staff member I trust."

Six months later:

Staff: "You don't trust me anymore."
Patient: "I guess I'll never get well."

This can go on for years, through repeated hospitalizations, insuring the continued employment of the staff members and a steady stream of customers. Others, who decide to cut out their "strange" behavior, turn over a new leaf and play the best game of Good Patient they can:

Patient: "I feel so much better. You certainly have helped me."
Doctor: "Thank you. I think you'll be ready to go home soon."

There are many doctors, though, who have "higher hopes" for their patients. Such doctors will strive for a change of character in their patients, and will keep them long enough for this to happen. The crucial conflict here is between the doctor and the patient over the nature of this "healthy" character. And, it should come as no surprise, the power lies in the hands of the doctor. The result of these games seems to be the perpetuation of hospitals—the doctors can claim to be effective, and those who see how "good" Johnny is now (compared to how "bad" and "mad" he was on admission) will not hesitate to send him back to the hospital should he become "bad" again.

People also evolve ways of dealing with day-to-day problems. They cheek their medications; they play endless games of Monopoly, casino, and gin; they try to get dope or alcohol. Playing the meaningless games is encouraged; smuggling dope and cheeking meds are not. All are tactics of survival, to combat boredom and mind-boggling medications.

Some hospitals will get rid of a patient who adamantly refuses treatment and is not too bad off. These are the more liberal places that don't want to waste their time on someone who doesn't want any part of them. I think they are rare.

I believe that one of the most powerful experiences of patients in the hospital is, paradoxically, the realization of their powerlessness. Many, many times I have heard patients talk about it: "I don't have a chance. I'll stay here forever. This place drives you crazy." I believe they are talking about the totality of their environment—the cards are stacked against them and there seems to be no way out. But, come to think of it, this experience is not confined to the mental hospital. I've had it myself when thinking about trying to change the world. It seems impossible—every effort I make will be turned around and transformed until it comes out to be a strengthening of the System. This feeling is very frightening and depressing. And rightfully so. The world, the System, is a collective creation, and cannot be re-created or changed by a single person. A single person simply doesn't have the power. This is a lesson I am learning and I believe many folks confined in mental hospitals learn it as a matter of survival. In terms of sheer force and resources, the doctors and staff have the power in the hospital (and considerable power, with the help of the police and the courts, outside the hospital). I think it is virtually impossible for an individual to beat the System. In the hospital, most people decide to play along, to negate themselves, in order to get out. On some level, they perceive that the staff and doctors need to be made to feel effective and powerful and good before they will grant privileges and freedom. Perhaps the luckiest person is the one who can play this role (the obedient, good patient) deliberately and consciously, with the purpose of getting out of the hospital. Most people have difficulty doing this because they insist on "being themselves," "being honest," etc. But sooner or later, most people who get out of the hospital do so by kissing ass. Not too obviously, of course. I believe this is how it is. And to anyone who was able to get out of the hospital without submitting, I say more power to you!

Discharge

A person is discharged from the hospital when others decide that the time is right. His or her money may run out (this happens often). Or the parents or family may take the person out. Or, most frequently, the psychiatrist discharges the patient when he or she is satisfied that the patient is "ready." And, most often, the patient is discharged to go back to the situation he or she came from. Mrs. H—— came in for depression following a suicide attempt. She was frustrated in her marriage—her husband was away four nights a week and would come home and demand sex quite abruptly. While in the hospital, she got shock treatments, insulin coma treatments and her (female) doctor suggested to the staff that we get her dirty books to help her overcome her sexual hang-ups. She was discharged and came back within a month. The situation was handled as if the illness resided in her. The forces at work on her in her environment (especially her husband) remained the same. Even in the case where someone shows remarkable "improvement," the risk is high that he or she will come back to the hospital.

There was a group of four or five patients who wanted to get a house together when they left the hospital. Of course this was not allowed; they were to be discharged one by one.

And of course, certain types of discharge plans are more acceptable to the doctors than others. You won't find many discharge orders that read, "Discharge to the care of his guru," or "Discharge to the care of the Black Panther Party." By the same token, you won't find patients getting "therapeutic passes" to go to demonstrations. They'll be lucky if they can get out to vote on Election Day! That's lucky? And, again, the decision-making process is out of the hands of the person most affected.

The Hospital in the Life of the Individual

Having been in a mental institution has a significant effect on the rest of a person's life. Ron was in and out of the hospital and was finding it harder and harder to get a job. Adolescents sometimes lose enough school credits while they are in the hospital to force them to go to summer school or to fall behind a whole year. For some, the mental hospital becomes the only situation in their lives that gives them what they need; bad strokes are better than none. Mrs. M—— has been in and out five times and sees the hospital as a place where she will be taken care of. And I've met other women for whom the hospital is the only place they can relax and get attention because they're usually so busy slaving away for their families without recognition. Yes, the hospital meets a need, but does not cure the problem. It can't. And by so doing, it preserves the status quo. The pressure is taken off the family, job, school, and so on to meet the needs of these people. At the other end of the spectrum, hospitalization is seen as something to be avoided at all costs. People who feel this way probably keep up an appearance of "sanity" and perhaps go to great lengths to avoid contact with psychiatrists. This of course is eminently rational behavior, though perhaps too costly to the individual. I'm sure it causes many people to "go straight" or at least straighter than they might have gone. By now the pattern should be familiar—reinforcing the dominant ethic, maintaining the status quo.

The Hospital in the Life of Society

How does society benefit by having mental hospitals? I have suggested that mental hospitals help to stabilize the society. Lots of research has shown how "scapegoating" stabilizes a group or community. This involves loading the evils of the society onto an individual and driving him or her away. Everybody feels better afterward (except one?) and before long you have folks who don't fit in anywhere else volunteering for the job of scapegoat. Bad strokes are better than none, as I said earlier.

The hospital tends to regroove people who have strayed from the desired path. I've described how passivity, docility, and dependence on authorities are traits that the hospital enforces in its inmates. Such attitudes in the hearts and minds of the people are necessary for society as we know it. Who benefits? Those in power. The capitalists and their servants, the politicians. Who suffers? The non-Anglo minorities, the workers, and everyone else, in one way or another. In terms of the society as a whole, institutional psychiatry seems to be a safety valve, taking the force and focus out of people's dissatisfactions.

It has also succeeded in making people afraid of their own inner workings. This you can see in everyday life. The embarrassment at a slip of the tongue. The funny looks you get when you say something crazy spontaneously. The jokes about being ready for the funny farm. People's reluctance to be alone with themselves. People's poverty of imagination and reliance on external, authoritarian sources (TV, film, advertising, newspapers) for their information and imagery.

I don't want to give the impression that fear of institutionalization is the cause of uptightness and repression. Rather it is one of the forces that keeps people in their place. All you have to do is talk to ex-mental patients to find out how afraid they are of going back to the hospital. And how this fear affects their day-to-day behavior: "If I lose my job (or miss a therapy appointment, or get too depressed, or too angry, or take drugs) the doctor will put me back in the hospital." And most people are afraid of and mistrust psychiatrists. Professionals interpret this as indicating that such people are afraid of themselves. First, I should point out that most people these days are afraid of and mistrust our "helping" institutions, hospitals and doctors particularly. And second, this fear is justified. Because these institutions are not organized and maintained to serve the people (though dedicated and well-meaning people may work in them) but to make a profit for a select few, fear of mental hospitals is realistic. Bad things will happen to you there! Beware! When people are first admitted to the mental hospital, they are afraid. Staff attributes this to fear of being in a new and strange place. But most people have a picture of mental hospitals that is very scary, and often true. It is a picture of people locked up, padded cells, restraints, burly attendants dragging screaming people down the hall. To what? Shock treatments, dark halls, lack of freedom, and the possibility of losing your mind and staying there forever.

Politics of Mental Health

Every society defines mental health by its dominant values. Large industries got interested in preventive and crisis-oriented medical care for their employees because they considered them to be machines whose breakdown and repair would cut into profits. The development of psychiatry within medicine has shown the same emphasis. Its main goal is to create healthy workers and healthy bosses. The oppressive relationship that exists between workers and bosses is not challenged. Men and women are helped to go back to their jobs, not to change them. This means, for the workers, that they reintegrate their personalities after a breakdown *in order to get back on the job and function well*. A rebellious worker, by these standards, is not functioning well because his primary responsibility is to produce. I can remember a man who worked in a steel factory who kept coming into the hospital because he was depressed and anxious. He was assigned to a permanent night shift, which made him very nervous. In the hospital, he was given a course of electroshock on each admission, presumably so he could return to work without anxiety. With workers being laid off and those who remained being forced to work harder (increased productivity which results in nothing but increased profits for the boss), his anxiety and the pressure put on him to be superefficient, are understandable. I believe the explanation for ex-mental patients' difficulty in finding work lies here. The boss thinks, "This guy may break down again and it will cost me too much to train a new man. So I won't hire him." The ex-mental patient is a poor risk economically. He or she cannot be relied upon to produce profits. And, conversely, capitalism *can* be relied upon to produce mental illness.

When people and their labor are reduced to sources of profit, conflict and alienation must result. Our task as therapists, then, is to educate people who experience this conflict as a mental breakdown about the real nature of it. There is a real conflict. Not an internal one. People need to be valued for their humanity, not their profit potential. And people now face the task of getting that need met. Not just in therapy groups either, but in their day-to-day life—work, home, community.

This analysis of the function of the mental hospital in society is incomplete and in need of documentation. My direct knowledge of the workings of the insides of mental hospitals supports it. More work needs to be done on the history of psychiatry within a capitalist state. But I *am* certain that we must look at the mental hospital in the broadest social context. It is not productive simply to muckrake—to get morally outraged at what goes on in mental hospitals. For any liberal reforms that come out of it will be in the context of a society that values its men and women for their ability to produce profits for the upper class, and views any kind of dysfunction as a threat to profit making.

Into the Future

What is to be done? In the hospital, if a patient, do whatever you can to get out and stay out. Kiss ass, run away, get a lawyer, sign out, whatever works. If a hospital worker, like me, keep your eyes and ears wide open and speak up about the contradictions you perceive. The fundamental fact about mental hospitals is their social reality, the power structure. The patients have no real decision-making power. Every interaction in the hospital happens within this context. We as workers are in a position of power, relative to the patients, and a position of powerlessness, relative to our superiors.

Of course, this advice goes only for those of us who can still stomach working in the hospital. We must, above all, not lie to the patients in our care. We must not contribute to the mystification process by trying to convince people they are sick, they are in the hospital for a good reason (the only good reason I know is that they want to be there to change their way of relating and/or to go through a crisis period), or that someone else knows best. With those folks in our care who are committed or otherwise forced to be in the hospital, I don't know what to do. Except perhaps, make clear to them their choices: (1) act "crazy" and stay in the hospital, (2) act "sane" and try to get out, (3) get further legal advice. It is also important to create an atmosphere among the staff in which criticism can flow freely and point up contradictions in daily practice (dehumanizing routines, manipulations, and controls). For example, a patient loses his privileges because he broke some rules. The staff's explanation: "He was asking for controls. He was telling us he needed more control." This is bullshit. The real reason is something like: "He broke the rules so we're going to punish him by taking away his freedom." This kind of contradiction can be pointed out to people. Another thing hospital workers can do is refuse to work with patients who don't want to be there and repeatedly to urge that such people be discharged. After all, you can't help someone who doesn't ask for help. There's not much point in "treating" people against their will, unless we have an interest in creating passive, obedient, resentful citizens.

Something else worth doing: work to have lobotomy, shock treatment without consent, and involuntary hospitalization abolished—no loopholes, no exceptions.

Many revolutionary organizations get started by meeting the peoples' needs where they live. The Black Panther Party and Rising Up Angry, to name two I'm familiar with, serve the people with free medical care (emphasis on preventive medicine), food, clothing, transportation, and have helped people organize against slum landlords, racist employers, and so forth. Many radical therapists are beginning to work in peoples' homes with families and whole social networks to find solutions within the community. No need to uproot someone and send him or her to the hospital, or downtown to some $400 a month office to see a shrink at $30 an hour. Therapy includes helping someone find a job, organize against a landlord, take a journey into themselves, eat sensibly, help others, raise consciousness. All Power to the People.

25. PETER DONOHUE:
Personal Account

Early on a chilly March morning in 1971, as I sat in an un-heated furnished room in a shabby rooming house in Jersey City, I spotted the "Attendants Wanted" ad in the classified section of the local newspaper. It had been a full month since my escape from the King County Jail in Seattle, Washington. Expenses crossing the country had used up most of the proceeds of a $622 robbery on the same day, and I now found myself running dangerously low on cash. I didn't want to alert the police to my presence in the area by pulling another robbery, so I decided to apply for the job.

Twenty minutes after boarding at Journal Square, the bus deposited me in front of the L—— County Mental Hospital in Secaucus, New Jersey. During the trip I pondered my "cover story." I decided to use the name of a boyhood schoolmate whom I knew to be still residing in Jersey City and in whose name I had purchased a phony driver's license the week before.

I crossed the highway, passed through the wide open gate and onto the grounds of the hospital. A uniformed police officer sat in a booth in the middle of the road, his nose buried in a magazine.

"Could you tell me where the personnel office is located?" I inquired.

My voice seemed to aggravate him. He glanced up at me and without turning his head he said, "Over there," snapping his thumb back over his left shoulder.

The officer's gruffy voice changed my attitude as I crossed to the building he indicated. I recalled the many stories I'd heard about "bug houses" while at Sing Sing and Attica. I fought to suppress an eerie feeling as I entered the front door. I tensed, preparing to deliver a crushing blow to the first maniac who attacked.

The immaculate appearance of the interior surprised me; walls spotlessly clean, decorated with painted daisies; floor highly polished; wooden benches and cushioned chairs neatly sprinkled about. Through a glass partition in the wall I viewed a humming office area. I tapped lightly on the glass. A gray-haired woman slid back the pane and gazed at me quizzically, not speaking.

"I'd like to apply for the attendant's job advertised in today's paper," I said softly.

"Oh, yeah," she muttered, pointing to a door back inside. "Come on in."

I rounded the corner and entered the office.

"Have a seat," another older woman stated from her position behind a desk. "Fill out this application."

I studied the form carefully, filling in the data I had memorized from the phony driver's license and social security card in my pocket. To the routine questions: "Have you ever been convicted or arrested for a felony?" and "Do you indulge in any narcotic drug or alcoholic beverage?" I wrote simply "No," laughing to myself at the possession of narcotics and armed robbery convictions which sent me to Attica. To make up for prison time, under "Previous Employment History" I wrote, "U.S. Air Force 6 years; Bellevue Hosp. Nurses Aid 3 years part time while attending classes at N.Y.U.; present night student Seton Hall University." I assumed the job was days; it wasn't.

"Seventy-five dollars a week paid every other week plus dinner," the woman stated when I handed over the completed application.

"Report to the basement of I ward at 4 P.M."

"Huh, er, tonight?" I asked dumbly, stunned at the quick decision.

"That's right, tonight!" she ordered. "You want the job, don't you?" and, without waiting for my reply, went on, "Four till midnight."

Apparently she wasn't reading the application.

"Oh," she remembered, "check with Dr. Williams across the hall." She ushered me out the door and into his office.

"New employee," she told the doctor.

room. Bart followed us in and latched the mesh-covered door behind him.

"Need four men up here," Mac said, plopping his feet up on the desk and leaning back in the swivel chair. "Never know when one of 'em might go off." He indicated the men moseying outside the door.

"Chambers there." He pointed at a middle-aged black man with one hand fastened to his waist by means of a leather cuff and strap. "He's a mean one. Don't ever turn your back on him—kill ya quick as that! ' He snapped his fingers dramatically.

A small, effeminate, forty-year-old man breezed by the door.

"Commere, Louie," Mac hollered, suddenly jumping up and rushing to the door. "Didn't I tell you to stay in bed?" he demanded threateningly, pulling Louie inside.

"I wanted to see the new men," Louie said with a lisp, looking over at myself and the younger attendant.

Mac threw a solid punch to Louie's chest, sending him reeling into the wall. He didn't try to block any of the blows Mac hammered into him with balled fists. Quietly he removed the cigar from Mac's mouth and kissed him full on the lips. Mac howled with glee, obviously familiar with the routine.

Louie then kissed Bart, who didn't seem to notice or care, and the younger attendant, too frightened to refuse. As he approached me I gently held him back with an extended arm, shaking my head "no" from side to side, unable to speak.

"He don't like you!" Mac screamed like a ghoul, laughing uproariously. Louie pleaded for a kiss. Mac yoked him into a corner and launched an unmerciful attack upon his chest. Still Louie stood with arms at his sides, not trying to defend himself. Finally he succumbed, sinking to his knees gasping for air. Mac roared, sticking out his chest like a belligerent ape. He made Louie crawl to the door where he kicked him in the buttocks, sending Louie spilling into the corridor. He laughed louder than before.

Not much later, as I sat in the office looking out at the "killers" roaming about, we heard the clatter of pots and pans outside the ward door.

"Come on," Mac directed, "let's feed these creeps."

Crossing the hall, MacInturf looked down at the two men still standing motionless facing the wall.

"Aw-right you two punks, git to bed."

Positioning us around the rickety table in the dayroom, sentry-like, MacInturf and Bart proceeded to feed the men, first taking the only stack of sliced cheese and hiding it in the office. Mac scooped a ladle of soup onto each greasy tray as the men filed past, Bart throwing on two pieces of bread and a slice of bologna. A pail of canned peaches stood on the end of the table. Some men scooped out handfuls, others didn't seem to notice. No eating utensils were issued.

Standing nervously at my sentinel post, I noticed a once glass-filled partition across the room. Three men sat hopefully looking at the serpentine line passing the food table from the bed-jammed room behind. Another man sat in a glass-removed space of the partition staring up at the ceiling, mouth wide open, saliva dripping from his lips. An identical partition/room was on the opposite end of the dayroom, with but one bed and a lone, burly figure pacing back and forth.

As the patients stepped away from the table, they slurped the soup from the tray, spilling most on themselves or the floor. An old man at the rear of the line filled trays for the three patients behind the partition, also making two trips with trays to the large dormitory down the hall.

The burly figure emerged, passed by Mac and Bart and filled each aperture on the tray with peaches.

"The Mad Russian," MacInturf snickered as the six-foot three-inch, two-hundred-fifty-pound man silently reentered his room.

Shortly after, the empty tray came sailing through the open doorway. Nobody but me even blinked as the tray clattered along the floor.

Chambers, one hand still cuffed to his waist, lapped the soup from the tray resting on a bench while kneeling on the floor.

Before long, the old man rounded up the trays and stacked them along with the pots and pans at the door. MacInturf slid them outside and the meal was over. The figure still sat with mouth agape in the partition, not having partaken of the meal.

Bart took me down to the not much cleaner central dining room where female patients served us an identical meal in an identical fashion, only we received cheese and a spoon. The other attendants ate heartily, not seeming to mind the poor quality of the food or the unsanitary conditions under which it was served.

A female nurse arrived on the ward at 8 P.M. and administered gigantic doses of liquid tranquilizers to each patient. Chambers refused to swallow the medication. Bart looped a towel over his head and twisted it in a fashion that brought Chambers to his knees, mouth wide open. Bart obviously knew how to handle an uncooperative man. The nurse poured the liquid down his throat.

The second and third nights on the job were repeats of the first, with MacInturf battering one or another drug-induced patient each night, usually knocking them to their knees and making them crawl. Chambers he knocked unconscious.

The fourth night I was assigned to K down ward and issued a small ring of keys.

"See ward boss Numiller," Ralph Lustre told me. "He runs things over there."

A different atmosphere prevailed in K down. Somewhat cleaner, a blaring television set was the main focus of attention, with most of the patients sitting numbly before it. A few patients gathered around me as I entered the ward, excitedly introducing themselves. A young boy about eighteen years old waved from a bench across the dayroom.

"What's that for?" I asked after crossing to him, pointing at the leather cuff securing him to the bench.

"I run," he said gaily. "My mother bring me back."

He was happy at my show of attention as I examined the cuff.

"I'm going again tonight," he laughed.

"How you gonna get out?" I inquired, genuinely interested. He stuck out his tongue, on the end of which was half a razor blade. He made a back and forth motion as if sawing at the leather. I couldn't help but like this kid.

Entering the office, Numiller motioned me to a chair in an affected manner. From appearance it was hard to tell he was a patient. Chubby, clean shaven, and well dressed, he had a healthy complexion as opposed to the pallor of all the rest of the patients. Black horn-rimmed glasses gave him an intellectual air.

"Anybody gives you trouble, just whack 'em," he said, swinging a large ring of keys in the air.

Patients on this ward ate in the central dining room, and I looked on as Numiller unlocked the door and led patients in and out, occasionally "whacking" someone with his keys. I had no idea what was expected of me. Numiller was in complete control. No supervisor arrived as he unlocked a drug cabinet and dispensed medication. My keys didn't fit the cabinet lock.

At nine o'clock he declared "lights out," turned off the television, and led the young boy runaway into the dormitory by a strap.

I spent the rest of the night skimming through magazines in the office.

The fifth night I was back in 5 up. The young boy runaway was now on this ward.

"I made it," he said, rushing to me as I entered the ward. "My mother brung me back."

I laughed with him over his escapade.

As I sat in the office a few minutes later, MacInturf entered the ward. I heard a commotion in the dayroom and quickly ran in.

"Escape will ya," MacInturf said, pounding away at the boy's chest and rib cage. The youth fell to the floor under the crushing blows, crying. "Escape now," he went on, leather cuffing both his wrists to his waist. The boy was a pathetic sight.

I decided to work at the hospital up until the first payday, one week away, then look for another job. The strip cells of Attica and Dannemora's dark cell I can handle; 5 up I couldn't. In the few days I worked there I came to realize MacInturf's description of the "killers" was just an excuse to vent his sadistic perversion. With the exception of ward boss Numiller, I saw no show of violence by any patient.

While the three other attendants were locked in the office, I roamed the ward. For the first time, I entered the large dormitory at the back of the ward. The incessant "drumming" I had heard since my first day was actually an elderly bedsore-covered man screaming "Die! Die!" over and over. For some reason the sound distorted before reaching the front area. A young, naked Puerto Rican sat on the edge of the man's bed gently patting his hand. Another Puerto Rican sat tossing scraps of bread into a filth-laden, foul-smelling corner. The stench was overpowering. I retreated to the dayroom area.

I spent the rest of the night in the dayroom, not once entering the office. I showed the boy how to open the simple locking mechanism of the leather cuffs with a file blade broken off my nail clippers. By midnight he could open them quicker than MacInturf could with his key. I also explained to him the procedure to follow in opening metal handcuffs with a paper clip, the means of my own successful escape from the Seattle jail.

Tuesday night, my first night back after two off, I felt somewhat relieved when Ralph Lustre told me I was working on K down ward. Numiller I could tolerate; I didn't trust myself with Mac-Inturf. Saturday was payday.

Everything was peaceful on the ward when I received a telephone call from Ralph Lustre about 8 P.M. "The Russian's going berserk," he hollered into the phone, "Get up to 5 up right away!"

The tone of his voice excited me, and I ran through the corridors, not bothering to lock any doors behind me. Two other attendants were waiting outside 5 up when I arrived, peering anxiously inside. MacInturf let us in, chomping on the inevitable cigar.

"It's the Russian," he said to one of the other attendants.

I hurried up the corridor and looked across the dayroom. The Russian was pacing back and forth in his room, seemingly oblivious to anybody or anything.

"He looks all right to me," I said to no one in particular outside the office.

"Won't take his shot," the nurse inside said, poised with a hypodermic syringe.

"We got more help coming," MacInturf said. "We'll get him down."

Apparently they had been discussing the possibilities of pinning the linebacker-looking hulk to the floor. So far there were seven of us attendants on the ward and "more help coming."

I walked back to the dayroom disgusted. The young boy runaway grabbed my arm and led me into the bed-jammed room across from the Russian. He had a mischievous grin on his face. He pulled a bed away from the wall and pointed to a door I hadn't noticed before.

"You got a key to that door?" he asked.

"I don't know," I said, rummaging the key ring out of my pocket. The fugitive camaraderie that attracted me to the boy was evident to him. He snatched the keys out of my hand and fumbled with the lock.

"That's the attic," he whispered softly, easing open the door. "I can get out through there."

I slid the keys into my pocket and walked back to the office somewhat contented with my trip to 5 up.

Five more attendants arrived on the ward, making us an even dozen, a dirty dozen.

The Russian stood determined in the doorway as the mob approached. Seeing any struggle would be useless against such overwhelming forces, he relented, backing into the room.

"Okay, okay," he said.

MacInturf swung before the others could register his peaceful surrender. The glancing blow brushed off the Russian's temple and he roared to life. Attendants swarmed all over him. He toppled to the floor where MacInturf snapped on a pair of metal handcuffs behind his back. The nurse administered the injection amidst the raining kicks and punches. The Russian continued to struggle futilely. Blood trickled from his ear. The medication finally took effect and the struggling subsided. After a few final blows the Russian lay motionless on the floor. An attendant slipped a black-jack into his pocket. The nurse didn't bother about the blood.

I stopped in K down long enough to get my coat and unlock every door my keys would fit. Passing through the corridors I tried my keys in every side door I encountered, leaving all I opened unlocked.

Outside, I scattered the keys all over the lawn. I crossed the road and passed through the gate. Damn that paycheck, I'll take my chances on a robbery.

26. CONSTANCE PAIGE:

Board up Bournewood Mr. Kaplan*

"One chimPANzee, two chimPANzee, three chimPANzee, four."

That's Dr. Leo Alexander, past president of the American Electroshock Association, present chairman of the Mental Health Committee of the Massachusetts Medical Society, counting out the seconds as he presses the button to administer shock treatments to his patients.

Actually Dr. Alexander's counting technique is legitimate, for the aim of the treatment is to induce and sustain a convulsion and the precise timing is not crucial. What is questionable about Dr. Alexander, however, is his overuse of electroconvulsive shock therapy (ECT). With his famous "triples"—three shocks a session—he gives some patients during a stay at the hospital many more than the 20 shocks recommended by the recent task force report on ECT commissioned by the Massachusetts Department of Mental Health.

Dr. Alexander is one of the more knowledgeable doctors staffing a private mental health facility in Brookline, Bournewood Hospital, exposed two weeks ago in the *Boston Phoenix* for its mistreatment of some patients (see "Shock Therapy: Pacification Program," *BAD*, 12/5/72). A subsequent investigation by this paper has revealed that Bournewood tolerates both malpractice and sadism, and further is violating several state laws in the following ways:

* SOURCE: *The Boston Phoenix* (December 19, 1972). Reprinted by permission of the author.

—Doctors sometimes fail to obtain from patients informed consent for shock treatments.

—At least one nurse functioned as a Registered Nurse before she was licensed.

—Aides sometimes dispense medicine and other treatment properly performed by nurses.

—Aides do not always obtain restraint orders and use restraint unnecessarily in some cases.

These charges could be grounds for suspension or revocation of the hospital's license.

The following account of Bournewood Hospital was culled from numerous conversations with present and former employees of the hospital, among them doctors, nurses and attendants, all of whom asked that their names not be published. The identity of patients has been disguised to assure their anonymity.

"Benign" Neglect

A portrait of Bournewood is best begun with an account of the neglect of some staff psychiatrists.

For instance, at least one of the doctors, Medical Director Arthur Stebbins, does not always honor the commitment and treatment procedures established by Massachusetts laws. The mental health reform act of 1970 allows a patient who voluntarily admits himself to a mental hospital to leave at will as long as he submits three days written notice of his intent. In order for the hospital to keep the patient after the three days are up, the superintendent must file a petition with the district court to commit the patient involuntarily. The *Phoenix* investigation could not determine whether this commitment procedure is followed to the letter, but the comments of a nurse suggest that Dr. Stebbins, at least, does not treat the three-day notice with much care. "Stebbins would rip up the notices before he would even talk to the patient. Most doctors would talk to the patient and the patient would rip it up. But he'd just rip it up and say to the patient, 'You never wrote one.' If they were lucid enough, the patients would get very agitated. Then he'd order them up to Female Ad (the acute ward). If they were given a treatment, they'd just forget about it (the three-day notice)." (One of the side effects of shock treatment is that patients often become extremely confused and forgetful afterwards.)

By comparison, an attendant at McLean Hospital reported that employees there treat three-day notices with almost religious respect.

Likewise aides sometimes give injections (or did last June, according to an aide who quit them), again a function legally performed only by a nurse. This happened in the treatment center, particularly on Saturday mornings, when some trusted aides stood in for overworked or absent nurses.

Even though Bournewood has recently hired more nurses, aides reported that there is not always a nurse for every building. Also, the nurses are not always on the wards, sometimes arriving anywhere from a half hour to forty-five minutes after the start of the three o'clock shift and leaving the ward for an hour or two during the afternoon or evening.

Despite their frustration with Bournewood, many of the aides interviewed were reluctant to criticize the hospital openly, many fearing they might lose their jobs. It is not just job insecurity, however, which prevents them from speaking out. Even more important is their concern that some of them could be prosecuted for having distributed drugs illegally.

Similarly some are worried about the restraint procedures used from time to time. Both male and female aides must respond to psychiatric emergencies for which many of them at Bournewood are ill-prepared. Like the cop on the beat who is suddenly expected to understand the intricacies of Supreme Court decisions, attendants must cope with violent or abusive patients without the prior training the hospital should be offering. Many of the attendants never learn, except by painful experience, appropriate ways to avoid using "restraints," the straps and other devices designed to secure patients out of control. Neither do many at first know restraining techniques or the legal implications of their duties.

Some attendants thus tend to overreact during crises, using restraints unnecessarily. In this they are encouraged by some of the psychiatrists.

A former Bournewood nurse who now works at another psychiatric facility in the Boston area described an incident which bears this out. One evening a woman was admitted and the psychiatrist admitting her argued that she did not need admittance to the hospital, an opinion the patient shared. Nonetheless, the woman was admitted. Her doctor, another psychiatrist, "marched her right up the stairs and said, 'Let's put her in restraints because otherwise she's going to take off.' She was given drugs and put in restraints and this kept her quiet—in other words, knocked her out for the evening till the treatment the next morning. After shock treatment, she didn't remember what had happened."

A male attendant who worked at Bournewood thirteen months until last August explained why he feels on-the-spot restraint is sometimes justified. "There are a lot of times when it's necessary. You get somebody who's off the wall and they may be pounding on the doors and then getting hostile and fighting and stuff. A lot of people can be hurt, including them. You have to remember that one of the side effects of ECT is confusion and memory loss. You can reassure these patients all you want and two minutes later they'll forget and be just as confused. Sometimes you can't wait around to get a doctor's orders. I know the state doesn't agree with it but there's times you have to say screw the state."

When asked whether it would be better at least to have a member of the professional staff always on the ward to oversee such crises, the aide answered, "That's nice too, if you have a nurse that happens to be handy."

It is true that in emergencies attendants must use restraints. However, state law prohibits use of restraints without written authorization in advance from the hospital superintendent or a doctor except "in cases of emergency such as the occurrence of, or serious threat of, extreme violence, personal injury, or attempted suicide." In questionable cases, then, aides are putting themselves in double jeopardy, having both to assess the seriousness of an emergency and to restrain patients, perhaps unnecessarily, without prior authorization.

Apparently some attempt is made to keep other patients away from the windows, but, in the words of one aide, "They'd look.

They would. Because they didn't know whether it was going to happen to them."

Doctors at Bournewood also are not always judicious about the candidates they choose for shock. As reported in the previous *Phoenix* article, Bournewood shocks a considerable number of adolescents. Said Dr. Spiegel of this practice, "Few people are willing to make a diagnosis of adolescents because they change so fast, and so to commit them to shock treatments is absurd."

Similarly, some homosexuals receive inappropriate ECT at Bournewood for their "affliction." Said a former attendant of a few of the homosexuals there, "There were a couple of young people put there. I didn't see anything wrong with them. They seemed happy the way they were. The only thing they would talk about was how depressed they were that their parents wouldn't listen to them and their doctors wouldn't listen to them.

"One person—I believe she was about 18 years old, told me her mother found a letter from one of her girlfriends, read it and found out she was a homosexual. She had her committed. From my personal observation, the girl seemed to be psychologically stable." His evaluation of this particular patient was confirmed by a psychiatric nurse who used to work at the hospital.

Psychiatrists outside of "shock shop" circles generally agree that there are only two indications for shock treatment. The first is for patients who are acutely suicidal; the second, for patients with debilitating depressions. Very occasionally acute schizophrenics receive shock profitably, or elderly patients who cannot tolerate drugs. Other than that, shock treatment should not be used—certainly not for adolescents, nor homosexuals, addicts and alcoholics —unless their primary diagnosis is depression and they are unresponsive to drugs and psychotherapy. Also, any patient who cannot be deterred *in any other way* from committing suicide can receive shock on an emergency basis.

Since the psychiatric community is still at odds about the appropriate uses for ECT, those Bournewood psychiatrists who use the treatment on patients for whom other doctors would not recommend it are probably safe from malpractice suits. And the medical—as distinct from psychiatric—care at Bournewood is usually excellent, further insulating these doctors from legal action. However, a couple of practices stand out that are not so proper. Occasionally patients due for shock are not given tongue depressors. These patients then bite their tongues and require emergency sutures. This is a definite instance of malpractice, and could be grounds for a suit.

Also it was reported that some doctors administer the treatment to patients who have eaten recently. The risk here is that the patient might vomit, and aspirate the food into the lungs. Aspiration can cause death, although none of the sources interviewed had ever heard of such a death at Bournewood.

Bournewood also may have violated some civil rights guaranteed by the mental health reform act. For example, last spring the hospital was told to install a pay phone for all patients not specifically barred from using it. An employee who worked there until Thanksgiving claimed that she never saw the pay phone.

Chronic Understaffing

Mistakes by some employees under the rank of doctor usually result from Bournewood's chronic understaffing. A registered nurse who worked at the hospital as chief nursing supervisor of her shift until last July, for instance, explained that she and one other nurse, Val Baghdlyan, were responsible for all three buildings and as many as 80 patients at a time on their 3 to 11 P.M. shift. Occasionally, especially during summer vacations, one of them would have to cover all the patients alone. This meant quite literally running from building to building, leaving almost no time to respond to patients.

Val Baghdlyan is now a night nursing supervisor. Up until October 3 of this year when she became a registered nurse, Ms. Baghdlyan was assuming the duties of a professional nurse without the proper certification, clearly violating the law. An alien, Ms. Baghdlyan had neither an LPN status nor the temporary certification required for a nurse trained out of the country, according to records at the state Board of Nursing Registration. Much to the annoyance of some other nurses, Ms. Baghdlyan was receiving $5 a week more than they, even without her certification.

Bournewood's sometime shortage of nurses means that the attendants are forced to shoulder heavy responsibility, without sufficient training by the hospital. (The highly respected McLean Hospital in Belmont provides a five-week training course for new attendants. Bournewood's receive a day's training, if that.) Some aides thus may have to recognize medical emergencies and distribute medications, responsibilities for which most are unequipped and none licensed.

A former aide (now studying respiratory therapy) who worked at Bournewood until last June described the scope of her duties for "meds":

"On our shift we had to go into the cabinet, check the orders, get out the medication cards, sort them, schedule the medication, look for the medication, check the label, pour the medication, give it to the patient and make sure he swallowed it—and if you had twenty patients, you couldn't really watch them all."

The hospital apparently discontinued this as a regular procedure last spring on the advisement of the Department of Mental Health. Several employees reported, however, that some longtime aides still give out medication on occasion.

Having aides dispense medication is illegal because it may be dangerous. Psychiatrist David Spiegel of the Massachusetts Mental Health Center explained why. "Basically aides have no training to recognize the properties of medication. There is no reason why they should know anything about counting out pills and they are more likely to make mistakes because the names all sound alike. There is no reason why they should recognize the symptoms of side effects—the bad reactions to medication—or situations in which patients shouldn't be given medication. For instance, sometimes patients get a drop in blood pressure just after taking a tranquilizer, or acute allergic reactions, in which case you would hold the next medication even when the order for it has been written. Suppose a patient has a heart attack? What the hell is a mental health worker going to know. Or if somebody looks a little pale and sweaty, the mental health worker will think they look a little pale and sweaty whereas somebody else might say they're going into shock."

Another psychiatrist disagreed with Spiegel. "I think that's really an elitist remark. At Boston State Hospital, anyway, those attendants know more about the side effects of medication than any resident when he arrives there." This psychiatrist works at Bournewood and feels the hospital's treatment of patients does not measure up to care given in "more academic settings." His argument suggests that one way to alleviate understaffing is by giving more responsibility to well-trained paramedicals. Perhaps he has a point, especially since the Bournewood employees who now give medications apparently are longtime, trusted aides. However, at this point in time, the practice is against the law.

The most recent law on the subject, the Controlled Substances Act of 1971, specifically bars anyone but an RN or LPN from administering medications, but a law enacted earlier, Ch. 112, Sec. 80B, allows certain workers, among them "therapists" and "technicians," to perform nursing duties "commonly recognized" as part of their jobs. David Vigoda of the Attorney General's office explained that usually specific laws like the Controlled Substances Act take precedence over more general laws. However, this particular case has never been tested in court.

Since attendants often are restricted neither by training nor, apparently, doctors, a few practicing sadists among them are given almost unlimited elbow room to mistreat patients. One attendant, ironically a priest, threw a young girl down the hall into a wall by her hair. In the words of another aide, the priest was "the golden-haired child" of the hospital administrators, and one of those attendants who always seemed to "restrain first and ask questions later."

Payola and Profiteering

The shortage of nurses and resulting dependence on aides sometimes poorly trained tells much about the hospital's actual purpose.

Bournewood is a corporation set up to make profits and owned by the retired psychiatrist Salomon Gagnon, whose son now works there. Free enterprise and competition imbue many aspects of the hospital's administration.

Bournewood's cook, for example, is given expenses for food from which he can pocket the excess after everything is purchased, according to testimony from an aide who got her information from several nursing supervisors and a kitchen helper. What the cook buys must not be too closely reviewed by the hospital's absentee dietitian, for the meals consist of "starch and starch," as one former employee put it. A typical menu (not generally posted) might include three slices of cold cuts and potato salad, or turkey à la king on bread with mashed potatoes. Rarely do patients receive fresh fruit or vegetables.

Bournewood goes to great lengths at times to deceive inspectors as to its culinary capacity. A former employee described one inspection day on which the inspectors and a few patients were served an elaborate meal that few others ever tasted. Meanwhile, some staff members had to eat in a back room standing or sitting.

(The hospital also beguiles inspectors in other ways. On inspection day, nurses are often reshuffled and beds rearranged so that sleeping arrangements appear less crowded.)

The hospital supplements regular pay with a "bonus" when the patient population is up. Every six weeks or so, employees who have worked there six months receive half a paycheck extra, and a whole paycheck extra after a year's service.

To add insult to injustice, Bournewood allegedly tries to skimp on the final paychecks of employees who have been fired. Several aides reported that their last checks were lower than they should have been, and one male attendant claimed that he was finally paid only after a lengthy and confusing court case.

The hospital's coffers are further filled by loyal patients who return again and again for treatments. A former nurse described a male teacher who has been admitted to Bournewood numerous times. An alcoholic, the man periodically commits himself to dry out, receiving a full complement of shocks in the bargain. He also spends most of his school vacations there. This particular patient is wealthy enough to afford his rather unique holiday.

In spite of Bournewood's understaffing, profiteering and legal violations, as well as overuse of shock and occasional malpractice, some of the doctors who privately express misgivings about the hospital refuse to complain publicly. One such psychiatrist explained that he didn't think these were matters for the popular press to expose. While conditions there may not be the best, Bournewood can be considerably less expensive than many other psychiatric treatment centers. Patients pay anywhere from $50 to $75 per day, on the report of several aides, which beats the $75 to $100 they might pay elsewhere. (This does not include the shock treatments themselves, which can run into some money at $25 a shot, but are usually covered by medical insurance.) At any rate, the argument goes, if people who can receive cheap treatment at Bournewood are scared away, they probably will have no other viable alternative for psychiatric care. This is especially dangerous for patients who might benefit from shock and are afraid to seek it out.

Stephen Rosner, Executive Director of the Massachusetts Association for Mental Health (a lay watchdog and lobbying group) expressed a similar concern. He also cautioned that "there are just not enough facilities, and state hospitals are such monsters that people don't want to send their relatives there. We get flak from families who want private facilities and the state Department of Mental Health licenses them out of desperation."

Another psychiatrist who works part-time at Bournewood agreed that psychiatric care is in short supply, but felt that public pressure is important, both to force changes at Bournewood and to inform prospective patients of what they can expect from shock treatment. "People should be able to select decent psychiatric care the way they choose any doctor. Doctors generally know what the best treatment is for medical ailments. In psychiatry we're really not that fortunate, so people still do have the option of going to different doctors who have widely differing opinions on how problems should be managed. It would be nice for patients to have an idea of exactly what's good for their heads and what isn't. That's what I think the value of articles like yours on Bournewood is. It's not necessarily in belittling Bournewood, but in educating people that their problems may not best be handled by shock treatments."

Hopefully news accounts have influenced people to think carefully before committing themselves or their relatives to Bournewood, and also to insist on their right to refuse treatment once there, without deterring those who are unusually depressed from getting help.

Apparently the press coverage has had yet another effect. The state Mental Health Department Inspector of Facilities, Robert Kaplan, has started an investigation into the hospital, after publication of the first *Phoenix* article and another by a *Globe* reporter.

Dr. Kaplan's conscience may be bothering him. As he quite candidly admitted in a phone interview, past inspections of Bournewood have been inadequate, owing in part to his limited authority and time. On the last tour, Kaplan was escorted by Myron Tuross, whose presence may have deterred both patients and employees from criticizing Bournewood. Kaplan has promised, however, that his future inspections will be more thorough. He also has requested and in some cases obtained conferences with the sources used by both the *Globe* and *Phoenix*. And his superior, Mental Health Commissioner Milton Greenblatt (who just last week resigned from his post), when read the list of complaints cited in this article, said "What you've told me is grounds for a thorough study."

Both hesitated to say, though, that they would suspend the hospital's license, one action possible under the circumstances. The other alternative—the one the department is most likely to take—is a strong recommendation that the hospital upgrade its standards.

Perhaps this means that Bournewood will receive closer scrutiny in the future and be forced to change. Or perhaps it means that the buck will pass from hand to hand and eventually end up right back in Bournewood's corporate executive's pockets.

27. CONSTANCE PAIGE:

Shock Therapy: Pacification Program*

> Toward the end of his life, recalling the first time he had tried the treatment on a human being, Professor Ugo Cerletti (the creator of shock treatments) remarked to a colleague: "When I saw the patient's reaction, I thought to myself: This ought to be abolished!"
>
> —Thomas Szasz,
> The Manufacture of Madness

Three weeks ago the *Boston Phoenix* ran a front page story about Wiswall Hospital in Wellesley which overuses and abuses electroconvulsive shock therapy (ECT) on mental patients. Wiswall is not alone. A subsequent investigation has revealed that a similar small private psychiatric hospital, Bournewood, in Brookline, has also been using and abusing electroshock, as well as violating a number of other commonly accepted psychiatric practices. At Bournewood:

—shock treatment often is used on patients for whom the therapy would not be recommended by most reputable psychiatrists in the Boston area;

—psychotherapeutic care is downplayed, the emphasis being on shock and shock alone;

—psychiatric aides are not properly trained;

—followup care is often minimal or nonexistent.

The case studies which follow were obtained in interviews with patients who have spent time at Bournewood and psychiatric personnel who have worked there. Most are still employed by the

* SOURCE: *The Boston Phoenix* (December 5, 1972). Reprinted by permission of the author.

hospital and all asked that their names be withheld. The names of patients have been altered or left out on request.

Abuse of ECT

George (a pseudonym) is a 17-year-old runaway. He had never been in a mental hospital until his mother brought him to Bournewood three weeks ago. Before he was admitted, George was seeing a social worker for his problems at school. He said he couldn't stand to be "closed in" and spent a good deal of time pacing the halls rather than attending classes. His situation at home was equally difficult, both for his family and himself.

The third time he ran away from home, he ended up at Project Place, where social worker Sherry Smith, who reported his case to me, became acquainted with him. Though George made friends at Place, he was unable to adapt to their program, and Ms. Smith finally sent him home, where he was seen on an outpatient basis by a psychiatrist at a prominent mental health facility.

George had repeatedly expressed interest in living in a "group home," a cooperative set-up for teenagers who live together with foster parents. He took an overdose of barbiturates and Ms. Smith feels that he was "trying to prove to his mother and me that he couldn't live at home."

Ms. Smith sees George's hospitalization after the suicide attempt as the mother's way of punishing the boy. "George's mother really dug the idea of shock treatments so that she could get back at him for all the trouble he'd caused her," Ms. Smith said.

Fortunately, a group of nurses and aides at Bournewood realized that George was not the proper candidate for shock treatment. They finally arranged with Ms. Smith to get him out before he received his scheduled ECT. He is now at another state mental health facility where he is receiving drug therapy and psychiatric counselling.

Crucial to the decision to administer shock to George was the Bournewood psychiatrist's evaluation that George is a paranoid schizophrenic. Although she admits that as a layperson she cannot diagnose the boy, Ms. Smith feels that George is "not the kind of person who is not relating to reality. He knows what day it is. He's just not as sick as that doctor thought he was."

Further, Ms. Smith feels that if George had been shocked, he would not have understood why. "He would have seen it in a punishing way, not in a therapeutic way. George is very resistant to any kind of help. Shock treatment would just reconfirm his feelings that he is hated."

George is not the only adolescent referred to Bournewood. A psychiatric aide who has worked at the hospital for nine months revealed that just last week there were six youngsters on the acute ward. Sometimes there are as many as fourteen at one time. During an interview, Robert Kaplan, Inspector of Facilities for the state Department of Mental Health, pulled out at random an inspection report for Bournewood from last July which substantiated this story. At that time, the hospital was treating ten patients under the age of 21.

The aide described these adolescents generally as "kids who seem normal. Some of the kids had a little grass and freaked out or their parents don't like their boyfriends or girlfriends." Some of them are depressed, but most, she feels, shouldn't be in a hospital at all, much less receiving shock treatments.

Her view is confirmed by a recent task force report commissioned by the state Mental Health Department. The report states unequivocally that shock should not be used on teenagers, no matter how depressed, unless an effort is made first to try other alternatives.

Not only the nurses and aides, but psychiatrists as well have complained about the handling of specific adolescents at Bournewood. One doctor who has worked at Bournewood for six months described a teenage boy admitted because he had been "involved with drugs." "The reason he was on drugs," the doctor explained, "was that he was depressed and had sleep disturbances—one of the indications for shock. But I certainly wouldn't have shocked him for it. I don't think he had an adequate trial of other treatments."

Inadequate Psychiatric Care

Bournewood also mistreats other, especially alcoholic, patients. Said one Bournewood aide of the therapy for alcoholics or problem drinkers, "They do nothing for them except dry them out. Sometimes they use shock treatments, if the patient has the money."

She described one woman, Mrs. R. (a pseudonym), who is a repeat visitor to Bournewood. Mrs. R. is 43 and "looks 80." According to this aide's description, Mrs. R. "hated it at Bournewood. She's an intelligent woman and most of the patients there are so confused that she couldn't make friends with any of them. She just sat around and read the paper and talked to the nurses whenever they had the time. Everyone on the nursing staff loved her. Her stays became longer and longer and she must have held the record for the number of times she'd come back—maybe 17 or so. Usually the hospital would let her out during the day and she'd go out and get drunk and then come back to spend the night."

Mrs. R.'s husband, a good-looking man in his mid-forties, was part of her problem. When his wife was home, Mr. R. insisted on keeping liquor around the house and often would offer her wine for dinner, after which she would invariably get drunk. He visited his wife faithfully in the hospital and "some people claimed he really loved her," but he also just as faithfully kept readmitting her to Bournewood, even after it became clear that the hospital was not really helping her.

Admittedly, Mrs. R. knew what she was doing to herself. "She always came to Bournewood drunk," an aide explained. "I don't think she ever came fighting. She knew when she got drunk it would be a pattern and she'd be coming back. She was very lonely at home and she loved to talk to people. Bournewood was kind of her second home. On the other hand, she knew also that she was killing herself."

Eventually the staff became so angry at Mr. R. for repeatedly maneuvering his wife into the hospital that he transferred her to Glenside, another small private hospital which also administers shock (but has a better reputation for psychiatric care than either Wiswall or Bournewood).

One of the reasons that patients like Mrs. R. never solve their problems is that they receive far too little psychiatric counselling. The hospital serves more a custodial than a therapeutic purpose, with the emphasis on physical rather than psychiatric care.

As described by a psychiatrist who has worked there several months, "What's detrimental to the patients is the fact that they don't get enough attention from the doctors. Bournewood is handled like a medical ward. The doctors come around and make rounds. If everybody's O.K., they leave. If someone has a specific complaint, that complaint is dealt with, but there is no attempt to form a relationship with the patient.

"The families are dealt with to a greater extent than the patients, especially at first. The patient is sort of the one who's left in the dark. The family is sort of doing everything and the physicians go along with this rather than helping the family and the patient get together on the decision as to whether to come there."

This opinion was substantiated by several people on the nursing staff. The Medical Director of the hospital, Dr. Arthur Stebbins, was singled out for particular criticism. The aides seemed to feel that he did not spend enough time with some of his patients. Said one aide, "He runs around shaking everybody's hand. We call it the Twenty-Five Dollar Handshake. Sometimes he's continually shaking hands for weeks, and then he goes without seeing them (the patients) for a long time."

According to testimony of both aides and doctors, however, poor medical and psychiatric care is not universal at Bournewood. Therapy—or lack of it—depends entirely upon which doctor is treating the patient. Many of the doctors are thorough and concerned about psychiatric as well as organic management of patients.

Another aide added that Dr. Stebbins does form a good therapeutic relationship with some of his patients. "If he cares for someone, he does get involved—someone who's been with him for years."

Training of Aides

The night supervisor of nursing, Val Baghdlyan, explained in a conference with a former Bournewood employee and this reporter, that nurses' aides at the hospital receive one day of orientation and are then put right on duty. In-service training is provided afterwards, but in at least one case, the training was not sufficient to acclimate one aide to her ward.

Jane Evans (a pseudonym), a nurse trained in England who had not yet received accreditation as a psychiatric nurse in the States, started working at Bournewood six weeks ago. Although Ms. Evans has worked as a full-fledged nurse in general hospitals, she had had little contact with psychiatric patients, and was hired as a psychiatric assistant. Her first assignment at Bournewood was to the "acute ward," a locked facility for the more violent, confused and intractable patients. According to her supervisor, her performance on the ward at first was excellent but she gradually became less "reliable." Eventually she was transferred to another ward and finally fired.

Ms. Evans' dismissal is currently being contested by lawyers. Ms. Evans feels, however, that her firing was "political." The longer that she worked at Bournewood, the more distraught she became about hospital policies, specifically the tendency to use shock treatment indiscriminately and the lack of psychiatric care for patients. She became increasingly outspoken about her doubts, eventually confiding to a patient's husband that she felt the patient was not getting the best treatment possible. The case came to the attention of the director of nurses, who accused Ms. Evans of "unethical" conduct, and summarily fired her.

What Bournewood describes as ethics Ms. Evans prefers to call inhumanity. She feels that her working relationship with patients was much more "human" than that allowed by Bournewood policy. "I didn't feel I was the keeper of anyone's soul. I'm a feminist and most of the women who came there came because they had been fucked over by men. I could understand that. The things they talked about I could identify with very easily. But how can you relate to someone if you aren't really listening to what they're saying and don't respond in a human honest way?"

Ms. Evans' claim that aides are not properly trained was seconded by another nurses' aide who worked at the hospital six months. "At one point they were handling training by having a part-time nurse take prospective aides around the hospital for eight hours. Then they were put on the ward. I didn't get any training. For the most part everyone doesn't even get talked to by the nurse, they just get stuck on the ward."

Followup Inadequate

David (a pseudonym) is 27 years old, the son of a prominent Boston-area psychiatrist. He has one sister, a performing artist, and one brother, a medical student, both of whom are successful. David is not, at least in the eyes of his family. He has neither a satisfactory job nor an acceptable girlfriend. What David does have, as described by his sister, is his own "weird world. Some people think he's brilliant and he's helped them. Others don't understand him because he does things like coming downstairs in his boarding house in his underwear because he forgets. David's a very vague personality in some ways, but it's not a tragic thing if you learn to live with it."

David had been in psychotherapy with Dr. Leo Alexander (see accompanying article) for some time. About a year ago Dr. Alexander changed David's drug order one day and David overdosed. The doctor and family both called it a suicide attempt and admitted him to Bournewood Hospital. David's father, although he long ago discontinued the use of shock treatment in his own practice, decided that they had tried everything else and they might as well try shock.

David received about twelve shock treatments during his stay at Bournewood. His sister visited him after he'd been there about a week. She described her impressions of him and the hospital.

"He was getting terrible headaches after the treatment—such great pain. He would mumble things—of course he was on Thorazine so he wasn't too coherent—like 'they're preparing me for life. I never was prepared for life before.' And then things like, 'Don't you think I'm aggressive?' I've never known anybody on Thorazine to be aggressive, and especially not in a situation like that.

"During the treatments and after, David forgot everything. It's very strange. I saw David about a week before any of this happened. I hadn't seen him in about a year. He seemed to be getting in really good shape. He was writing and working as a dishwasher. He could relate to people in a much more relaxed fashion than he ever had or than he can now. He was living in a boarding house at the time and the woman who owned it was a nurse who really liked him. She was scared for David. She didn't think anything was wrong with him.

"He used to write these little fables—they were quite nice. Now he's forgotten his writing and his yoga and all his good things. They took that all away from him."

David's sister is reluctant to make a judgment about the longterm effects of the treatment. She did say, however, that David was released from the hospital "without a personality, without a memory, without even knowing where the bathroom is."

David's evaluation of the treatment is harsher. "Shock treatment leaves a person very passive for quite a time. When you're in that passive position, it satisfies everybody. The psychiatrist thinks you'll do what he wants. The parents think, 'Ahah, he's going to accept my good advice.' It works out for everybody except the patient, who after a while awakes from this and realizes how much he's been messed up."

David remembered little of his followup treatment. "Supposedly I did have some, and apparently what it consisted of was trying to make me parrot certain phrases. I was supposed to come back dynamic, aggressive, obedient."

Asked if aggressiveness and obedience weren't contradictory, David replied, "In the mind of my psychiatrist (Dr. Alexander), they weren't. Any good quality you might have rests on obedience."

David reiterated that the object of the therapy at all times was to mold him. He had saved from his stay at Bournewood a sheet of paper Alexander had given him. On it was Rudyard Kipling's poem *If* ("you'll be a man, my son"). With the poem were four instructions:

1. Get physically fit and remain so.
2. Concentrate on the task at hand. Strive to eliminate idle purposeless activity, both physical and mental.
3. Clarify every issue and be master of every act. Know why you act. Remember and forget as necessary.
4. Control your reactions to mass opinions and emotions.

David recalled that there was some followup treatment after all. "The main thing was how it was done. Dr. Alexander deluded himself into thinking I was in a better state when I was in a worse state. And I thought everything was O.K. too. I wasn't thinking. I thought everything was going smoothly and I couldn't remember anything. I accepted everything. I was pliable. I was obedient to authority."

And now?

"Well, it's possible that this will all have some longterm benefits. Anything's possible. It's possible that death could have longterm benefits too."

Shortcutting the Shock Shops

As explained in the Wiswall article (see "100 Shocks . . .", *Boston Phoenix*, 11/14/72), little can be done to correct the situation at Bournewood (or Wiswall). The state has jurisdiction only over the physical plants, staff qualifications, and civil rights of patients. If the doctor in charge of inspection feels that certain clinical practices are unjustified or inappropriate, he can advise the hospital to change its procedures, but cannot back the recommendation with any legal reinforcement.

Likewise the medical profession is hamstrung. Specific doctors can be defrocked by local, state, or area medical societies or psychiatric associations, but the process is cumbersome and must be initiated by patients. Suits can be brought against doctors or the hospital, but again the patients must agree to them first. Apparently this recourse has been considered by local physicians who look askance at the flagrant violations at Wiswall particularly, but Bournewood, with its modicum of good doctors as well as its sampling of bad, has not yet come under the same scrutiny.

The competent doctors working there do not seem to be speaking out publicly against the place. But they do feel frustration. One psychiatric resident "moonlights" there (a commonly accepted practice for psychiatrists-in-training who need an outside source of income to pay for their own psychoanalysis). He expressed his outrage at Bournewood and the system in general in these comments: "It's very ironic that the money that is paid to the very well-trained analysts to treat the future topflight psychiatrists in Boston comes from income gained from working at places like Wiswall or Bournewood or Glenside or St. Elizabeth's. We are being paid for giving very bad treatment at these hospitals, so that we can buy treatment for ourselves that's much better, so that in the future we can give much better care to our patients. I guess that's a commentary on how things are done in our society."

The Task Force report recently completed by the Department of Mental Health will probably lead to a set of guidelines regulating the use of shock treatment, but it will be some time before these can be implemented. Legislation is also being planned, to be sponsored jointly by state Senator-elect Chet Atkins and former Boston Municipal Court judge Charles Francis Mahoney. The bill if passed, also will take time to implement.

Meanwhile, Wiswall and Bournewood and a number of other local "shock shops" remain virtually unrestricted, exercising indiscriminate use of shock treatments.

Bournewood: Symptom Not Cause

In reviewing these cases, as well as accounts of many, many other patients at Bournewood and Wiswall, it became obvious that while sometimes these patients left the hospital more able to cope, occasionally even liberated from their problems, more often they were merely calmed momentarily, only to resume their old life styles and problematic behavior. This is the substance of an argument now raging within the psychiatric profession: whether these so-called treatments actually deal only with symptoms and not causes, and thus cannot cure the patients. Dr. Alexander's claims notwithstanding, the case can be made that in only very specific and limited circumstances is shock treatment beneficial.

There is a larger question, troubling not only to shock advocates and the psychiatric profession as a whole, but to all of us. In effect, *all* the shock treatments, and in fact most treatment administered—whether it be electroshock or drugs or even psychotherapy—on any psychiatric ward tends to subdue the patients. Where once lunatic asylums were hellholes of rage and violence and terror à la *Marat/Sade,* now they are more often stage sets of loneliness and boredom and despair, artifacts of a civilization that has nowhere to go when things get rough except to the hospital. Pacification programs—ECT and drug therapy and the like—are necessary to keep the inmates in check until they are ready to resume their worldly roles. If sometimes pacification produces remissions, well, all the better.

Unfortunately this is not always the case, and the reasons are not hard to find. Interviews with many mental health workers revealed that most of the patients they see—regardless of bizarre "symptoms" of "illness"—are reacting to untenable living situations. Patients are sent by families no longer able to deal with them, families appalled by sexual exploits or drug experimentation or misbehavior at school.

28. PRISON SURVIVAL CENTER:
Fred

No anthology on mental institutions today would be complete without a statement of what goes on in the psychiatric wards in the prison system. Here, the control is complete. Here, the analogy between mental hospitals and prisons becomes identity: they are one and the same.

This pamphlet from the Prison Survival Center (Dorchester, Massachusetts) makes the point quite clear.

Let's not always allow the prison administration to sensationalize the fact that prisoners do kill prisoners for reasons too easily explained. Let's look at the killing of prisoners by the administration, the guards, and the prison itself, let's look at just one.

—Kumasi

I met Fred Billingslea in the Los Angeles Central County Jail around April of 1966. We met in a dayroom at a card table in a game of tonk. There was nothing different about Fred from any other prisoner in that jail except the individual personality, place, and date of birth, and so on—things that give men their own identification.

Fred was also in the guidance center at Chino with me during May and June of 1966. He got along with everyone, had few arguments, and I don't remember him having a fight. He played basketball and boxed a little, but what was new to him, as he explained during a later conversation we had shortly before his assassination in Quentin (Feb. 25, 1970)—was his interest in book reading. He told me how he was surprised and impressed because he heard me arguing and negating the historical context of a book one day, that he had always taken for granted that textbooks held the truth, all of it, without a typical slant in the point, one that would indoctrinate and orient the student to its classical establishment position. (In this case I had been arguing about the treatment American history books had been giving blacks; this was before black studies was introduced to the school curriculum.) So Fred became a bona fide bookworm, studying and examining every book and subject he could get his hands on—I never asked him what he was doing because to me it wasn't unusual and at the time, I didn't know his motive; it could have been the same as mine for all I knew. But other prisoners thought it was peculiar because Fred didn't only read, he carried a load of books down the corridor, through the chow line, in the dayroom, everywhere but into the shower—and he always kept one open and concentrated on its pages even when walking. He was cool, and had the rhythm and gesticulations and outward emotional movements common to black people but slightly exaggerated, so everyone began to call him Triple Hip, meaning not only was he hip, but triple hip.

In June of 1966 I went to Tracy and Fred went to Soledad about the same time. We didn't run into each other again until 1969 when he stepped into F-wing, fresh off the bus, returning from Vacaville. He wasn't the same, either in appearance or character. His peculiarity was more exaggerated than before, his movements were slow, very slow and awkward, but he still maintained a taste of coolness. He was larger but his athletic build was gone, his back was hunched, his face was bloated and his eyes seemed to look without seeing. His speech was stumbling—he fumbled and grasped for words—but he could still smile and we talked about the time and events that had passed between.

Fred told me he had been to Vacaville and that the doctors had given him various kinds of medicines and treatments (among them was Thorazine and Prolexin) and the most dreaded treatment of all to all of us—the electroconvulsive shock treatment! I asked him why he allowed them to give these drugs and treatments to him and Fred said that if the doctors decide to give them to you,

you can't refuse and if you do refuse, there are inmates there they call greenshirts who are employed as restraining agents. Five, six, or as many greenshirts as it takes will run into your cell and beat you into submission or unconsciousness, and then the doctor will come in and shoot you with a needle. It only takes a few seconds before every muscle in your body relaxes and all you can move is your eyes. Then they take you somewhere, strap you to a table, put a bit in your mouth and electrodes on your head, and shock you into convulsions.

During the shock treatment you lose consciousness, some say the heart stops temporarily, and the person, the victim, has the feeling of experiencing death. When consciousness is regained, there are long periods of severe headaches and the victim neither remembers his name or what has just taken place, and it's been said that until the victim is reoriented he does not remember his friends or even his family on sight.

He is fed Thorazine, and sometimes Prolexin, which slow his movements and speech to the point that to raise a spoon from his tray to his mouth takes five to seven seconds, ten paces are taken in twenty to twenty-five seconds—one looks like a film in slow motion. Others laugh and mock and tease one another about being the next victim, but there are some of us who would rather know death.

Fred also told me that he allowed them to experiment on him with new drugs that he didn't even know the name of, or even their purpose. I personally pulled a patch from Fred's shoulder resembling a large Band-aid that had some kind of medicine or chemical or something on it. They put it on and then test and examine your biological, metabolical, and psychological reaction to it. They have some that they put on different parts of the body; they scrape particles from the eye, take samples of skin, blood, urine, hair. It's a real human test lab and Fred thought nothing of it because he said they paid him a few dollars for each test. I asked Fred if he didn't consider he was being used for a guinea pig, that if even the doctors did not know beforehand what his body reaction would be to the test, that a bad reaction could possibly cost him his life? Did he ever think that they could be experimenting with what might in the future be used against all of us as a secret weapon, or that it might be used on other people elsewhere in the world in struggles against colonialism and imperialism, or that drugs might replace guns as a subduing force and tool of repression? Fred said he had not thought of it that way, that so many of the prisoners in Vacaville had been under these treatments that it seemed to be part of the program. It was accepted; they had all been bought. But Fred began to understand this logic: there never was and there will never be any human concern for the prisoner shown by the guards, the doctor, the administration, or any other tool of the confining elements.

I told Fred how much he had changed, how he was no longer the athlete he had been, how what they had given him had even affected his weight, how his speech and his manner were such that I was the only one in the joint who would rap to him besides the brother who came down from Vacaville with him and who felt he was crazy. I told him to refuse the medicine, to resist their attempts to destroy his mind, but like he said, he couldn't. Besides, one has the feeling of being "high" under the influence of these drugs and thousands of prisoners mistakenly pretend something is wrong with themselves to secure a prescription from the doctor.

One day Fred is missing from Soledad's mainline; the rumor spreads among our circle that Fred was taken in the night to Vacaville again.

The next time I see Fred is in B-section, San Quentin's dungeon lockup—a cesspool of madness where war veterans, ex-policemen, drunks, and the emotionally unstable man the gunrails day and night, pointing their rifles and carbines at prisoners, shooting at and around them while they sleep, while they shower, while they fight, while they play, always maintaining a coldly calculated atmosphere of horror and death.

They use any excuse to beat a prisoner. But first they must manipulate him into the position of committing himself verbally. An officer—we call them pigs in accord with their conduct—will enter a cell and read a prisoner's mail, ramble through his personal effects, family pictures, personal writings, books, and so on. The pig will bend a picture, leave a footprint on a letter, destroy legal affidavits pertaining to the prisoner's case that he has been working on for weeks and that have a deadline for submittal to the courts. All these will be shuffled, misarranged with the rest of his cell in order to evoke a heated response from the prisoner when he returns from the yard.

A few words are exchanged, enough to constitute an argument, to constitute a violation of inmate behavior, to constitute a threatening attitude, and the pig returns with the "goon squad." Ten, fifteen uniformed pigs, armed with tear gas, clubs, towels, and cuffs will line up in front of a one-man cell. There will be a few moments of intimidation and harassment evoking more responses from an already enraged prisoner. Then comes the tear gas, sprayed or shot into the cell with either a .38 caliber or a twelve gauge "gas gun." If it is shot, the noise and the blast itself has an effect on the prisoner. At first he thinks he's been shot because all this time there is a gunman armed with a carbine and a pistol backing the others from a gunrail straight across from the cell, on the opposite wall and they don't expose the gas guns at first. They maneuver the prisoner up to the bars and then suddenly they come from his blind side and shoot him in the face. The blast knocks him backward, burns the skin off his face, blinds him, and while he is falling backward screaming from surprise and the shock of the blast in his eyes, they unlock his cell gate and rush in upon him, as many as can fit themselves in that cell, climbing, falling over each other, clubbing one another in the process of getting to this "loud-mouthed" prisoner. They beat and drag him to another cell, a strip cell where he'll live without his property, without his clothes, without his bed, or anything but himself and the memory of that beating if he survives—for days, months, maybe years.

B-section is never quiet. It is impossible to explain everything that goes on in an endless fashion and how the only difference between night and day is the lack of meals and lights. Some things go on in prison that prisoners cannot explain. We keep saying to one another, "Man, they wouldn't believe this out there on the street—even I wouldn't believe it if I had not seen it!" So I will not waste any time attempting to explain the most hilarious and unexplainable scenes.

One night, February 25, 1970 Fred began to scream vindictives from his cell, but everybody screams in B-section. The only difference is that most of us who do the screaming and competing with a few hundred voices and learning to distinguish the difference between the others and the one answering you is that we usually know what we're screaming about. Fred didn't. The drugs I told him to refuse had finally dissolved Fred's mind. In B-section he seemed completely incoherent. There were still moments when his conversation made sense, but if he talked extensively his words would trail off and he would be speaking completely out of context.

Everyone knew what Fred had been through—San Quentin is full of men whose minds have been destroyed rather than their bodies; the prison knows the sophisticated way to kill. Since the prison needs labor, prisoner labor, it would not be in the interest of the administration to kill all the prisoners. So, many are killed mentally and spiritually—it's a slower death that the administrators do not have to claim credit for. If a mind is subjected to enough stress, the brain will go on strike. The subject refuses to function on his own accord and it is in this state that he is most suggestible and remote. Between periods of stress, laxatives and comforts are supplied; the subject receives gifts of pacification. Fish to a captive seal, under the stress of his newly attached leash; meat to a falcon, whose resistance to captivity and the change in his life has not yet been stifled; and to a man, you supply many things, because he is more intelligent, but the crisis remains, and when the crisis is repeated and patterned to perfection, it becomes a weapon in the hands of a vicious tyrant.

During this spell of incoherence that overcame Fred that night, more than twenty pigs came to his cell with tear gas, mace, and clubs. They intimidated him, practicing the choke holds they would use on him to get him out of his cell. One of them had a small tube resembling a small fire extinguisher and their first move was to empty this in Fred's cell. Fred went to the back of his cell and started a small fire that, as it appears, he kept going in front of him. The fire seemed to counteract the gas for a while—it didn't seem to affect the rest of us too much. So the pigs left and returned with another tube of gas which they sprayed into Fred's cell. Everyone was yelling at the pigs by now: "Leave him alone, pigs!" and "If they come in, fight 'em, Fred!" "Pigs, if you jump on him, you got to jump on every one of us in B-section." Whites, blacks, chicanos, everyone was on Fred's side. Fred said nothing to no one; it was not clear just what he was doing in the corner of his cell, whether or not he was even conscious. Different people called to him, asked him to give some sign of being all right in there; meanwhile more threats were shouted at the pigs. Another tube of gas arrived and was emptied in Fred's cell just like the two that preceded it. About ten minutes later Fred began to speak. He spoke rapidly, in a whimper. "Let me out, let me out, let me out, please let me out, please I can't stand it no more."

But another tube of gas was emptied into Fred's cell and by now all of B-section was filled with gas and even the prisoners around the corner in A-section were beginning to feel the effects of it and were wetting towels and putting them across their faces and hiding under pillows that were covered by blankets. (Another practice, if you are in a closed cell with a door, an outer door beyond the bars, and the cell is full of gas, is to put a pillow atop the commode and bounce on it until the water goes down, and then stick your head in it and put something, a blanket or whatever's available, over your head. It's the only air, it's foul, but it's fair, fairer than gas.)

Back to Fred. By this time the pigs had called the hospital. We don't know what transpired on the phone, but two greenshirts wearing inmate attendants' uniforms, one black, one white (I won't give their names because they are still awaiting payment of the highest debt, under the code of retribution) came to Fred's cell and were admitted into the cell to subdue Fred so as to exempt the pigs from the blame. Everyone yelled and threatened those attendants. Their names were finally thought up and they were called by name and told that if they jumped on Fred for the pigs, they could hang it up. They jumped on Fred anyway and dragged Fred out by the balls! Fred was taken downstairs by the pigs once those attendants got him out of the cell. There was the sound of tumbling going on all the way down and it was obvious that the pigs were doing their thing—beating, pushing, and throwing Fred down the stairs.

About twenty minutes later, word came up from the prisoners on the first floor that Fred had been carried out on a stretcher with a blanket over him. Word spread from cell to cell, tier to tier, from the first tier to the fifth. Then there was silence in B-section for the first time in many nights and it lasted all night. Warden Louis Nelson announced Fred's death on the radio, both public and institutionwide. His story was that Fred was disturbing other inmates in B-section by making noises and setting fire to his cell (a concrete cell), and that correctional officers were called in to his cell to remove him, and because he refused to come out on his own accord force was necessary. Tear gas was used first in order to subdue and quiet Fred, who, Warden Nelson explained, was a psychotic, and then the warden apologized, saying how deplorable it was that San Quentin did not have the facilities to accommodate psychotics—there was a need for hospital space in order to make this possible. He said that Fred put up a struggle with the officers that was so intense that at one point an officer was kicked all the way down the stairwell, and that Fred's death was not the result of a beating as the rumor around San Quentin had it, but that he died of asphyxiation due to the fire he had set in his cell and that it was "complicated by tear gas." Again he apologized and asked all the black prisoners who didn't believe him to consult some officer in the yard whom they could confide in and ask him for the truth.

The matter was determined to be an atrocity—one of a long list of atrocities committed against us in captive detention. The guilty party was not an individual, but a system, as always, that employs individuals to carry out its duties and to bear the responsibility along with the consequences themselves. The individual pig who has become perverted by making himself an instrument of this system alone must bear the consequences of a mistake the system made and handed down. But it may not always go like that, for retribution is without boundaries for us, the dispossessed.

A few days after Fred's death, a "random pig" was hit (knifed), not deliberately but by mishap; this mishap, which did not cost him his life, possibly saved the life of another pig. In return for a random hit, a random search was begun by the rest of the pigs and eventually (it always is an eventuality with us), a man was picked from the population of men inside San Quentin to stand trial.

This was James McClain, whose trial was later to be terminated in the Marin County Courthouse shootings on August 7, 1970—a day of heroic revolutionary endeavors, a day that marked not the end for the men, the revolutionary cadres who died, but marked the beginning of the end of the confining element. There are some who will try to bottle up the action at Marin as a criminal act of banditry. But then, there are some of us who know how to recognize history the day and time it is being made, who don't wait on it to be shown in print on the pages of a textbook. "We are those who, at the fire's center, plan for the new world to rise out of the ashes," as William J. Pomeroy says. We know, as Ralph Featherstone plainly wrote: "To look at a watch and know the time of day is to be able to read. To see what time it is in history, our history, and act accordingly, is to be revolutionary."

V. PATIENTS' RIGHTS

Introduction

This brief section shows a bit of the movement for mental patients' liberation, and for the rights of mental patients. The movement is basically progressive. Most of the groups are militant and many have begun to link the experiences of mental patients with the experiences of other groups oppressed by capitalism. These groups should be supported. Hopefully, more and more of these groups will come into existence. The fusion of what they've learned from their own experience with a growing, militant class-consciousness can develop, through struggle, into a powerful movement.

29. MENTAL PATIENTS' CIVIL LIBERTIES PROJECT:

Patients' Rights Manual

An Outline of Patients' Rights

The items listed below are a brief summary of *some* of the rights and issues discussed in the following article. Read the *whole* Manual to get the *whole* idea.

AS A PATIENT IN THIS MENTAL HOSPITAL, YOU HAVE A RIGHT TO:

—be treated with dignity and respect;

—privacy;

—a safe, clean, and wholesome environment;

—be free from seclusion and restraints except on a doctor's written order, for specific reasons and for a limited time—and never for punishment;

—communicate with persons outside the hospital;

—sell things you make and keep the money;

—be released as soon as hospital care is no longer necessary or, if a voluntary patient, on proper notice;

—be informed about your treatment in words you understand;

—refuse treatment;

—read and make changes in all printed forms you are asked to sign;

—refuse to be used for teaching purposes and for research purposes;

—be informed of all hospital and ward rules;

—freedom of speech;

—at a commitment hearing, receive at least five days' notice, to have the help of an independent doctor on your side, to present your own witnesses and your own evidence, to have a lawyer, to appeal.

THE BEST SAFEGUARD OF YOUR RIGHTS IS YOU; STICK UP FOR YOUR RIGHTS!!!

Patients' Rights Manual

People who are patients in mental hospitals are entitled to basic human, legal, and civil rights. This Manual is written for you, so that you may better understand patients' rights. Among other rights, you have the *right to know your rights*.

I. In-Hospital Rights

A. Seclusion and Restraints

A Pennsylvania state law (Section 422 of the Mental Health and Mental Retardation Act of 1966) *prohibits the use of mechanical restraints* such as straps, sheets, and jackets on patients within the hospital *except* when required by the person's medical needs, but only when used according to state regulations.

Haverford State Hospital policy allows *restraints or seclusion* to be applied only on a doctor's *written order,* for specific reasons and for a limited time. If you are secluded or restrained, you have the *right to be told the reasons* and to give your side of the story.

Restraints and seclusion should be used by hospital staff only as a last resort to protect people's physical safety. It may *never* be used as *punishment.* If you are upset and a nurse or aide suggests seclusion or if you yourself wish to be alone, you have the right to be placed in the visitors' room, the music room, or your own room if that will serve the purposes of seclusion.

You have the *right to get in touch* with the Mental Patient Civil Liberties Project *immediately* if you feel you have been secluded or restrained improperly. *"Immediately"* means even while you are in seclusion or restraints. Tell the nurse, aide, or doctor that you wish to speak with us. If he or she refuses, or you are unable to reach us, you may get in touch with us as soon as you can.

B. Other Rights By State Law

Another state law guarantees seven *specific rights* to patients. They are:

1. the right to have reasonable opportunity *to communicate* with any person outside the hospital and to be furnished with *writing materials* by the hospital.

2. *the right to sell* things you make and keep the money.

3. *the right to be released* as soon as hospital care is no longer necessary. Voluntary patients, of course, may leave on request or on up to ten days' written notice.

4. *the right to be employed* at a useful occupation.

5. *religious freedom.*

6. *the right to send sealed letters* to any member of your family, your lawyer, the state welfare department, the hospital director, and the court, if any, which committed you. When a lawyer or a representative of the welfare department speaks with you, you have the *right to be alone and speak privately* with him or her.

7. *the right to* request the welfare department to arrange and pay for (if you can't afford it) *an examination by an independent doctor.* This request may be refused only if you make it less than six months after you entered the hospital or one year after you have had a previous examination in this way. *Forms* for making the request are available from the Mental Patient Civil Liberties Project.

C. Constitutional Rights

As a person living in this country, you are guaranteed certain rights by the United States Constitution. These are not lost just because you are a resident of a mental hospital. Constitutional rights include: *freedom of speech, freedom of assembly, freedom from unreasonable searches and seizures, freedom from cruel and unusual punishment, freedom from involuntary servitude, the right not to be deprived of life, liberty or property without due process of law, the right to equal protection of the laws and the right to vote.* So far, the courts have had very little opportunity to examine and explain exactly how these Constitutional rights apply in the mental hospital situation. The Mental Patient Civil Liberties Project is glad to answer any questions you may have and help with any problems that come up.

Courts in some states have held that a person hospitalized for alleged mental illness has a Constitutional *right to treatment.*

Vital to a patient's dignity and bodily integrity is a *right to refuse treatment;* however, such a right has yet to be fully recognized as applicable to mental patients. A New York federal court decided that the First Amendment religious freedom of a Christian Scientist mental patient outweighed the hospital's interest and desire for her to have drug treatment. The court upheld her right to refuse. If traditional religious belief is sufficient to justify refusal of medication, then it would seem Constitutionally required, the Mental Patient Civil Liberties Project believes, to treat similarly any situation where the patient's feelings against medication are sincerely and deeply held. Also, the Project believes that just as anyone may refuse an operation or medical treatment that a medical doctor recommends, so should a mental patient be able to refuse psychiatric treatment.

You also have the Constitutional *right not to be punished for* what the hospital says is your *"illness."* You have the *right to be informed of all* hospital and ward *rules.* You should not be punished for breaking a rule you didn't know about. You should not be punished severely for breaking a minor rule.

D. JCAH Rights

The Joint Commission of Accreditation of Hospitals (JCAH) is a national private organization which *sets standards* for all types of hospitals. Haverford is accredited by JCAH and has agreed to meet their standards for psychiatric hospitals. Some of the JCAH standards include those rights already mentioned above; *some* additional protections are listed below. Words in quotation marks are the exact words of the JCAH standards.

1. The hospital must *"acknowledge the dignity and protect the rights* of all its patients."

2. You have the *right to be informed about your treatment* in words you understand.

3. You have the *right to privacy*—including access to an area where you can be alone when you want to, a place to keep personal possessions and clothes with locked storage space, privacy in the bathroom, confidentiality between you and your therapist. Staff should show their respect for your privacy by knocking on doors before entering your room.

4. You have the *right to a safe, clean and wholesome environment.*

5. "Provision should be made for *patient-community meet-ings*."

6. "Patients should be allowed to conduct *private telephone conversations* with family and friends and to *send and receive mail without undue hindrance*."

E. Some Other Rights

1. The hospital often uses *printed forms* that they ask you to sign for many purposes including, for example, commitment and consent to treatment. You should *never sign* such a form *without reading* it carefully *and understanding it*. You have the right to ask that it be explained and you may make changes in the form before signing it.

2. When a medical doctor is treating your body, you have the right to be treated in privacy and to be shielded from the eyes of those who aren't caring for you. In the mental hospital, *what is said to you or about you* should likewise be *shielded from* the ears of *other patients and those not treating you*.

3. Information from your *medical record* should not be released to outsiders without your specific consent.

4. You have the *right to refuse to be used for teaching purposes or research* purposes. Although teaching and research have traditionally been done on poor people, often without their consent, economic status or the fact of being a patient in a state hospital does not impair your right not to be a medical lesson or guinea pig.

II. Getting In and Out

Most people at Haverford come into the hospital *voluntarily under Section 402 or Section 403* of the Act. You have the *right to choose which kind of voluntary patient you want to be*.

Section 402 permits patients to *leave* the hospital *"at any time."* Your request to leave does not have to be in writing.

Under *Section 403,* you may commit yourself voluntarily for up to *30 days*. At the end of each commitment period, you may commit yourself for a further period. In order to be released, you must give *written notice* to the hospital director; after you give this notice, the hospital may not keep you for more than 10 days.

(If you are *under 18,* the law says that your parents or guardian may bring you into the hospital under *Section 402 or 403* "voluntarily" even if you actually don't want to become a patient.)

Section 405 provides for *temporary emergency commitment.* When a person appears "by reason of his acts or threatened acts, to be so mentally disabled as to be *dangerous* to himself or others and *in need of immediate care"* he or she may be taken into custody and to the hospital for *up to 10 days.* Unless a petition for a Section 406 commitment has been filed and unless the person's behavior still fits into the above "dangerousness" definition, it is illegal to keep someone in the hospital for more than ten days under Section 405.

The following *seven paragraphs* deal with *Section 406.*

Section 406 provides for *involuntary civil commitment* by order of a court. Someone (usually a relative) signs a petition asking that the potential patient (you) be committed to the mental hospital. The court then issues a warrant, sets the time for a hearing and notifies interested persons. Delaware County court *rules require that you receive written notice at least five days before the hearing,* in most cases.

You have the *right to a lawyer* at the hearing. If you can't afford one, the Public Defender will represent you at no cost. It is hoped that the Mental Patient Civil Liberties Project will be able to provide legal assistance in certain cases at commitment hearings. *As soon as you know that there will be a commitment hearing, contact a lawyer.* You have the right to present evidence and witnesses on your own behalf, to speak in your own behalf and to cross-examine witnesses for the other side.

The court rules give you the *right to an independent psychiatric examination before the hearing* to help you prepare your case. If you don't have enough money, the court will appoint the doctor. If this doctor thinks you should be committed, he can't be forced to say so in court. If he thinks you should not be committed, you can have him testify for you in court.

Hearings are usually held twice a week before a "master" appointed to make recommendations to the court; the master's recommendations are usually followed. The master can recommend commitment for a definite or indefinite time; he may also order outpatient care, partial hospitalization, or release you completely and dismiss the petition. You have the right to suggest and argue for the type of care you think you should receive. If less restrictive care than total hospitalization will serve the purpose, then you have a *right to the least restrictive alternative.*

There are usually *two hearings.* At the *first* one, the person who wants you committed, the petitioner, explains the *facts* upon which he or she is basing the petition. The master decides whether or not this evidence is sufficient; if not, you will be released. If the evidence is sufficient, the master may commit you for up to *ten days for psychiatric evaluation.* Then, a *second* hearing is held at which a hospital psychiatrist will state the *hospital's diagnosis and medical opinion.* The master will then (after opportunity for cross-examination and for your case to be presented) decide the case.

It is not unusual for many of your *rights to be ignored or unrecognized* at commitment hearings. *If that happens,* speak to the lawyer or the master immediately and ask for an explanation. You may also consult with the Mental Patient Civil Liberties Project for assistance.

People committed under Section 406 remain hospitalized until the hospital decides that treatment is no longer necessary or until a court orders their release. Every person committed by the court has the *right to appeal* to higher state courts. You have this right even if you cannot afford to pay the costs of appeal.

About *criminal commitments:* Persons charged with crimes or found not guilty by reason of insanity may, under certain circumstances, be placed in a mental hospital. If you are in that situation and have questions or need help, please feel free to contact the Mental Patient Civil Liberties Project.

III. WHAT TO DO ABOUT PROBLEMS

1. *Habeas Corpus*—If the procedure leading to your commitment were insufficient or illegal or if continued hospitalization

is not needed, you have the *right to be released* after a hearing on a habeas corpus petition. This is part of *Section 426* of the Act. For any unconstitutional deprivation of liberty, the Constitution guarantees the right of habeas corpus.

2. *Civil Liability*—If a person or agency "falsely, corruptly, maliciously or without reasonable cause" gets you committed, he, she or it may be held liable for resulting damage.

3. There are circumstances in which the conditions of hospitalization or particular treatment may entitle you to sue for violation of your Constitutional rights, the federal civil rights acts or other laws.

4. Any patient wishing to challenge his or her hospitalization may request *free assistance without cost from the Mental Patient Civil Liberties Project.* You may at any time contact *your lawyer, the Public Defender* of Delaware County, *Delaware County Legal Assistance* or the *Court,* if any, which committed you. The hospital staff has an obligation not to hinder but to assist you in making such contacts.

5. At Haverford State Hospital, the Mental Patient Civil Liberties Project is an *independent* group which has agreed to provide *legal and advocacy services* for patients. Under the agreement, you have the *right to get in touch* with the Project *at any time,* even if you are in seclusion, restraints or otherwise restricted. You may not be punished or treated differently for asking for the Project's services.

The Project will try to help any patient who feels that his or her legal, civil or human rights have been violated, by acting as patient-advocate with hospital or other officials or, when appropriate, by legal action.

30. DAVID FERLEGER:

Mental Patient Civil Liberties Project*

The purpose of this paper is to describe the theoretical basis for a mechanism to protect the rights of users of hospital psychiatric services in the context of an organization now operating at a state mental hospital. The model discussed is one which could be utilized and further developed by social workers and consumers, especially those involved in community organization activities.

Almost half a million persons are confined, about 90 percent of them involuntarily, as patients in public and private mental hospitals. Having established purportedly due process procedures to get people into these institutions, society has been content to leave their "treatment" in the hands of the professionals. Such dependence on the psychiatric profession may be as unwarranted and as dangerous to the rights and liberties of the inmates involved as is dependence on the penal professionals in the prison setting. Methods must be found to protect the rights of those incarcerated as mental patients without the present almost exclusive reliance on those who manage the institutions.

Mental hospitals have the potential (often realized) of totalitarian control over patients' lives. The effect is totally pervasive. The patient is dependent upon the institution for food, clothing, medical care, recreation, companionship—in short, for all the physical and emotional sustenance of life. In addition, the mental hospital exercises plenary de facto legal power over its inmates, usually with no court adjudication of incompetency. It decides whether or not the person is capable of handling spending money

* SOURCE: *The Radical Therapist,* vol. 3, no. 3 (November 1972).

or other property, and how much. It limits or censors his or her mail. It decides who will be allowed to visit the patient, and when. It decides whether the patient will live on a locked ward or in an open building and whether the patient will have the "privileges" of walking the grounds, taking a trip to town, or visiting his or her family and friends. The hospital decides whether the patient will stay there or leave, despite the fact that the great majority of mental patients have no behavior problem which would limit out-placement.

Conditions in mental hospitals are notoriously bad; minimal standards are frequently violated. The abysmal quality of care and the related difficulty patients have in obtaining desired adequate treatment are fundamental problems and it would be blind to think of remedying civil liberties questions without aggressively addressing this situation. But even where a hospital provides high quality care there are difficulties. There is an inherent conflict of interest between the hospital and the patient on many matters. The patient may be interested in optimal freedom to come and go, to socialize, to have visitors and activities, to be free from arbitrary transfers and punishments and searches. The hospital's interests may be in administrative convenience and quietude. It is clear that a mental hospital does not stand in a position to be an impartial protector of its patients.

The Mental Patient Civil Liberties Project, Philadelphia, Pennsylvania, is a unique endeavor which combines legal and advocacy services with a community organizing approach. Its director is a lawyer and its staff consists of law students, volunteers, and social work personnel. Unlike the few other efforts nationally which provide access to legal help for mental patients, the Project does not work within the traditional legal-aid framework of one-to-one problem solution with occasional test-case litigation. Because the Project's goal is to develop means through which persons confined in mental hospitals gain greater control over the factors which shape their institutional lives, the Project works with patients collectively in an effort to make the mental hospital accountable to those who consume its services. Thus, "consumer accountability." As further discussed below, the work of consumer-oriented social workers and consumers themselves is crucial to the legal work of the Project.

The Mental Patient Civil Liberties Project is based on a model which does several things:

1. It recognizes that mental patients are in critical need of protection of their civil liberties and assistance in organizing to assert them.

2. It recognizes, as does psychiatric opinion, that "competency" among mental patients is a very flexible concept. The mind may be lucid in every aspect except a very narrow one. Or the patient may be subject to occasional lapses of coherency while at other times retaining his or her full maturity and abilities. Or the patient may not be "ill" at all.

3. It respects individual freedom and dignity and the critical importance of permitting individuals to make the decisions central to their lives. It recognizes the right to be different.

4. It recognizes that the more a mental patient is protected, the more he or she must be enabled to protect himself or herself from overprotection. The most complete protection is the total institution. It is in the total institution that the most serious efforts are needed to guarantee actual availability of services theoretically offered and the continuing citizenship and autonomy of the inmates.

Patient Organization

Powerless and oppressed people have never effectively gained power or tempered oppression except through a process of awareness of their common situation, organization, mutual cooperation, and struggle toward collectively-determined goals. Though the particular development varies depending on the existing social and historical conditions, the above process is familiar to the United States in the history of union organization, the civil rights movement, the growth of the National Welfare Rights Organization, and the women's movement.

Mental patients and people associated with them are beginning to "get their heads together" in forming an awareness of their plight and a perspective on what needs to be done about it. This growing movement will be a significant force in determining the future of our society's treatment of noncriminal deviant behavior. It is important that people become involved in assisting hospitalized mental patients as they begin to work among themselves and with or against the institution to make it more responsive to their needs.

The Mental Patient Civil Liberties Project has as a primary purpose fostering the establishment and growth of patient self-organization within a selected target institution, Haverford State Hospital, Haverford, Pennsylvania. Interaction between the Project and its client-patients assumes many forms running a gamut which includes, for example, discussions with and advice to patients on an individual and group basis, assisting at meetings, planning publications (e.g., a rights handbook and a patient newspaper), facilitation of contact with public and press, acting as an intermediary to the hospital administration and institution for legal action on behalf of the patients. Unlike the traditional caseworker for the hospital, a social worker involved in these activities would take the lead from the patients' desires rather than from what the psychiatrist or hospital superintendent feels is best for the patients.

The organization of a patient union or committee within an institution could serve a variety of functions with reference to the protection of civil liberties and enlargement of the patients' sphere of autonomy. Stronger, more competent patients could be trained to serve as a grievance committee for the other inmates. The union could assert a governance role, certainly on issues which do not involve psychiatric judgments and possibly on some of those issues as well. Power to deal with "disciplinary" problems, now absolutely in the hands of staff and attendants, might be shared with a patient committee. A patient committee could provide a forum for fact-finding where a patient disputes allegations which have been made against him or her. In addition to advocacy and governance, such a union, by its very existence, would reduce the total de facto authority which mental hospital administrations now exercise in extending and withdrawing civil liberties to and from the patient.

Advocacy and Legal Services

Any individual living in an institution with total authority over his or her life needs an ally and an advocate to assist when inevitable conflicts of interest arise. The Project provides advocacy with undivided loyalty to the client-patient's self-determined interests. There is a deliberate avoidance of the traditional medical "best interest" approach which presently characterizes the relationship of the psychiatrist and the committing court to mental hospital patients. Functioning in conjunction with the patient organization activities described above, the advocacy role of the Project utilizes the time and talents of law students, working through accredited law school clinical programs, to provide legal representation for patients and to provide in-hospital advocacy to spur and expedite hospital response to complaints and requests.

It is basic to the structure outlined above that the community organizing and the legal services play reciprocally reinforcing roles, that each builds on the other and that each is necessary to the success of the other.

Conclusion

The ideology and activities of the Mental Patient Civil Liberties Project are suggested as a model for social work community organizers (functioning in conjunction with legal services personnel) to contribute to the transformation of mental hospitals into institutions more responsive to the needs of the people they serve. This development would not only increase the autonomy of the client population but would create a mechanism whereby the civil liberties of mental patients could be protected.

Appendix

Mental Patients' Liberation Groups

Cleveland, Ohio

Patients Rights Organization, 2108 Film Building, Rm. 707, 44114

Harrisburg, Pa.

Mental Patients Liberation League, c/o Thomas O'Grady, 1209 N. 2 St.

New York City, N.Y.

Mental Patients Liberation Project, 56 E. 4 St.

Mental Patients Political Action Committee, c/o J. Shupack, 450 E. 63 St.

Mental Patients Resistance, 11 Polhemus Place, Brooklyn

Minneapolis, Minn.

Mental Health Patients Liberation, c/o Claudia Keagy, 3356 10th Ave. So., 55407

Edison, N.J.

Mental Patients Liberation Project, 117 Evergreen Rd., Greenfield Gdns., 08817 (24 hr. phone 201–548–0429)

Philadelphia, Pa.

Mental Patients Liberation Project, Box 1745, 19105

Portland, Oreg.

Mental Patients Liberation Project, c/o Mike Gallagher, 1626 S.E. 39th Ave.

Richmond, Va.	Insane Liberation Front, c/o T. Carwile, 104 N. Harvie St.
Syracuse, N.Y.	Mental Patients Liberation Project, c/o Carole Hayes, 211 Wellesley Rd.
Washington, D.C.	Mental Patients Liberation Project, c/o George Brewster, 3407 Wessynton Way, Alexandria, Va. 22309
Vancouver, B.C.	Mental Patients Association, 1982 W. 6th Ave.
London, Eng.	Mental Patients Union, 97 Prince of Wales Road, NW5

Research, Legal, and Publicity Groups

Auckland, N. Zealand	Campaign Against Psychiatric Atrocities, c/o R. Povall, Box 6899
Baltimore, Md.	Community Mental Health Legal Services of the Legal Aid Bureau, 341 N. Calvert St., 21202
Berkeley, Calif.	LAMP, 2014 Channing Way
Los Angeles, Calif.	Mental Patients Rights Panel, c/o Richard Fox, 1888 Century Park East, Suite 225, Century City, 90067
Philadelphia, Pa.	Mental Patient Civil Liberties Project, 121 S. 18th St.
St. Louis, Mo.	Patient Advocacy Legal Service, Washington University Law School, 63130

74 75   12 11 10 9 8 7 6 5 4 3 2 1